Death
and the Disinterested
Spectator

AN INQUIRY INTO THE NATURE OF PHILOSOPHY

Death
and the Disinterested Spectator
Spectator

AN INQUIRY INTO THE NATURE OF PHILOSOPHY

Ann Hartle

State University of New York Press

Published by
State University of New York Press, Albany

For information, address State University of New York
Press, State University Plaza, Albany, N.Y., 12246

Library of Congress Cataloging-in-Publication Data

Hartle, Ann.
   Death and the disinterested spectator.

   Bibliography: p.
   Includes index.
   1. Philosophy.   2. Death.   3. Plato.   Phaedo.
4. Augustine, Saint, Bishop of Hippo. Confessions.
5. Descartes, Reneé, 1596-1650. Discours de la méthode.
6. Immortality (Philosophy)   7. Science—Methodology.
I. Title.
B72.H335   1986   101   86-14447
ISBN 0-88706-285-7
ISBN 0-88706-284-9 (pbk.)

10   9   8   7   6   5   4   3   2   1

Contents

Preface   1

Introduction   5

Chapter I: Socrates: Penelope and the Bee 11
   The *Phaedo* as Apology; Comedy, Tragedy, Philosophy; Actor
   or Spectator; Hubris and Irony; Truth and Deception: A.
   Socrates, B. Phaedo, C. Plato; Transition: From Philosophical
   Courage to Christian Hope

Chapter II: Augustine: The Look of Pity 85
   Confession and Apology; Laughter, Tears, Trembling and
   Wonder; Actor or Spectator; Pride and Humility; Truth and Self-
   Deception; Transition: From Christian Hope to Modern
   Certitude

Chapter III: Descartes: Occupation and Pre-occupation 137
   The *Discourse* as Apology; Laughter, Tears, Trembling, and
   Wonder; Actor or Spectator; Pride and Humility; Truth and
   Certitude; Transition and Return

Chapter IV: Conclusion: Death and the Disinterested Spectator 191
   Compassion and Distance; Wonder and Death; The Strange and
   the Familiar; The Fable of Certitude; Philosophy and the Divine:
   From Disinterested Spectator to Compassionate Actor;
   Cartesian Presumption, Socratic Victory; Idle Talk and Endless
   Toil; Weaving the Shroud

Notes. 221

Works Consulted. 253

Index 259

For Bob

Le soleil ni la mort ne se peuvent regarder fixement.

—La Rochefoucauld

And pray to God to have mercy upon us
And I pray that I may forget
These matters that with myself I too much discuss
Too much explain
Because I do not hope to turn again
Let these words answer
For what is done, not to be done again
May the judgment not be too heavy upon us

—T.S. Eliot, *Ash Wednesday*

Preface

Each semester for several years I taught a course entitled "Philosophy of Man" at St. Francis College. Its purpose was to examine the question about the nature of man, i.e., the question about the manner of human being. Among the works we studied were Plato's *Phaedo*, Augustine's *Confessions*, and Descartes's *Discourse on Method* because these works discuss such issues as the relation between soul and body and the immortality of the soul.

My reading of these works led me to see that the question about the nature of man cannot be separated from the question about the nature of philosophy, that activity which claims to be the highest, that way of life which claims to be best for a man. I also began to see *internal* connections among the *Phaedo*, *The Confessions*, and the *Discourse*. By this I do not mean anything that depends on somehow proving that Augustine read the *Phaedo* and that Descartes read *The Confessions*.

It is often claimed that Augustine is a kind of Platonist and that Descartes is indebted to Augustine for his first principle, the *cogito*. This claim is based on a perception of the kinds of internal connections which link the *Phaedo*, *The Confessions*, and the *Discourse*. My own interpretation of these works shows that they are indeed to be understood in relation to each other but not because they are in fundamental agreement or because they constitute a sequence of "development" or dependence within the history of philosophy. Rather, as Socrates defines himself in contradistinction to the natural philosophers and Sophists, so Augustine understands himself, not as a Platonist, but as having rejected a version at least of the Platonic notion of philosophy, that is, the claim that it is a *divine* activity. Augustine's encounter with the Platonic books teaches him "the difference between presumption and confession." Descartes's project in the *Discourse* is radically and self-consciously different from Augustine's confessing. Descartes's grounding of certitude in the *je pense, donc je suis* is, from Augustine's point of view, the greatest presumption. But the project of the mastery of nature which follows from this first principle could not have occurred without the Christian notion of the divine. Descartes's occupation belongs to man as man but presupposes the Augustinian understanding of God as compassionate actor.

The first three chapters of this book are presentations of my interpretation of the *Phaedo, The Confessions,* and the *Discourse* respectively. On this level, they are relatively autonomous chapters. At a second level, the internal connections among the three works are displayed and, at decisive points, articulated. The fourth chapter is an attempt to deal more directly with the question concerning the nature of philosophy, presupposing the interpretations presented in the first three chapters and linking these three chapters more explicitly.

It might be asked whether other philosophical works would have also served as a kind of background for my own reflections on the nature of philosophy and perhaps have led me to different conclusions. For example, the discussion of the philosophical life in the *Symposium* presents the philosopher, not as beginning from or striving for the stance of the disinterested spectator, but rather as being driven by the *erotic* pursuit of wisdom. I chose to begin from the *Phaedo* and to follow out its presentation of the philosophical life because it is there that the claim that philosophy is a preparation for death is made and displayed most explicitly. But, given this beginning, would not Boethius's *On the Consolation of Philosophy* be the most appropriate way into the medieval perspective on this claim? There, the question I am concerned with is discussed explicitly. It seems to me that the specifically *Christian* response to philosophy's claim is not made in Boethius's work at least in the way it is in Augustine's account of his torment in the face of death in *The Confessions*. And Descartes's response to philosophy's claim presupposes Augustine's uncertainty in the very attempt to overcome that uncertainty. Finally, in Descartes's *Discourse* the modern search for certitude shows itself as grounded in the desire for power against death. This search for certitude has been reduced, in our own century, to the desire for clarity and distinctness and precision which is the limit of the analytic movement. My reflections on the nature of philosophy are intended to pose again the Socratic claim that philosophy, by its very nature, is a preparation for death.

Finally, in speaking about "my own" reflections on the nature of philosophy, I do not claim anything like "novelty." I cannot separate what is precisely my own from what has its beginning in my thinking about the *Phaedo, The Confessions,* the *Discourse,* as well as the other works on which I rely in my fourth chapter. In this sense, I hope that this book will show that the study of the history of philosophy is not simply reducible to the study of intellectual history. It seems to me that anyone who today wishes seriously to raise the most fundamental philosophical questions must inevitably be drawn back into the history of philosophy. At best, we raise again the oldest questions.

I am grateful to friends and colleagues who have helped me in bringing this work to an end. Much of what I have written here concerning comedy and tragedy goes back to conversations with my husband, Robert. From beginning to end he has encouraged, read, criticized, and even typed. Donald Phillip Verene read the first version of the manuscript, and his suggestions are reflected here in several important ways. Gerald Galgan, friend and former colleague, was unsparing with his time, insightful in his criticisms, and invariably encouraging. I am grateful to William F. Edwards for his comments on the first version of the chapter on Descartes and to James Gouinlock for his suggestions concerning the chapter on Descartes and the concluding chapter. Donald Livingston, Gilbert Meilaender, and Carl G. Vaught raised questions about my project which helped me to be clearer and to express myself more clearly about it. I am very grateful for their help. Rose Bode and Patricia Redford typed the original version of the manuscript, and I thank them for their skill and patience.

I am indebted to the National Endowment for the Humanities, to the Earhart Foundation, and the Institute for Educational Affairs for their generous support.

Note on the Texts

I have used Burnet's edition of the *Phaedo* and have consulted the Loeb and Grube translations. The Latin text for Augustine's *Confessions* is the Loeb edition. I have relied almost exclusively on Warner's translation of *The Confessions* and I have followed Warner's practice of italicizing Augustine's quotations from Scripture. References to Descartes are to the sixth volume of the Adam and Tannery edition of the *Œuvres de Descartes* (spelling modernized) and to the first volume of the English edition by Haldane and Ross. The translations, however, are principally mine. A reference such as (AT 3; HR 82), for example, means (page 3 of Volume 6 of Adam and Tannery; page 82 of Volume I of Haldane and Ross).

Introduction

After Philosophy has dismissed the Muses of poetry and has reminded Boethius of her presence at the death of Socrates, she makes this speech:

> He who has calmly reconciled his life to fate, and set proud death beneath his feet, can look fortune in the face, unbending both to good and bad: his countenance unconquered he can show. The rage and threatenings of the sea will not move him though they stir from its depths the upheaving swell: Vesuvius's furnaces may never so often burst forth, and he may send rolling upwards smoke and fire; the lightning, whose wont it is to smite down lofty towers, may flash upon its way, but such men shall they never move. Why then stand they wretched and aghast when fierce tyrants rage in impotence? Fear naught, and hope naught: thus shall you have a weak man's rage disarmed. But whoso fears with trembling, or desires aught from them, he stands not firmly rooted, but dependent: thus has he thrown away his shield; he can be rooted up, and he links for himself the very chain whereby he may be dragged.[1]

The consolation of Philosophy is the speech that takes away fear and thus conquers proud death. But Philosophy has Muses of her own. She heals Boethius with her songs. And in charming away fear, she must also chase away hope.

My book began as a study of philosophical "disappointments" and became a questioning of philosophy's claim to console in the face of death. The burden of the text is an interpretation of three works: the *Phaedo*, Augustine's *Confessions*, and Descartes's *Discourse on Method*. What these works have in common, that is, what first led me to link them, is that they are in some sense "autobiographical." Each recounts a "turning point" in the life of the author, a struggle or disappointment with

5

philosophy that turned the author in a different direction. As I tried to understand the significance of these turning points, two things began to make themselves clear. One cannot write an autobiography without saying or implying something about one's death, that is, without facing one's death. And, then, it began to seem that these three works are not, after all, autobiographies. The *Phaedo* is a myth, *The Confessions* is a prayer, the *Discourse* is a fable. Philosophy has Muses of her own.

When Philosophy consoles in the face of death, she is defending the philosophical life. She reminds Boethius of what he has been and of what he is: "Do you remember that you are a man? . . . Can you say what is a man?" When Boethius answers that man is an animal, reasoning and mortal, Philosophy knows the cause of his sickness: "You have forgotten what you are. . . . You are overwhelmed by this forgetfulness of yourself."[2] Boethius's "forgetfulness" is a version of the sickness to which the philosopher is most susceptible from within, and of the attack to which philosophy is most often subjected from without. This is the suspicion that philosophy is "mere words."

The *Phaedo, The Confessions,* and the *Discourse* are defenses of the activity, indeed of the worth of the lives, of the authors. The defenses are, in one sense, the same in each: the kind of life presented is a life that leads to immortality. But in the *Phaedo* and the *Discourse* this defense must be seen in its poetic context. The "immortality" that is promised is an imitation of an activity done in *this* life. In *The Confessions,* death is presented as having been truly overcome. The defenses that are given in the *Phaedo* and the *Discourse* are accomplished by means of a deliberate lack of precision concerning the distinction between theoretical and moral excellence. But in the *Phaedo* this is a blurring of the distinction which preserves both terms. In the *Discourse,* the distinction ultimately collapses: Descartes attempts the radical reorientation of philosophy as such toward the practical.

In this respect, Augustine is much closer to the ancient than to the modern position: the life of contemplation, the activity of "useless" prayer (especially the prayer of praise) is actually displayed in *The Confessions.* Yet, Descartes's radical reorientation of philosophy could not have taken place without the change in the notion of the divine that is manifested in *The Confessions.* Descartes's reorientation presupposes the Augustinian notion of the divine as actor, as compassionate actor, in contrast to the classical philosophical notion of the divine as disinterested spectator.

This classical notion is inseparable from the view that philosophy is a divine activity that is done by human beings. Nowhere is the philosophical tension between divine and human so strikingly displayed as in Socrates, especially in the *Phaedo*. Here, philosophy is defined as the separation of soul and body, as the practice of death. This definition appears to dominate the entire discussion. But another definition is also presented and then seems to be forgotten: Philosophy is the greatest music. The philosopher "sings charms" everyday to charm away the fear of death. Descartes's fable too exerts its power through its "charm." The soothing message of the *Discourse* is that pain, misery, ignorance and even death can be overcome.

The possibility of this Cartesian overcoming of death depends upon the securing of an unshakeable point, an Archimedean point, from which the world can be moved. Yet the position of analytic philosophy today is one of embarrassment at its own powerlessness. At most it is the observer of the power of science. And the only causes of wonder are the man-made things, especially those which imitate the human. Descartes's "defense" of philosophy really brings about its destruction: it is left with nothing worthwhile of its own. In the *Discourse*, Descartes completely identifies himself with the accusation that philosophy is "mere words." By identifying the good and important with the useful, Descartes reduces philosophy to the position of a pleasant diversion.

Thus, modern philosophy can only end in what Husserl has called "the despair of one who has the misfortune to be in love with philosophy."[3] And this despair finally takes the form of the withering of philosophy to a kind of precise powerlessness such as we find articulated by Gilbert Ryle:

> I conclude, then, that there is, after all, a sense in which we can properly inquire and even say "what it really means to say so and so." For we can ask what is the real form of the fact recorded when this is concealed or disguised and not duly exhibited by the expression in question. And we can often succeed in stating this fact in a new form of words which does exhibit what the other failed to exhibit. And I am for the present inclined to believe that this is what philosophical analysis is, *and that this is the sole and whole function of philosophy.* But I do not want to argue this point now.
>
> But, as confession is good for the soul, I must admit that I do not very much relish the conclusions toward which these conclusions point. I would rather allot to philosophy a sublimer task than the detection of the sources in linguistic idioms of recurrent misconstructions and absurd theories. But that it is at least this I cannot feel any serious doubt.[4] [Emphasis added.]

To claim that "transmutation of syntax" is the sole and whole function of philosophy is not simply modesty. It is ultimately the acceptance of the view that philosophy is "mere words." And if this is so, then philosophy is indeed defenseless because trival.

The defense of philosophy presented in the *Phaedo* is precisely a defense against the accusation that philosophy is "idle talk." Philosophy is indeed a "sublimer task" than the transmutation of syntax. But it is also an "endless task." The *Phaedo* invites us to distinguish between "endless" and "futile." To make this distinction is to do something which must be distinguished from the detection of a source in a linguistic idiom of a recurrent misconstruction or absurd theory.

My intention, then, is to pose once more the question of the nature of philosophy, especially insofar as that nature is revealed in the claim that the philosophical life is a preparation for death. That is, I want to ask whether philosophy has any real power. In what way and to what extent is the activity of philosophy an overcoming of death?

The claim that philosophy overcomes death and leads to immortality is inseparable from the claim that philosophy begins in wonder. Wonder entails a stepping outside of the everyday immersion in action, in the web of means and ends which has to do with preservation. In this respect, wonder is the assumption of a more-than-human stance. It is the posture of the disinterested spectator. But, at the same time, in the very act of escaping the demands imposed by mortality, philosophy presupposes that mortality. Thus, the proper task of philosophy is to be a meditation on death. It is in this task that its power is revealed.

Here we begin to see the vulnerable position in which philosophy is placed by the very questioning of its power. Insofar as philosophy begins in wonder, insofar as it seeks simply to know, it is necessarily useless. It is not a means to an end, but is itself an end. To require a defense of it is to require that it show what it has accomplished for us, that is, that it demonstrate its usefulness as a means to some end other than itself.

My attempt to deal with these questions (against the background of the *Phaedo, The Confessions,* and the *Discourse*) leads to two related conclusions. Philosophy does not herself console. In order to defend herself, she needs the arts of rhetoric and poetry. Indeed, she must "sing charms every day." The *Phaedo* is a myth; the *Discourse* is a fable. This inability to console of herself is the ultimate powerlessness of philosophy. Death is not overcome, the immortality of the gods is not achieved.

The prayer of Augustine is indeed a consolation which even claims to have its consoling power not from myth but from the Truth itself. But the very need for this consolation shows that Augustine's position in the face of death is one of hope. And hope is neither courage nor certitude.

In the distinctions among courage and hope and certitude the true power of philosophy can be made manifest. Philosophy is not an escape from death but it is a preparation for death. Socrates, on the day of his death, appears to be the disinterested spectator of his own death. But this god-like separation of soul and body is, at the same time, a courageous ruling of the body. Socratic meditation on death is not the search for certitude about the immortality of the soul. It is not the search for knowledge either as the end of the detached observer or as the means of the moral agent in the face of death. It is the search for wisdom and, therefore, at the same time, a preparation for death. Precisely if, and only if, philosophy does not seek to be useful, to be a means to some other end, it has its proper effect. Socrates's death is a display of the real power of philosophy as the search for wisdom.

Socrates: Penelope and the Bee

The *Phaedo* as Apology

The *Phaedo* is another apology and is meant to be compared with the *Apology of Socrates*. In one sense, the two dialogues mirror each other as opposites, yet they are ultimately concerned with the same questions. Together and in contrast with each other they reveal Socrates's understanding of the nature of philosophy. And what forces itself on us at once is that, whatever the nature of philosophy as practiced by Socrates may be, it is always vulnerable, always under attack, and always in need of defense.[1]

That the *Phaedo* is intended by Plato to be taken as another apology is clear from the early part of the dialogue where Simmias and Cebes accuse Socrates of being too eager to die. Socrates takes what they say as an "accusation" against which he must defend himself as if he were in a court of law (63b). The conversation here is playful in contrast to the serious, if ironic, speech of the *Apology*. Although some of those present on the day of Socrates's death were also present at the trial, the audiences are, on the whole, very different. This contrast between friendly and hostile audiences suggests one possible way of putting the accusations against which Socrates must defend himself: in the *Apology* he is defending himself for being with others, for sharing himself with everyone indiscriminately, and in the *Phaedo* he must defend himself for being apart from his friends, for separating himself from others.

Another way of expressing the accusations against Socrates is in the explicit manner of the *Apology* itself. There Socrates replies to two groups of accusers: the old, that is, public opinion over the years, and the new, that is, Meletus, Anytus and Lycon who have brought the formal indictment against him. Public opinion, built up over the years, holds that

Socrates is a natural philosopher and a Sophist. In the *Apology* Socrates replies to the first of the old accusations by simply denying it: no one has ever heard him talking about things in the heavens and things under the earth (19d). He replies to the charge of sophistry by distinguishing himself from the Sophists in several ways. He says that he does not claim to teach, he does not take money for what he does, he does not go from city to city and remove the young men from their fellow citizens in order to instruct them in private. The *Apology*, however, also presents us with less obvious responses to these accusations. Socrates's account of his own life, his own activity, as it must be distinguished from both natural philosophy and sophistry, is his response at another level.

The *Phaedo* is also a reply to the charges of natural philosophy and sophistry, a kind of redoing of the *Apology*. The section of the *Phaedo* that is actually labeled an apology begins at 63b and ends at 69e. This is only a small part of the dialogue and consists of Socrates's explanation of why he is not afraid to die, indeed, why he seems quite cheerful on the day he is to die. But, as in the *Apology*, there are more and less obvious lines of defense. The *Phaedo* as a whole, and at least on one level, continues to address itself to the reasons for Socrates's cheerfulness in the face of death. Socrates's explanation of why he is not afraid to die is an account of the life of philosophy, a life that he distinguishes, throughout the dialogue, from natural philosophy and sophistry.

That Socrates might be replying in the *Phaedo* to the charge that he is a natural philosopher is not a surprising claim. In the section of the dialogue where he presents a kind of autobiography (96a-100a), he tells those present that he had been very interested in the "history of nature" as a young man but had been disappointed in this pursuit and had abandoned it. The claim that Socrates is also replying in the *Phaedo* to the charge that he is a Sophist is initially more surprising. But the fact that this reply is less obvious does not mean that it is less important or less central to the dialogue's meaning. Indeed, the distinction between Socrates and the Sophists is the point, the center, to which the *Phaedo* is constantly leading us and to which we will return.

Comedy, Tragedy, Philosophy

It has often been noted that, in reading a Platonic dialogue, the actions of the characters must be taken into account: a dialogue is not a treatise. Certainly the *Phaedo* presents us with dramatic action. The entire dialogue leads up to and is always looking ahead to Socrates's drinking the poison. The *Apology* culminates in two separate actions: the jury votes first to find him guilty, and then to sentence him to death.

Part of what it means to say that the Platonic dialogues are dramatic is that they allow us to see the passions, that the passions at work in a dialogue or deliberately excluded from it must also be taken into account in the interpretation of the dialogue. In the *Apology*, Socrates's defense of the life of philosophy provokes anger, the same anger that caused his prosecutors to bring him to trial. Socrates says this himself in two ways: when his audience shouts at him he asks them not to be angry with him, and in his account of his questioning of the politicians, poets, and artisans he says that his interlocutors often became angry.

Now it does seem undeniable that Socrates is deliberately provoking anger in the *Apology* or, at the very least, he does nothing to moderate the anger that he knows is building. This is true even in the speech he makes between the time of his conviction and his sentencing. The *Apology* thus becomes a demonstration of the causes that brought him to trial. The dialogue that is so unusual in being a kind of formal speech by Socrates in a court of law is, in its provocation of anger, an illustration of the response he usually encounters, a response which confirms his analysis of why he is on trial at all.

The anger that Socrates says he provoked by his questioning (23c) might be characterized as anti-philosophical. Those whom he questions become angry at him instead of at themselves when they are shown to know little or nothing about matters in which they think themselves wise. The instance of this in the dialogues that turns out to be most relevant for the *Apology* is the scene in the *Meno* where Socrates makes Anytus reveal himself as a fool. Anytus, of course, comes back in the *Apology* as one of the prosecutors, having displayed his anger in the *Meno*. One instance in the dialogues which makes a striking contrast with this kind of response to Socrates's questioning is in the *Theaetetus*. Theaetetus is shown to be ignorant of what knowledge is, but he is never angry at Socrates for this revelation. Indeed, at the end of the dialogue Socrates refers to Theaetetus as having become even more gentle than he was before through the questioning of Socrates.

What distinguishes Theaetetus from Anytus is that Theaetetus is "philosophical." This point is made quite explicitly at the beginning of the dialogue and culminates in Socrates's description of himself as a midwife. Theaetetus feels anxiety when he thinks of certain questions. This anxiety is wonder, and philosophy begins in wonder. Socrates's function as midwife is to help Theaetetus deliver an opinion, a definition of knowledge, which they will then examine to see if it is true or false. Theaetetus is grateful to Socrates for this service and does not become angry with Socrates because his own opinions are false. Like Socrates, Theaetetus wants to know that he does not know.

The metaphor for Socrates's activity that is used in the *Apology* and that must be contrasted with the midwife metaphor is, of course, that of the gadfly. And the gadfly metaphor is perfectly apt for what happens in the *Apology* where anti-philosophical anger dominates the hearers, and the brief exchange with Meletus, instead of causing Meletus's humiliation, only further inflames the spectators. There is also a metaphor for Socrates's activity presented in the *Phaedo*, a metaphor that is hardly noticed but which complements the gadfly metaphor and even recalls Meno's characterization of Socrates as a torpedo fish. In the section of the *Phaedo* that deals with the hatred of argument, Socrates compares himself to a bee (91c) or, more precisely, he says that he does not want to go off like a bee leaving his sting in his friends. This metaphor and the context in which it is placed are central to my interpretation of the *Phaedo* and I will return to them later. What chiefly concerns us now is the role of the passions in the dialogue and the relevance of the presence or absence of certain passions for an understanding of the Socratic practice of philosophy.

The anger which so dominates the *Apology* is absent from the *Phaedo*. We not only infer its absence, we are told that it is absent. At the end of the dialogue the servant of the eleven comes and stands beside Socrates and says: "Socrates, I shall not find fault with you, as I do with others, for being angry and cursing me, when at the behest of the authorities, I tell them to drink the poison. No, I have found you in all this time and in every way the noblest and gentlest and best man who has ever come here, and now I know that your anger is directed against others, not against me, for you know who are to blame" (116c). We learn from Socrates that he and this unnamed man have talked sometimes while Socrates has been in prison and we realize that his knowledge of Socrates is the result of these conversations. What the man's remarks show is not that Socrates is incapable of anger or feels no anger, but that the anger which he does feel is directed toward those who deserve it. The man's remarks also indicate that Socrates is most unusual in this respect. It is easy to imagine and not at all surprising that men who are about to be executed might not be especially precise about the distribution of their anger. The surprising thing is not the failure of the moderation of anger in this circumstance but rather the evidence of its being controlled. Thus, it may not be correct to say that anger is absent entirely from the *Phaedo*. The brief speech of the servant of the eleven implies its controlled, hidden presence.

Far more surprising than the absence or control of anger is the absence or apparent absence of fear. This is so surprising as to be almost incredible. We are forced to doubt the veracity of Phaedo's account. Fear of death is so thoroughly excluded from Phaedo's report that his final description of Socrates as good, wise, and just, excludes the virtue of courage, precisely the virtue that would ordinarily account for the manner of facing death that Phaedo has just reported of Socrates. This exclusion of the fear of death also begins Phaedo's report: Socrates seemed happy, fearless and noble.

Phaedo is less surprised at Socrates than he is at his own feelings. Of course, Socrates's conduct and appearance are the cause of Phaedo's strange feelings. What Phaedo finds most strange and "wonderful," is that he did not feel any pity. Pity is the fitting and the usual response to being present at the death of one's friend and because it is usual, Phaedo wonders at its absence. Also absent was Phaedo's usual pleasure in discussion. As customary, their talk was of philosophy but their customary pleasure was missing (58e-59a). What Phaedo did experience was a strange feeling, an unaccustomed mixture of pleasure and pain, when he thought that Socrates was going to die. And all of those present, he says, felt the same way. This unaccustomed mixture of pleasure and pain shows itself in their sometimes laughing and sometimes weeping.

We see from Phaedo's opening description of their feelings that Socrates does not provoke the passion of pity. He is not pitiable even in the face of imminent death. The *Phaedo* is not a tragedy. This is made clear not only in Phaedo's opening description of their feelings but also in his remarks at the end of the dialogue. When they saw Socrates drink the poison they could no longer control their tears. But Phaedo is careful to say that he did not weep for Socrates; he wept for himself, for his own misfortune in losing such a friend (117d).

Of course, we have no direct knowledge of what Socrates's feelings were on the day of his death. He is presented in Phaedo's account as cheerful, happy, and without fear. This absence of fear makes Socrates seem inhuman. We cannot, I think, overlook the impression that a man who shows no fear in these circumstances must be grossly insensitive. Or, if he is not lacking the ordinary human feelings, then he must have a firm, unshakeable belief in the immortality of the soul, absolute certitude that death is not the end of his existence. As we will see, Socrates does not lack the ordinary human feelings. But neither does he have a firm and certain conviction that the soul is immortal. What, then, can account for his extraordinary behavior in the face of death?

As noted above, the *Phaedo* is surely a dramatic representation of Socrates, but it is not a tragedy. The most striking proof of Socrates's fearlessness is the manner in which he actually drinks the poison: "He took [the cup] and very gently, Echecrates, without trembling or changing color or expression, . . . he raised the cup to his lips and very cheerfully and quietly drained it" (117b-c). There is no hint of "overcoming" here. It is made to look easy. This is why no pity is evoked. And throughout the dialogue Socrates never cries. He does laugh and smile several times. And he jokes so that the others laugh in spite of themselves (64b, 77e). The conversation is about death and so the jokes are about death. The overwhelming impression is that Socrates is completely untroubled on the day of his death.

Again, this makes Socrates seem inhuman, extraordinary. That is, he seems to be either above or below the human, more than human or so grossly insensitive as to be monstrous. Indeed, Socrates's own insistence throughout the dialogue that this day is no different from any other day for him only strengthens this inhuman impression. When Simmias and Cebes hesitate to pursue the possible objections to the claim that the soul is immortal, Socrates laughs and says: "Simmias, I should have hard work to persuade other people that I do not regard my present situation as a misfortune, when I cannot even make you believe it, but you are afraid that I am more fretful now than I used to be" (84e). And he drinks the poison as if it were merely wine. It is precisely Socrates's ordinariness here that is so extraordinary. And as his gentle rebuke to Simmias reveals, he expects his friends to expect his customary behavior. But even they are surprised. For Socrates, the question about the soul has *always* been urgent and serious. For those present, the question has *suddenly* become serious.

There is constant movement in the *Phaedo* between the ordinary and the extraordinary, the customary and the surprising, the familiar and the wonderful. This is the movement of philosophy. But the wonderful is always the human. The characters in the *Phaedo* do not wonder at things in the heavens and things beneath the earth. They wonder at Socrates and he wonders at them. Socrates's last words to them (apart from the final words to Crito) are an expression of his surprise at their uncontrolled weeping: he addresses them as "you strange men." And in the central section, on the hatred of argument, Phaedo tells Echecrates: "I have often wondered at Socrates, but never did I admire him more than then" (88e).

Phaedo and those others present at Socrates's death wonder at him and continue to be surprised at his conduct because, even though they know him well and indeed are his friends, they do regard him as human, not as a god and surely not as a monster or an insensitive brute. Phaedo's final description of Socrates is of "the best and wisest and most righteous *man*." [Emphasis added.] Socrates is extraordinary but he is, nevertheless, a man. Is he, then, really totally free of the fear of death?

The gods, of course, are totally free of the fear of death: they are "the immortals." And the gods in Homer, for example, do not cry. They do laugh, often in ridicule. Socrates's laughter on the day of his death and his making jokes about death seem, in a way, god-like. He comes close to showing contempt for death. But there are at least two places in the dialogue where we are given a glimpse of something else, of a human appearance uncovered and covered again in the twinkling of an eye. In the section on the hatred of argument Socrates gives us a hint of his private, otherwise hidden state of mind: "For I fear that I am not now being philosophical about this particular question, but am contentious, like quite uncultured persons. . . . I shall not be eager to make what I say seem true to my hearers, except as a secondary matter, but shall be very eager to make myself believe it" (91a). There is a hint of struggle here, a suggestion of overcoming. And near the beginning of the discussion of the immortality of the soul, Socrates says: "I do not think that anyone who heard us now, even if he were a comic poet, would say that I am talking idly and speaking about things which do not concern me" (70b-c).[2] There is laughter in the *Phaedo* but there is no lack of concern about death. The laughter may in fact be, as laughter so often is, a cover for deep concern.

The laughter and tears of the *Phaedo* are not the laughter and tears of comedy and tragedy: Socrates is neither pitiable nor ridiculous. But to say that the *Phaedo* is neither comedy nor tragedy is not to deny that it is poetry. From its internal myths and mythical speech about Hades to its overall poetic form it is, as Aristotle calls the Socratic conversations, an imitation by words alone, an imitation of action.[3] But this is poetry in the service of philosophy, poetry as useful, as the "handmaiden" of philosophy. And the action that is imitated in the dialogue is not the death of Socrates but the rule of soul over body.

Again, the degree to which Socrates rules his body—to the extent that he does not even tremble or turn pale—seems either incredible or inhuman. Trembling and turning pale come close to being involuntary.[4]

We would certainly not hesitate to judge a man brave in the face of death simply because he trembled or turned pale. In this sense, Phaedo presents Socrates as more than heroic and, we cannot help thinking, as more than human. But the overwhelming proof of Socrates's humanness is that he *does* really die. In this, he is perfectly ordinary.

The tension between the ordinary and the extraordinary in Socrates, the tension between the commonness of death itself and the extraordinary manner in which he faces death, is one way of raising the issue of inequality among men. The members of any other animal species are, in any important sense, equal. But the human species includes a remarkable range, both morally and intellectually. Our own century is hardly lacking in instances of depravity and cruelty so great as to be considered lower than bestial. It also has its heroes who have risen above what could be expected of even a decent man. In terms of intelligence, the inequality between the philosopher and the non-philosopher has been held by some to be so great that philosophy has been called a divine activity.[5]

There is surely a strong tendency in the *Phaedo* toward characterizing philosophy as divine. In what is clearly mythical speech about reincarnation, the soul of the philosopher enters into communion with the gods after death. The other members of the human species pass into other species, depending on the lives they have led, and some even become men again. This mythical speech takes into account the wide range of possibilities included in the animal species 'man' (81e-82c).

But there is another sense of the divine in the *Phaedo*, a sense that does not, at least explicitly, limit itself to philosophy or to the soul of the philosopher. This sense of the divine is introduced at the very end of the argument that attempts to prove the immortality of the soul by linking it to the uncompounded and unchanging. Almost as an afterthought, Socrates associates the soul with the divine and the body with the mortal because the soul rules the body (80a). The condition in which the soul rules the body is the condition in which "the soul and the body are joined together." That is to say, our present condition, the condition of life, is that of the soul ruling the body. In this the soul is "like" the divine.

The point I wish to focus on now is illustrated in part by the contexts in which these two passages about the divine appear. These discussions of the immortality of the soul, when considered together with the other discussions of immortality, reveal the fundamental difficulty that emerges in the *Phaedo* with respect to any attempt to defend the claim that the soul is immortal.

It is possible, I think, to divide the discussions of immortality into two kinds: mythical speech and arguments. The mythical speech about immortality in the *Phaedo* usually, if not always, distinguishes the philosopher from all other men. For example, only the soul of the philosopher can commune with the divine (82b-c); the philosopher need not fear death (67e-68b); the purified soul of the philosopher will dwell with the gods (69c).

The major arguments for the immortality of the soul are three: the argument based on "opposites come from opposites" (70c-72a), the argument linking the soul to the uncompounded (78b-80c), and the argument that hinges on the claim that an opposite can never become its own opposite (100b-107a). (I omit here the argument based on the claim that knowledge is recollection, regarding it, for the time being, as a supporting argument for the claim that the soul existed before entering the body. I also omit the arguments refuting Simmias's claim that the soul is a harmony.) Of these three major arguments, two share an insurmountable difficulty, a difficulty not noted by Socrates's interlocutors but actually pointed to by Socrates himself. The first and third arguments both prove the immortality of everything that ever was or is alive. They cannot be limited to human souls. If the proof for the immortality of the soul is made to rest on what must be true of life, on what necessarily belongs to the living, it cannot distinguish between men and mosquitoes or between men and weeds.

Socrates is well aware of this. Indeed, he says it quite clearly at the very beginning of the first argument, the argument based on the principle that opposites come from opposites: "If you wish to find this out easily, do not consider the question with regard to men only, but with regard to all animals and plants and, in short, to all things which may be said to have a beginning" (70d).[6] These two arguments prove too much. They amount to the claim that nothing ever really dies. The second argument is in principle not exempt from the same difficulty. It is rescued because in the chain that connects the soul to the uncompounded, Socrates inserts two specifically human links: the "forms" as they function in discussion (78d-e), and the soul's likeness to the divine insofar as it rules the body (80a).

It must also be noted that these three arguments differ in strength. The first is said to arrive at a conclusion that is "necessary" (72a). At a crucial point in the third argument Socrates asks Cebes if it has now been "proved" that the soul is immortal and Cebes agrees that it has been proved and even "quite satisfactorily" (105e). The second argument, the only one of the three that attempts to locate the specifically human, is the weakest. After Socrates has linked the soul to the uncompounded, he asks: "Can we say anything else to show that this is not so?" (80b). When Cebes can say nothing to show that it is not so, Socrates leads him to conclude that the soul is entirely indissoluble, "or nearly so" (80b). What is also characteristic of this second argument is that it rests only on the likely: the soul is most *like* the divine and immortal and simple and unchanging (80b). The likely is the probable. And Simmias, in a different context, comments on the inferiority of arguments based on mere probability: "Those arguments which base their demonstrations on mere probability are deceptive, and if we are not on our guard against them they deceive us greatly, in geometry and all other things" (92d).

The argument that does address itself most directly to the indestructibility of the *human* soul is the weakest; there are no claims made for the necessity of its conclusion. And, again, the stronger arguments prove too much. It is only the mythical speech of the *Phaedo* that distinguishes between good and bad souls, promising punishment to the wicked and happiness to the good (see for example, 81d-82c).

There is at least one conclusion to be drawn from this discussion concerning the immortality of the soul, a conclusion that will be decisive for my interpretation of the *Phaedo*. The arguments for the immortality of the soul are not very good arguments, and, since Socrates himself refutes them within the dialogue, we can infer that Socrates is aware of their weaknesses.[7] There are also several points to be emphasized. The only argument for immortality that does introduce the specifically human is based on the probable. The two senses of the divine, the practice of philosophy and the rule of soul over body, are two characteristics of the human as distinguished from other animals. And the tension between ordinary and extraordinary in Socrates's death is a manifestation of the tension between the animal and the specifically human, or divine.

This last point leads us to consider again the issue of inequality among men. This issue is addressed in mythical speech and in Socrates's refutation of Simmias's claim that the soul is a harmony. In the mythical speech, the souls of the bad are said to pass into the bodies of the appropriate beasts. The souls of the good are of two kinds: those who have practiced the political virtues called justice and moderation without philosophy, and the philosophers, who are wholly pure. The former pass into a gentle species such as that of bees, wasps, or ants, or even into the human species again. The latter enter into communion with the gods (81d-82c). What this account does is to locate the human— the "most human" of all the human possibilities—at the level of political virtue practiced without philosophy, but instead practiced out of habit (82b).

In Socrates's refutation of Simmias's claim that the soul is a harmony, the issue of inequality is also addressed, and in a twofold manner. The second part of Socrates's refutation is the argument that if the soul is a harmony then it follows that all souls are equally souls and that all souls are equally good: "According to this argument, then, if all souls are by nature equally souls, all souls of all living things will be equally good" (94a). Socrates's refutation of Simmias, then, contains the implicit refutation of two of his own arguments for the immortality of the soul: these arguments must regard all souls of all living things as equal. And the last part of Socrates's response to Simmias contains a possible refutation of his own argument that the soul is uncompounded, or without parts. This part of his response is based on the soul's rule over the body: Socrates argues that the soul cannot both rule the body and be the harmony of the body. As an example of the soul's ruling the body he cites the passage in Homer where Odysseus, still hiding his identity, observes what is happening in his household:

> He struck his breast, and thus rebuked his heart:
> "Endure, my heart, you have endured worse than this."
>
> (XX.17,18)

The soul opposes the body and tyrannizes over it, sometimes inflicting punishments such as gymnastics and medicine. It also speaks to desires, passions, and fears, "as if it were one thing speaking to another thing," as the passage from Homer illustrates (94d).

The description of the soul's rule here may be an implicit refutation of Socrates's linking the soul with the uncompounded, depending upon whether the soul is really ruling the body or itself. That is, the desires, fears, and passions are here relegated to the body and this is the tendency throughout the *Phaedo*. Man is two (79b), soul and body. Not only the bodily appetites but also fear and anger are treated as belonging to the body. This amounts to a very Cartesian-like identification of soul and nous.[8] (I do not mean to imply that nous is the equivalent of Descartes's 'mind'.)

The division of man into two and the relegation of all passion to the body does allow for an uncompounded soul. It also has the effect of placing the soul "in" the body as a pilot in his ship. But the kind of opposing and ruling that characterizes the soul's relation to the body in the *Phaedo* is quite different from the opposing and ruling of the soul in the *Republic*.⁹ There the soul does have parts; the passions are not relegated to the body, and when the soul rules them it rules itself.

The rule of the soul over bodily appetites is tyrannical. That is, hunger cannot be persuaded to go away. The soul must force itself and the body not to eat, but appetite does not disappear. Hunger arises within the body and is caused by the body. But fear and anger, the passions identified as the "spirited part" in the *Republic*, are not caused by the body. They do not occur without some intelligence. Their beginnings are in the realization that one is threatened or unjustly treated. Certainly they are felt in the body and manifest themselves in ways that are visible through the body. But the spirited part, and in some sense even the bodily appetites, are "shared" by body and soul.

Fear and anger, the passions of the "third," spirited part of the soul, are the dominant passions of the *Phaedo* and the *Apology*. Even if Socrates is truly without fear, the others are not. The whole discussion of the immortality of the soul is prompted by their fear of death. After Socrates presents the argument based on the claim that opposites come from opposites, he says to Cebes: "'I think you and Simmias would like to carry the discussion further. You have the childish fear that when the soul goes out from the body the wind will really blow it away and scatter it, especially if a man happens to die in a high wind and not in calm weather.' And Cebes laughed and said, 'Assume that we have that fear, Socrates, and try to convince us; or rather, do not assume that we are afraid, but perhaps there is a child in us who has such fears. Let us try to persuade him not to fear death as if it were a hobgoblin'" (77d-e).

Cebes's response here indicates the manner in which the soul rules the passions of fear and anger. The spirited part of the soul is not ruled by force as the bodily appetites are. It is ruled by persuasion, by speech. This is precisely what Odysseus does in the passage cited by Socrates. He speaks to his "heart" and controls his anger.

The exchange between Socrates and Cebes about the fear of death brings us back to our starting point. Here is Socrates, joking about dying on a windy day, and Cebes laughing, perhaps in spite of himself and from embarrassment, covering his shame at being afraid. We can understand why Phaedo would say, at the beginning of the dialogue, that he felt no pity for Socrates and, at the end, that he wept for himself and not for Socrates.

Nevertheless, there may in fact be some tragic element in the *Phaedo*. There is at least an inclusion of tragedy to be contrasted with the exclusion of comedy. After he has finished relating the long myth at the end of the dialogue, Socrates compares himself to a man in a tragedy: "You, Simmias and Cebes and the rest, will go afterwards, each in his own time; but I am now already, as a man in a tragedy would say, called by fate" (115a). The exclusion of comedy occurs toward the beginning of the dialogue when it becomes clear that those present wish to continue talking about death and the immortality of the soul. Socrates says: "Well, I do not think that anyone who heard us now, even if he were a comic poet, would say that I am talking idly and speaking about things which do not concern me. So if you like, we must examine the matter to the end" (70b-c). Socrates is referring, of course, to Aristophanes, who is also mentioned in the *Apology* on account of his portrayal in *The Clouds* of Socrates as a natural philosopher.

Laughter does occur several times in the course of the dialogue: Socrates himself laughs and smiles, and the others also laugh. But Socrates excludes comedy almost from the beginning. Socrates never weeps in the dialogue and he rebukes the others for their tears after he drinks the poison. But he allows a hint of the tragic to enter the end of their discussion.[10] Phaedo, the witness, excludes the feeling of pity: indeed, this is the first thing he does in his report of what happened on the day Socrates died.

We must leave open the question of whether there is tragic action in the *Phaedo*. And we must now raise the question of whether there is heroic action. Socrates's reference to Odysseus shows us the hero overcoming himself, talking to his anger, the anger provoked by his having been treated shamefully in his own household. The reference to Odysseus is complemented by a reference to Penelope. Socrates is speaking in mythical terms about the soul of the philosopher, the soul freed from the body, purified, and thus prepared for communion with the divine: "The soul of the philosopher would reason in this way, and would not think that philosophy should set it free, and that then, being set free, it should give itself back again into bondage to pleasure and pain and practice the futile [endless] task of Penelope" (84a).[11]

These two references are complementary in that the first shows the rule of soul over body (or over itself if anger belongs to the spirited part of the soul) and the second is about the separation of soul and body, which is philosophy. The first concerns heroic action, the second concerns the practice of philosophy. Of course, the comparison here with Penelope is to make the point that the philosopher should *not* be like Penelope, engaged in futile [endless] toil. But there is, as we shall see, a sense in which the philosopher is like Penelope, a sense in which Penelope's weaving and unweaving mirrors what is happening in the *Phaedo* itself.

The notion of toil points to another heroic figure who plays an important role in the imagery of the *Phaedo*. Heracles, the man who by his own strivings became a god, is the hero introduced in the section concerning the hatred of argument. Here Socrates and Phaedo together, like Heracles and Iolaus, do battle against the monster that threatens all of them, the evil that Socrates calls "hatred of argument." It is this section of the dialogue that gives the whole its name. Their battle against this monster recalls the very beginning of the dialogue where Phaedo tells Echecrates why Socrates's execution was delayed: the Athenians were celebrating the annual festival, in honor of Apollo, commemorating Theseus's slaying the Minotaur and saving the fourteen Athenian youths. The purpose of Plato's including the Theseus legend in the *Phaedo*, indeed opening the dialogue with it, may very well be to set the stage for the action of the dialogue as Socrates's saving those present from the monster of the fear of death.[12] But the greatest evil that can happen to a man, as Socrates says later in the dialogue, is to become a misologist, a hater of arguments. This, I think, is the true battle of the *Phaedo*, a battle that Socrates thinks he wins. And this victory makes the *Phaedo*, for Socrates, a successful apology. The analysis of the section concerning the hatred of argument and its place in the dialogue as a whole will be central to my subsequent discussion of the Socratic practice of philosophy. What I wish to focus on now is, again, the notion of heroic action, the question of whether there is heroic action in the *Phaedo*.

It is certainly plausible to identify Socrates in the *Phaedo* with Theseus and Heracles. Socrates himself suggests the latter comparison. The dialogue also allows for comparison of Socrates with Odysseus, who, in the passage cited by Socrates, rules his "heart." But the least obvious and perhaps most important comparison with a named figure may be with Penelope, in spite of the fact that Socrates says the philosopher should not be like Penelope, engaged in futile toil.

The figures of Odysseus and Penelope, as noted above, complement each other in the *Phaedo*. Odysseus is presented as ruling his passions, as an instance of the rule of soul over body, and Penelope as an example of what the philosopher should not do and does not do because his soul is freed from the body. These two figures reflect the two senses of the divine mentioned in the dialogue.

If we further consider Socrates's reference to Penelope we realize that it is not entirely accurate to characterize her work as futile. It would be futile if she were really trying to finish the weaving, to produce a completed product. But this is not Penelope's *real* task. Her true purpose is to put off the suitors, and at this she is successful. She succeeds not by doing battle with them but by deception. The weaving is done openly, the unweaving is concealed. Socrates himself is famous for his concealing; an essential element of the Socratic irony is deception, a kind of feigned ignorance and false modesty. And Socrates almost never indicates to his hearers whether he agrees with what is being said, even when it is being said by himself. We saw an instance in the *Phaedo* where he surely knows that the argument is seriously flawed, even states its implicit refutation, but allows his interlocutors to accept it and does not explicitly raise any objections.

The context for Socrates's saying that the philosopher should not be like Penelope has to do with the freedom from pleasure and pain which philosophy gives to the soul of the philosopher. The philosopher should not undo this by giving himself back into bondage. Such an undoing would make philosophy a futile toil. Socrates is speaking here as if the kind of separation from the body practiced by the philosopher could be accomplished once and for all and need not be constantly repeated as the term "practice" suggests. But the notion that freedom from pleasure and pain is achieved and preserved is contradicted by what happens near the beginning of the dialogue. Socrates's legs are in pain because of the fetters and when he is released the pain is replaced by pleasure.

There is another sense in which this scene contradicts the claim that the philosopher is not engaged in an "endless task." This sense is expressed in what Socrates says about the pain and pleasure he feels: "What a strange thing that seems to be which men call pleasure. How wonderfully it is related to what seems to be its opposite, pain" (60b). Socrates, on the day of his death, still feels pleasure and pain and still wonders about it. Philosophy begins in wonder and then seeks to replace wonder with knowledge.[13] But the philosopher does not wonder once and for all. He is always slipping back and being caught again in wonder. He is always undoing what he has done; in Socrates's own words, he is always going back to the beginning (107b).

Socrates, then, is indeed like Penelope. In the *Phaedo* he weaves and unweaves arguments and conceals the unweaving. He is also like Odysseus who conceals himself while he controls his passions. But there are certain things that cannot be concealed. Socrates can hide his thoughts, can even deceive about what his thoughts are, but when he takes the cup of poison his hands and his face are visible. Those who are witnesses can see if he is trembling and turning pale.

Actor or Spectator

Phaedo reports that Socrates did not tremble or turn pale when he took the cup and drank the poison. As noted above, trembling and turning pale come very close to being involuntary: we would not call a man a coward in the face of death simply because these things happened to him. Socrates's behavior appears inhuman. He really seems to be completely free of the fear of death. And his laughter and joking throughout his last conversation with his friends gives the impression of a kind of inhuman detachment from the imminence of his own death. Laughter, at least some kinds of laughter, presupposes a certain detachment and distance from what is laughed at. Socrates appears to be a disinterested spectator of his own death, calmly and dispassionately talking about death in the hours before he is to die. The manner in which he excludes comedy allows us a glimpse of what is being concealed: his imminent death is something that "concerns" him. But the overwhelming impression, deliberately created by Plato in Phaedo's report, is that of Socrates as the disinterested spectator of his own death.

The stance of the disinterested spectator is the initial philosophical stance. The initial move from pre-philosophical life to philosophy requires a putting aside of private concerns, of ordinary human concerns, the cares that human beings have in common. This is why philosophy begins as natural philosophy or physics: the human has no special place.

The disinterested spectator removes himself from the immersion in the everyday life of means and ends which is the life of action. It is not surprising, then, that natural philosophy should be more concerned about stars, sun, and all things in the heavens than it is about what is underfoot. This, of course, is what happens to Thales, and the housemaids come out and laugh at him. But there is another, complementary story about Thales. He has his revenge. His ridiculous star-gazing enables him to corner the olive market because he foresees a drought.

These two stories about the first philosopher raise a question that can be raised with respect to Socrates, especially as he is presented in the *Phaedo*. What is the relationship between theory and action? Or more specifically, what is the relationship between Socrates's thoughts and his actions on the day of his death? Before addressing this question directly, some preliminary observations on the difference between Socrates and the natural philosophers need to be made.

In the *Apology*, Socrates denies that anyone has ever heard him talking about things in the heavens and things beneath the earth. He characterizes knowledge of such things as "more-than-human wisdom," and, although he does not assert that knowledge of this kind is impossible for man, he denies that he himself has this knowledge. The inhuman stance of the disinterested spectator of the heavens is the divine stance; natural philosophy attempts to achieve the divine perspective on the world. Socrates's wisdom is only "human wisdom."

It is said that Socrates brought philosophy down to earth, that he turned to ethical matters.[14] Certainly, the Platonic dialogues are concerned with human things, with matters directly related to human action and which all men care and worry about. The *Phaedo* provides us with a perfect example of this: every man must face death, his own and that of his loved ones. Simmias says at the beginning of the discussion: "Well, do you intend to go away, Socrates, and keep this thought to yourself, or would you let us share it? It seems to me that this is a good which belongs in common to us also" (63c-d).

All of those present on the day of Socrates's death must themselves face death. The only difference is that Socrates must face it on that day. And Socrates treats this difference as unimportant, nonessential. The mood that Socrates seeks to create is one of complete ordinariness. He rebukes Simmias for hesitating to raise objections to the argument for the immortality of the soul: "You are afraid that I am more fretful now than I used to be" (84e). Nothing is changed by the fact that this is the day he will surely die.

We can say at least tentatively, then, that Socrates's reorientation of philosophy, his turn to matters of the greatest concern to human beings, is not entirely or simply an abandonment of the stance of the disinterested spectator. Matters of the greatest concern to human beings are precisely those matters which arouse the greatest and strongest passions. In the *Apology* Socrates speaks about justice without becoming angry; in the *Phaedo* he speaks about death without showing fear. Initially we might say that Socrates seems to take the stance of the disinterested spectator, but with respect to human things.

It would also be true to say that Socrates's turn to human things does not mean an abandonment of metaphysics. He was certainly disappointed with natural philosophy and in particular with Anaxagoras (98b). But the context for his brief "autobiography" in the *Phaedo* shows that his turn to human things is not equivalent to a turn away from all things. Socrates is responding to Cebes's claim that the soul may outlive several bodies but that eventually it too perishes: "It is no easy thing that you seek, Cebes; for it is necessary to investigate completely the cause of all generation and destruction. Now I will tell you my own experiences about these things if you wish" (95e-96a).

Socrates, on the day of his death, is still investigating the cause of all generation, destruction, and being. He is not carrying out this investigation in the manner of the natural philosophers; he has a way of his own. More importantly, he is not seeking the same *kind* of cause: "I am going to try to show you the kind of cause with which I have been busying myself" (100b). And, finally, each of the three major arguments for the immortality of the soul deals with the whole of nature. The last, immediately following the story of the turn from natural philosophy, even introduces the being of numbers.

Having said that Socrates does not abandon the stance of the disinterested spectator, that he seems to take this stance with respect to human concerns, we have to consider another tendency in the dialogue which, at least at first, appears to be in tension with this stance. The tension can also be seen in the passages concerning Odysseus and Penelope. In the Odysseus scene we see the soul ruling the body. The reason for Socrates's reference to Penelope is to show that the philosopher must separate soul from body, must be free from pleasure and pain.

These two apparently very different versions of the relationship between soul and body are both put forward explicitly and often throughout the speech of the dialogue. At the risk of oversimplifying, we can say that the separation of soul from body is what the disinterested spectator strives for, and that the rule of soul over body is what the moral agent strives for, and what is most strikingly displayed in the hero. (I am putting aside for now the whole question of the status of what, in the *Republic*, is called the spirited part of the soul.)

The two versions of the relationship between soul and body strike us at first as very different, if not contradictory, because the notion that soul and body are separable implies that man is two, that soul and body are two distinct things, whereas the notion that the soul rules the body implies a union and suggests inseparability. Of course, as Socrates says in the Odysseus reference, soul ruling body and opposing it also means that they are distinct, but they must be united and need not be separable.

Separation of soul and body and rule of soul over body are both characterized as divine in the *Phaedo*. But only the first makes communion with the divine after death possible. Only the philosopher is purified to the extent that he is free from the body. Rule of soul over body is not necessarily identified with the life of philosophy as such. But the man who is virtuous by reason of habit, without philosophy, does not commune with the gods after death (82a-c).

What all of this is leading to is the conclusion that there are two kinds of moral virtue: the virtue of the philosopher, and the virtue of those who practice moderation and justice out of habit, without philosophy or nous. In fact, we need not rely upon only the mythical speech about rewards and punishments after death in order to find the distinction. In the early section of the dialogue that is explicitly labeled an apology, Socrates argues that only the philosopher is *truly* virtuous. He is speaking here especially of courage and moderation or self-restraint: "'You know, do you not, that all other men count death among the great evils?' — 'They certainly do.' — 'And do not brave men submit to death, when they do submit to it, through fear of greater evils?'—'That is so.' — 'Then all except philosophers are brave through fear and terror. And yet it is absurd to be brave through fear and cowardice.' . . . Courage, and self-restraint, and justice and, in short, true virtue exist only with wisdom (*phronēsis*)'" (68d-e; 69b).

What is being asserted here is that there is a necessary connection between true moral virtue and philosophy. This is indeed an apology for the practice of philosophy; one could hardly think of a better way to justify the practice of philosophy to society, and one wonders why Socrates did not make this argument at his trial. In any case, he does make it here in the *Phaedo* to his friends, to the friends of philosophy, who accept it without anger. It should also be noted that true virtue, the virtue of the philosopher, is also, to some extent, the result of habit: the philosopher is not afraid of death because he has been "practicing."

At least on the level of appearance, the necessary connection between philosophy and moral virtue is displayed by the drama of the dialogue. Socrates attributes his calmness and even cheerfulness in the face of death to his having lived the philosophical life. That he does not tremble or turn pale when he takes the cup is his successful apology for the practice of philosophy. That he was condemned to die at all is due to the failure of his apology to the city of Athens.

As noted above, the toil of Penelope can only be called useless if her task is really to accomplish the weaving. Her true task is to hold off the suitors, and at this she succeeds by deception. What the *Phaedo* seems to present us with is a weaving and unweaving of arguments, the "futile toil" of philosophy, but also with complete success at the task of holding off the fear of death. We cannot help wondering whether or not there is deception at work here also. The connection between philosophy and moral action, between theory and practice, is not quite so simple as my discussion thus far has allowed it to seem.

Socrates appears in the *Phaedo* as a spectator, the (almost) disinterested spectator of his own death, and he appears as an actor, taking the cup and drinking the poison without trembling or turning pale. And throughout the dialogue he seems to conduct himself as if there were a causal link between theory and practice. That is, there are strong indications that Socrates faces death cheerfully *because* he believes that the soul is immortal.

Socrates never openly argues in the *Phaedo* that the soul perishes with the body. He always argues that the soul is immortal and he refutes the objections of Simmias and Cebes when they are not convinced of this. The fact that Socrates always takes only that side of the argument creates the impression that this is what he truly believes, and, thus, that his action at the end of the dialogue is simply consistent with and follows from the arguments for the immortality of the soul.

If we consider the first of what I have called the three major arguments for immortality, we see that Socrates begins from myth: "Let us consider it in some such way as this, by asking whether the souls of men who have died are in Hades are not. There is an ancient account, which we remember, that they go there from here and come back here again and are born from the dead" (70c). And, in fact, this metaphorical way of talking about the soul, as if it were "in" Hades or "in" a body, runs throughout the dialogue. To speak of the soul this way is to speak of it as if it were a body. This is one of the first assumptions of the speech of the *Phaedo* that must be "carefully examined" (107b).

Socrates begins the second argument by explicitly linking argument and action in a causal relationship: "Must we not ask ourselves some such question as this? To what kind of thing is it proper to undergo scattering, and for what kind of thing should we fear it, and for what kind of thing should we not fear it? And after this must we not inquire to which of the two the soul belongs *and fear or not fear for our souls depending upon the answers to these questions?*" (78b) [Emphasis added.]

The third argument, the response to Cebes, begins: "It is no easy thing that you seek; for it is necessary to investigate completely the cause of all generation and destruction" (95e). In order to show that the soul is indestructible, they must first investigate the cause of all destruction and then see whether or not the soul is a kind of thing that can be affected by that cause. Although Socrates does not explicitly repeat the connection between argument and hope or fear, it would be appropriate to introduce the third argument in the same way as the second: "And after this [investigating the cause of all destruction] must we not inquire to which of the two the soul belongs [that is, whether it is destructible or not] and fear or not fear for our souls depending upon the answers to these questions?"

Again, the impression is that Socrates's actions, in which he shows no fear, are based on what he knows about the indestructibility of the soul. But, as we saw earlier, the arguments for the immortality of the soul are all unwoven within the dialogue itself. The first and third are each undone by taking one of Socrates's own beginning remarks and showing that the argument leads to a totally unacceptable conclusion. That is, Socrates himself tells us that the arguments based on life simply must include all animals and plants (70d): the unacceptable conclusion is that nothing ever really dies. The second argument, linking the soul to the uncompounded, is undone if the example of Odysseus really shows that the soul has parts, as Socrates discusses it in the *Republic*.[15]

That the arguments for the immortality of the soul do not provide absolute certitude is even made explicit at the end of the third major argument. Although Simmias cannot find anything wrong with the argument he still cannot help having some doubt about what has been said. Socrates answers: "Not only that, Simmias, but our first assumptions ought nevertheless to be more carefully examined, even if they are trusted by us" (107b). It is necessary to go back to the beginning again, like Penelope at her endless task.

The initial impression of a direct, causal connection between theory and action, then, simply fades away. Socrates does not act as he does in the face of death *because* he is certain about the immortality of the soul. There is instead a gap between theory and action in the *Phaedo*. This gap can perhaps be best expressed as the gap between the uncertainty of the arguments and the certitude of action: the arguments are "shaky," but Socrates does not tremble.

Another way of putting this conclusion is to say that there is a kind of coexistence of doubt and sureness, doubt in thought and sureness in action. This gap, or coexistence, is most acute, of course, in Socrates. The others feel some uncertainty about the arguments but do not see the unweaving, and their actions at the end are uncertain and changeable. Socrates is more sure in both ways: he is fully aware of the difficulties in the arguments but completely unhesitating in taking the poison, even to the point of not waiting as long as he might have.

If Socrates's certitude of action is not based on certitude of belief, or rather on certain knowledge, then what can possibly account for it? There are two responses that could simply sidestep the question. Perhaps Socrates's certitude of action is based on other arguments not made in the *Phaedo*, arguments that he keeps secret and does not share with them for their common good (63c-d). The other possibility is that Phaedo is lying and that Socrates did at least tremble and turn pale. It seems to me that the only way to eliminate the first explanation would be to show that there could not be any argument that would definitively prove the immortality of the soul, that the nature of argument is such that no such proof is possible. With respect to the suspicion that Phaedo is lying, I am not sure how that could be confirmed with perfect assurance. But there are two things that would lend weight to the view that Phaedo is not reporting what really happened. If it could be shown that he is hiding the truth at some other point in the dialogue, then we would at least be open to the possibility that he is hiding the truth about Socrates's end. And if it could somehow be shown that no man could possibly act in the face of death as Phaedo reports of Socrates, then we would have to regard Phaedo's report with some uncertainty of our own.

If either of these two responses is correct, then there may be no gap between theory and action in the *Phaedo* that needs to be accounted for. There are either hidden, certain arguments upon which Socrates's unhesitating actions are based, or Phaedo is concealing what really happened. There seems to me to be no evidence in the dialogue that Socrates is concealing a better argument for immortality than the deficient ones he is presenting. Rather, the evidence is that he is concealing his own fear of death. I am referring to the two glimpses we are given into the fact that he is not a disinterested spectator of his own imminent death.

There is, however, reason to think that Phaedo is willing to conceal: there is evidence that his report is less than totally frank. This raises the question of whether Phaedo's account *is* really a report.[16] Phaedo, we must be aware, is not a disinterested spectator. True, he is a witness to what happened: this is the point of the very first lines of the dialogue. Echecrates asks him: "Were you with Socrates yourself, Phaedo, on the day when he drank the poison in prison, or did you hear about it from someone else?" Phaedo answers, "I was there myself, Echecrates" (57a). And he gives his assurance that he will try to tell them "everything from the beginning" (59c).

The evidence of Phaedo's willingness to be less than frank, or to be more than a reporter, concerns an instance in which, I think it can be shown, he hides his own identity. In the third argument for the immortality of the soul, Socrates relies heavily on the notion that an opposite can never become or be its own opposite. After he has insisted on this point with many examples, Cebes seems completely convinced and ready to hear the rest of the argument. Phaedo tells Echecrates: "Then, hearing this, one of those present—I don't remember clearly who it was—said: 'By the gods, did we not agree earlier in our discussion to the very opposite of what is now being said, that the greater comes to be from the smaller, and the smaller from the greater, and that opposites simply come to be from their opposites. But now it seems to me we are saying that this would never happen.'" (103a). There is reason to think that the one who makes this objection is Phaedo himself, and, of course, he would not have forgotten that. The evidence for this identification is found in the section concerning the hatred of argument. There we learn that Phaedo is sitting at Socrates's right hand on a low stool beside his couch and that Socrates's seat was much higher than Phaedo's (89a-b). When the objection is made later, in the third argument, Socrates bends his head on one side and listens. Then he says: "You have spoken up like a man" (103b). In the section concerning hatred of argument, Socrates had recruited Phaedo in the battle, comparing them to Heracles and Iolaus.

Now, I do not regard this identification as completely convincing. But if Phaedo is in fact attempting to hide his identity as the objector, then we cannot expect complete conviction. There is a kind of half-hiding that is being done, ultimately by Plato, and half-hiding means that we will not have total clarity or illumination. But what possible reason could Phaedo have for not wanting to reveal himself to Echecrates as the objector? The same reason that Socrates has for covering over the objection when it is raised.

The objection is not a trivial one.[17] And even if Socrates's very brief answer to it is satisfactory, he hardly allows those present to entertain the notion that the first and third major arguments for immortality might be in contradiction with each other, might "unweave" each other. While Socrates is giving his very brief answer he is looking at Cebes's face. And instead of discussing the objection with the care it merits, Socrates simply pushes ahead, saying to Cebes: "Are you troubled by anything of what this man says?" Cebes's answer is designed to leave room for discussion of the objections: "No, not this time; though I do not deny that many things do trouble me." But Socrates skips over the opening and reasserts the conclusion to which the unnamed man had objected: "Well, we are altogether agreed upon this, that an opposite will never be its own opposite" (103c).

The immediate reason for Socrates's playing down the objection is that he wants to achieve agreement. The words 'agree' and 'agreement' are used so often in this section of the dialogue that we cannot help noticing their frequency. Socrates is striving to unite the hearers in the argument. The one note of discord is brushed aside. Now as Phaedo relates the conversation to Echecrates, he hides his identity as the objector because he has become the ally of Socrates, the Iolaus to Heracles. But the real battle is against the hatred of argument as such and not against any particular argument for the destructibility of the soul.

My reason for introducing the hatred of argument here is to show that Phaedo is an actor in the dialogue, Socrates's partner in action, and not simply a spectator giving his report. And if my identification of Phaedo with the unnamed objector is correct, we see that the *true* task of Socrates, and thus of Phaedo also, may be accomplished by, and may indeed require, deception.

Part of this deception may be Phaedo's description of Socrates's taking the poison without trembling or even turning pale. Of course, I am not entitled to argue that because Phaedo *may* be concealing his identity at one point in the dialogue he is surely deceiving us about Socrates's end. And even if it were certain that Phaedo concealed his own identity it does not follow that he is deceiving us about anything else. But we are entitled to some small suspicion that Phaedo's report is not totally accurate. For the report itself pushes credibility to its limits: it is really difficult to believe that any man could control himself to the extent to which Socrates is said to have done. And when we add to this the weakness of the arguments for immortality, our suspicion grows.

Nothing of what I have said thus far is sufficient to allow the conclusion that there really is no gap between theory and action in the *Phaedo*. The suspicion that Phaedo may not be simply reporting does not justify sidestepping the question: If Socrates's certitude of action is not based on certitude of belief or on certain knowledge, then what does account for it? The answer provided by Socrates in the section identified as his apology seems to be the only other possibility: "Other men are likely not to be aware that those who really engage in philosophy in the true sense of the word practice nothing but dying and death. If this is true, it would be absurd to be eager for nothing but this all their lives, and then to be vexed when that comes for which they have been eager and been practicing for so long" (64a). To say that the philosopher practices dying means that the philosopher separates soul from body, as much as it is possible to do so. And death is the separation of soul and body.

The philosopher's separation of soul and body is the freeing of himself from bondage to the body's pleasures and pains. In the reference to Penelope, Socrates speaks as if this freeing could be done once and for all. But the notion of "practice" implies that it is done over and over, like

Penelope's endless task. And Socrates's own pleasure and pain in his legs at the beginning of the dialogue show that he does still commune with his body.

If we then take Phaedo's account of Socrates's drinking the poison as an accurate report, it seems that we must conclude that Socrates's conduct is due to the practice of philosophy. But this does not mean that philosophy has given him certitude about the immortality of the soul, a proposition in terms of which he acts, suiting his actions to the content of the assertion. Philosophy has left him with uncertainty and doubt. We can only conclude that Socrates acts out of habit, not from knowledge. What happens, then, to the distinction between those who practice virtue out of habit without philosophy and those who are "truly" virtuous because of the separation of soul and body? Both ultimately act from habit, but the philosopher is said to be striving to separate soul and body while the other kind of virtuous man is striving to rule his body, as the reference to Odysseus shows.

The two versions of the relationship between soul and body presented in the *Phaedo*—the soul separating from the body and the soul ruling the body—are both senses in which the soul is said to be divine. And they seem to be quite different relationships. But what the *Phaedo* shows, on the literal level, is that in the philosopher the separation of soul and body and the rule of soul over body are inseparable. That is, what we see in Socrates on the day of his death is that *in this life*, while the separation of soul and body is not complete and not accomplished once and for all, the extent of the separation of soul and body is the extent to which the soul rules the body. Separation and rule are the same action. The separation of soul and body as complete purification is said to make the philosopher suitable for communion with the divine. But this is precisely the point: separation of soul from body to this degree and in this manner is, for Socrates, more than human and not achievable once and for all. This is more-than-human wisdom, which he contrasts with his own "human wisdom" in the *Apology*.

Those who practice philosophy in the true sense of the word are always striving to release the soul from the body (64a). But what 'striving' means is that this release is not accomplished, only approached. *This* life is the condition for philosophy, and it is the condition of the soul together with the body. All of the talk about the condition of the soul after death serves to point up more clearly what the condition of the soul is in this life.

But Phaedo, especially in his description of Socrates's taking the poison, does not show us any struggle in Socrates. We see no effort at overcoming, no hesitation. Phaedo does not feel pity and he does not call Socrates courageous. He calls almost no attention whatever to the rule of soul over body in Socrates. We are given only the briefest glimpses of Socrates's concealing a struggle within himself. In the section concerning hatred of argument, Socrates admits that he wants to win the argument. Winning the argument means conquering himself. Socrates is not the disinterested spectator of his own death. No man can be the disinterested spectator of his own death. The question of the immortality of the soul cannot be, *for human beings*, a "merely" theoretical question. The stance of the disinterested spectator with respect to such questions is the divine, not the human stance.

Hubris and Irony

The two senses in which the soul can be said to be divine, separating from body and ruling body, are exemplified in the philosopher and the hero, in Socrates and Odysseus or Heracles. Heracles, by his own strivings, became a god. The descriptions of the strivings of the philosopher in the *Phaedo* are of a kind of heroic attainment of freedom from the body so as to be suited for communion with the divine. But Socrates's descriptions of his own activities do not really match what he says, usually in mythical speech, about the philosopher's strivings. That is, Socrates appears far more modest.

Hubris is the attempt to go beyond the human, beyond what is appropriate to man by nature. In discussing the science or knowledge called "first philosophy," Aristotle expresses the view that such knowledge is beyond the human: "Evidently then we do not seek it for the sake of any other advantage; but as the man is free, we say, who exists for his own sake and not for another's, so we pursue this as the only free science, for it alone exists for its own sake. Hence also the possession of it might be justly regarded as beyond human power; for in many ways human nature is in bondage; so that according to Simonides 'God alone can have this privilege,' and it is unfitting that man should not be content to seek the knowledge that is suited to him" (*Metaphysics* I. 2). In this passage, the divine character of first philosophy is based on its uselessness, on its being "for its own sake." The knowledge that is suited to man, then, is useful knowledge.

It is because human nature is in many ways in bondage that useful, as distinguished from free, knowledge is the kind for which man is fit. One of the first claims that Socrates makes in the *Phaedo* is that "we men are one of the possessions of the gods" (62b). He is speaking of the reasonableness of the prohibition against suicide: we do not belong to ourselves. What is said here in the language of the "mysteries" is in fact shown to be the case, in at least one important respect, by what happens in the dialogue. The sheer fact of death, our ultimate powerlessness to prevent it, is a demonstration of the fact that we do not own our bodies, at least not in the way we own other bodies. Insofar as owning means doing what we want with something, disposing of it as we wish, both sickness and death are proof that our power over our own bodies is very limited.

From the beginning of the *Phaedo* Socrates is presenting himself as obedient to the gods, as not guilty of hubris, and as "keeping his place" as a man. Even before the discussion of the prohibition against suicide, he explains his writing poetry as a following of the command received in a repeated dream: "I thought it was safer not to go away before making sure that I had acquitted myself by obeying the dream and composing poems" (60e-61a). In the *Apology* Socrates presents his activity, indeed his life, as a service to the god, as a working out of the command of the god Apollo whose oracle is at Delphi. And insofar as the discussion in the *Phaedo* as a whole can be looked upon as "telling stories" (61d-e), it can be seen as a carrying out of the command received in the dream, the command to "make music," which Socrates interprets to mean myth.

Socrates defends his activity in the *Apology* by arguing that it is useful to the city. Indeed, he claims to be the god's gift to the city, given for its good, and that he therefore deserves only good from the city. The gadfly is useful but annoying. And we see in the *Apology* itself how annoyance is expressed in anger. In order for Athens to treat Socrates justly, giving him the good he deserves, the passion of anger would have to be controlled. The defense of philosophy as a truly useful activity could be seen as an attempt to skirt the charge of hubris. That is, in the *Apology*, philosophy is presented as useful and thus as fitting for man. In fact it is presented as most fitting: "The unexamined life is not a life for man [not a human life]." Socrates is most careful to distinguish his wisdom from more-than-human wisdom. But the defense of human wisdom provokes anger and ultimately fails.

In the *Phaedo*, the activity of philosophy is also presented as useful: only the philosopher is truly virtuous. Separation of soul and body entails rule of soul over body. And the virtuous individual is useful to the city. The Socrates who drinks the poison in the *Phaedo* is the same Socrates who stayed at his post at Potidaea, Amphipolis and Delium (28d-e) and "ran the risk of death." Socrates's death, his self-execution, is done in obedience to Athens (98e).

There is a contrast which begins to come to light now, a contrast which may be seen most clearly within the *Apology*. If we compare what Socrates says he will die for and will not die for, we see that he will die in obedience to Athens in battle but he will not obey its command to stop his activity. Yet he dies as penalty for that activity and thus dies in obedience to Athens. The comparison has another aspect. Socrates defends himself in the *Apology* for not having ruled Athens (31c-32a). His defense is that, had he gone into politics, he would have been put to death long ago. His "voice" held him back, thus keeping him alive for the practice of the activity by which he has done so much good for Athens. Socrates is defending himself for not being the philosopher-king. He rules himself but not the city. He cannot rule the city's anger. But in the *Phaedo* he does rule the fear of death, his own and, to some extent, the fear of those present.

These last considerations bring us back to the question of hubris, for one of the greatest manifestations of hubris is contempt for the irrational in human life.[18] A man who thinks or acts or tries to act as if he is immune from the power of the irrational within or outside him thinks he is above the human and is soon brought down. The references to dreams and to mysteries, the care that Socrates takes to carry out what he interprets as the command in the dream, the reverence for the mystery expressed in the prohibition of suicide, all convey the impression of Socrates's respect for the place of the irrational, for its power which inspires fear and caution.

The final stage of Socrates's brief presentation of the story of his life is dominated by fear and caution: "It seemed to me that I must be *careful* not to suffer what happens to those who look at the sun and watch it during an eclipse. . . . I was *afraid* of that and I *feared* my soul would be altogether blinded if I looked at things with my eyes and tried to grasp them with any of my senses" (99d-e). The beginning of the argument that immediately follows is also filled with references to fear and caution and safety: "I think this is the safest answer I can give" (100d); "You would, I think, be afraid that some opposite argument would confront you" (101a); "Would you not be afraid of this?" (101b); "You would be afraid to say that ten is more than eight by two" (101b); "For you would have the same fear" (101b); and "You would be afraid, as the saying goes, of your own shadow and of your lack of experience; so you would cling to that safe hypothesis" (101d-e). [Emphasis added.]

Socrates's turn to argument is here presented as safe and reliable, with no risks, no overconfidence. His fear of being blinded cannot fail to bring Oedipus to mind.[19] Apollo dominates the *Phaedo* but Dionysus, the god of tragedy, is present although unnamed.[20] Socrates's turn to argument is in some sense a "being brought down." He begins the story of his life with an account of his initial fascination with natural philosophy: "I thought it was a glorious thing to know the causes of everything" (96a). But he finds that he is by nature unfit for this kind of investigation: "I was so blinded by this investigation that I unlearned what I and others also thought I knew before" (96c). Then he becomes very eager to read the books of Anaxagoras, but his wonderful hope is quickly taken from him (98b). His own "way" is presented as a kind of settling for second-best, a compromise and an acceptance of limits.

The irrational is present in the *Phaedo* in yet another way. And the manner of its presence in this particular way is revealing. After Socrates has gone through the first major argument for the immortality of the soul—the argument that opposites come from opposites—Cebes provides additional support for the conclusion that the living come from the dead and that therefore the soul must have existed before being born in human form. This is the section of the dialogue where the "learning is recollection" thesis is examined.

What is striking about the way this section begins is Socrates's very forceful and indeed almost rude steering of the discussion away from mathematics. This is especially puzzling because the "form" which is featured in the discussion is equality, a notion perfectly suited for discussion in terms of mathematical objects.

When Cebes mentions the learning is recollection thesis, Simmias cannot remember how the thesis is proved and asks to be reminded. Cebes responds with what could easily be taken as a summary of what happens in the *Meno*: "One very good proof is this: When men are questioned, if someone puts the questions well, they answer correctly of themselves about everything; and if they had not within them some knowledge and a right account of the matter they could not do this. That this is so is shown most clearly if one takes them to mathematical diagrams or some other such thing" (73a-b). Before Simmias can say anything, Socrates jumps into the conversation, steering it forcefully in another direction: "And if you are not convinced in that way, Simmias, see whether you agree when you look at it in this way" (73b). He even insists that Simmias is not convinced: "You doubt that what is called learning is recollection?" That Socrates is forcefully steering the discussion becomes more obvious from Simmias's response: "I do not doubt but I want to learn just what we are talking about, to recollect. And from what Cebes undertook to say I am already remembering and being convinced; nevertheless, I should like to hear now the way you were intending to explain it" (73b-c). In spite of the fact that Simmias *is* remembering the proof on account of Cebes's reminder, Socrates completely drops that line of argument and begins his own account from perception.

It seems quite clear that Plato is inviting the reader to think of the learning is recollection thesis as it is presented in the *Meno*.[21] He brings it to our attention and then has Socrates push it aside and suppress it. The deliberate exclusion of mathematical diagrams is puzzling not only because of their appropriateness for the discussion of "equality itself" but also because of the Pythagorean overtones and undertones present throughout the dialogue.[22] Simmias and Cebes are themselves Pythagoreans and Echecrates is also a Pythagorean: the Pythagorean presence is felt on two levels. By bringing the mathematical to our attention and then abruptly putting it aside, Plato leads us to compare the treatment of the learning is recollection thesis in the *Meno* and the *Phaedo*.

The most striking difference between the two has to do with the "forms": they are omitted in the *Meno* and are all-important in the *Phaedo*. The account in the *Phaedo* is reminiscent of the divided line segment of the *Republic* in its movement from images to originals to forms. But again, this comparison makes even more puzzling the omission of mathematicals from this section of the *Phaedo*: mathematical objects play a crucial role in the movement up and down the divided line, providing the link between visible objects and the forms. When we compare the presentations in the *Meno* and the *Phaedo* we see one feature of Socrates's exchange with the slave that may explain, at least in part, why Socrates steers away from it in the *Phaedo*. The line which the slave learns about is the diagonal of the square, a line which is incommensurable with the side and is thus irrational in length. The exclusion of the *Meno* account may be an exclusion of the irrational, but an exclusion that is made conspicuous. This, then, amounts to suppression, a covering over, and not a complete absence.[23] The irrational is the unsayable. That is, it has a name which serves to "point" to it and which fixes it in relation to something else, but there can be no account of it in itself.[24]

What we catch in the *Phaedo*, then, are glimpses of the irrational, as of something that is being half-hidden. The overall impact of the dialogue is the suppression of the irrational, but it is allowed to break through here and there showing one of its many heads. The suppression is especially noticeable in the tendency to regard man as "two" (soul and body) rather than as "three" (the division of the *Republic*). In the argument for the immortality of the soul that connects the soul with the uncompounded, Socrates asks Cebes: "Are we anything else than soul and body?" Cebes replies: "Nothing else" (79b). The two other main arguments which treat the soul simply as the bearer of life also regard man as two. But the most significant instances are the definitions of death and philosophy, and the refutation of Simmias's argument by reference to Homer.

The definition of death which Socrates presents toward the beginning of the dialogue is one of the "first assumptions" of the whole discussion and is never called into question: "Is death anything else than the separation of the soul from the body, and is being dead this, that the body comes to be separated from the soul and is apart, itself by itself, and the soul is separated from the body and is apart, itself by itself? Is death anything other than this?" (64c). The definition is accepted and becomes the foundation for the treatment of soul and body throughout their conversation. Philosophy is then defined in terms of death: "Those who are philosophers in the right way practice dying. . . . They are in every way set at variance with the body and they desire to have the soul itself by itself alone" (67e). The *Phaedo assumes* the separability of soul and body; it assumes that soul and body are two distinct "things."

Further, the thrust of the discussion in the dialogue is to relegate the passions to the body. We considered this briefly with respect to the example of Odysseus. Socrates interprets this scene as an instance of the soul ruling the body and not as an instance of reason ruling the spirited part. And in his explanation of how philosophy is the separating of soul and body, Socrates mentions explicitly the so-called bodily pleasures and the senses which the philosopher takes leave of in taking leave of the body (64c-65c); he does not mention the spirited part at all. The soul is treated as simply *dianoia*. Speaking of the soul only in terms of thinking or reasoning is characteristic of Socrates's discussion of philosophy and the philosopher. Speaking of the soul simply in terms of life is characteristic of two of the major arguments for immortality. We are presented, then, with two extremes: the soul as reason or thought, the highest activity of men, and the soul as life, what is common to all animals and plants. This is typical of the pushing to extremes that one finds throughout the dialogue.

To say that man is soul and body and then to assign fear and anger to the body is to close the soul to the irrational. In the language of the third argument for immortality, the irrational is not "admitted" into the soul

(103d, 105a). But this way of speaking is ultimately forced into distortion: ordinary human experience is pushed out of shape. This, I think, accounts for the fact that we cannot help doubting the accuracy of Phaedo's report of Socrates's taking the poison.

The more we are led by the discussion to the extremes, the more the spirited part of the soul comes out of its half-hidden place and assumes a crucial role in the interpretation of the dialogue. That is, the place of the fear of death in the *Phaedo* strikes us all the more forcefully because of the distortions created by its apparent absence in Socrates. This apparent absence makes Socrates seem more than human. His joking about death looks like hubris. But there *is* fear in Socrates in the *Phaedo*.

The complementary passion of the spirited part, anger, is very obviously present in the *Apology*, not in Socrates but in the jurors. The cause of this anger is explained to them by Socrates but in such a way as to provoke more anger. The *Apology* is most ironic. Irony at first appears to be a kind of opposite of hubris: *eirōneia* is self-depreciation, the opposite of boastfulness. But the modesty here is false modesty, mock modesty. It really means the opposite of what it pretends: the hearer or observer is supposed to think the opposite of what is being said. How, then, are we really to understand Socrates's claim in the *Apology* that his wisdom is to know that he does not know, that his wisdom is merely human wisdom as distinguished from more-than-human wisdom?

Socrates's account of his activity is sure to infuriate just as the activity itself is. In recounting his questioning of the politicians, he speaks as if he is naive, perplexed by the reaction to his questioning: "And then I tried to show him that he thought he was wise but was not. As a result, I became hateful to him and to many of those present" (21d). One way to characterize the activity of Socrates as he presents it in the *Apology* is as a humiliating of others, a "bringing down" of those who appear to themselves and to others as somehow better and wiser. The one being questioned suddenly appears ridiculous and becomes an object of laughter. Socrates's service to the god (23b) can thus be viewed as his helping put men in their place. Another way of expressing this is to say that Socrates's activity is that of unmasking, uncovering the truth. He does this by removing the appearance of wisdom, making the false appearance disappear.

We begin to see the public nature of Socrates's activity in a somewhat different light. All of this humiliating and unmasking is done publicly, indiscriminately, in the presence of spectators. In contrast to the Sophists, Socrates's activity is open to all. But what is revealed is the ignorance of others in spite of Socrates's insistence that he, too, is ignorant. For all the appearance of openness and publicness, Socrates himself is hidden. He is the most public and at the same time the most hidden of men. He uncovers others while hiding himself. This gives him the reputation for being a busybody, one who questions others relentlessly but never lets anything of himself slip out. There is annoyance on the part of the one being questioned because the questioner is in the superior position. For all his assurances that he too is ignorant, Socrates in the Platonic dialogues never appears ridiculous.

I do not mean to imply that because Socrates's modesty is a false modesty he is really guilty of hubris. Even his description of himself as the god's helper in putting men in their place does not amount to hubris. Hubris has to do with man's place in relationship to the divine. Socrates's irony, his incessant unmasking of others, his being a gadfly, have to do with his relationship to other men and in particular his fellow citizens. What Socrates is affirming in the *Apology* is that he is indeed wiser than anyone else; he is the wisest of men.

So there is, on the one hand, the denial that he has "more-than-human wisdom" and, on the other hand, the affirmation that he is the wisest of men. His wisdom is "merely" human wisdom. Yet for all his claims to be the servant of the god and to be carrying out the command of the god in questioning others, Socrates originally undertakes his activity as a way of investigating the god. His first response to the oracle is doubt; he is puzzled at what the god could possibly mean. Then he sets out to investigate the god and to show that the oracle is wrong (21b-c).

Of course, he cannot interrogate Apollo directly. He must work out the meaning of the oracle among men, who are accessible to him. And at the end of the *Apology*, when he presents two possible accounts of what death might be, he says: "And the greatest pleasure would be to pass my time in testing and examining the people there, as I do here, so as to find out who among them is wise and who thinks he is when he is not" (41b). In this description of life in Hades, he presents himself as questioning demigods, heroes, poets, but not gods.

If we compare this account of what he expects after death with the mythical speech about philosophy in the *Phaedo*, we see two different versions of what philosophy is. And these two different versions dominate the two dialogues. In the *Apology*, Socrates presents his activity as a kind of sharing, a constant being among other men. This is precisely what he defends himself for. In the *Phaedo*, the speech about philosophy is always about the separation of soul and body, a separation that implies separation from other men. And this is precisely what he defends himself about in the *Phaedo* (63a-69e). Death, too, is a separation not only of body and soul but also from other men. This is how those who remain experience it.

The first defense fails. In the *Phaedo* he says: "I will try to make a more convincing defense before you than I did before the judges" (63b). Is the *Phaedo* a successful defense? In a way, the question hinges on the role of the spirited part of the soul. The failure of the *Apology* is a failure to rule anger, not his own but that of the many. The success or failure of the *Phaedo* as an apology depends upon whether or not Socrates is able to rule the passion of fear, both his own and that of his friends. This would perhaps be a more modest victory, limited and temporary. Looked at in another light, it is an attempt to rival the gods in their contempt for death.

Truth and Deception

It is precisely Phaedo's description of Socrates's drinking the poison that forces us to be suspicious of the accuracy of his report, to suspect that he is not simply a reporter. But this is not the only level at which we have to be suspicious. There are, I think, three such levels that must be identified and distinguished. The first level is that of the conversation and events of the day of Socrates's death: this is what Phaedo is supposedly reporting. The second level is that of Phaedo's reporting, his exchange with Echecrates which contains his supposed report. The third level is that of Plato's writing, his presentation of Phaedo's exchange with Echecrates. None of these levels is external to the dialogue. The text itself tells us something about each.

The most important issues that are raised by identifying and distinguishing these levels are the issues of truth and deception. At each level, the question about truth shows itself in a somewhat different way and always along with the suspicion that we may be being deceived. That is, the suspicion about deception prompts us to ask what truth can mean in the dialogue. Of course, we could not even be suspicious if the deception were complete, if the truth were completely covered over. What we have is a half-hiding: we are given the briefest glimpses which suddenly give us a different perspective on what is before us.

Socrates

In considering the first level, the accuracy of Phaedo's report has to be accepted at least provisionally, as a working hypothesis. This means, for example, that we take as given the description of Socrates's drinking the poison. At this level, then, there *is* a gap between theory and action, between the uncertainty of the arguments and Socrates's sureness of action, and it is a gap that needs to be accounted for. But before we look at this level as a whole in order to ask about truth and deception, we must consider what is said about truth and deception in the course of the conversation that took place on the day of Socrates's death.

Socrates presents two of what I will call "approaches to truth" in the *Phaedo*. It is possible that they may be linked in some way but initially they strike us as quite different. Each is presented along with its opposite. The first approach, which I will call "the approach of sight," is described against the background of mythical speech about purification and is consistent with the notion of philosophy as separation of soul and body. It follows immediately upon the claim that the soul of the philosopher, because it is pure, enters into communion with the gods when it departs from the body at death. This approach to truth is presented in contrast with its opposite:

> The lovers of learning know that when philosophy gets hold of their soul it is simply imprisoned in and clinging to the body and is compelled to examine things through the body as through prison bars, not itself through itself, and that it is wallowing in every kind of ignorance. And philosophy sees that the most dreadful thing about the imprisonment is the fact that it is due to the desires, so that the prisoner is himself most of all the accomplice in his own imprisonment. The lovers of learning, then, I say, know that philosophy, taking hold of the soul when it is in this state, encourages it gently and tries to set it free, pointing out that investigation through the eyes and the ears and the other senses is full of deceit, and persuading it to withdraw from these, except insofar as it is compelled to use them, and exhorting it to gather and collect itself within itself, and to trust nothing except itself and its own thought of beings and to believe that there is no truth in that which it sees by other means and which varies in varying conditions, since everything of that kind is visible and apprehended by the senses, whereas the soul itself sees that which is invisible and apprehended by thought (*noēton*). (82d-83b)

The second approach, which I will call "the approach of argument," is presented in the final stage of Socrates's story of his life. It is this approach, then, with which Socrates most closely identifies his own activity. Its opposite is discussed in the section of the dialogue concerned with hatred of argument. Socrates has just explained his dissatisfaction with natural philosophy. Now he will present his own, second-best way of seeking causes:

After this, then, since I had given up investigating things, it seemed to me that I must be careful not to suffer what happens to people who look at the sun and watch it during an eclipse. For some of them ruin their eyes unless they look at its image in water or something of the sort. I thought of that and I was afraid my soul would be entirely blinded if I looked at things with my eyes and tried to grasp them with any of my senses. So I thought I must take refuge in arguments and examine in them the truth of things. . . . However, this is the way I began: I assume in each case some argument which I consider strongest and whatever seems to me to agree with this, whether about cause or anything else, I hold as true, and whatever disagrees with it, as untrue. (99d-100a)

In order to illustrate his "method" he presents the third major argument for immortality. Or rather, he discusses his turn to argument as a prelude to the argument for immortality, since this whole section of the dialogue is a response to Cebes's objection. The context for the story of his turn from natural philosophy to argument is the investigation of the cause of all generation and destruction in order to see if the soul is destructible. The third major argument for immortality begins from the existence of the "forms," the "itselfs." This is the *logos*, then, which he is accepting as "strongest" and against which he will test whatever else is said.

That these two approaches to truth are meant to be taken together is made strikingly clear by the manner in which Socrates characterizes their opposites. If the soul is not purified by philosophy, if it remains in bondage to pleasure and pain, it suffers "the greatest and most extreme evil" (83b-c). When Cebes asks what this evil is, Socrates explains: "That is that the soul of every man, when it is greatly pleased or pained by anything, is compelled at the same time to believe that what caused the feeling is most distinct and most true, but it is not" (83c). The objects to which he is referring are mostly the visible objects. When this occurs the soul is most completely in bondage to the body "because each pleasure and pain nails it as with a nail to the body and fastens it on and makes it bodily so that it believes the things are true which the body says are true" (83d). The soul of the philosopher must not give itself back into bondage after it is set free, like Penelope unweaving the web that she wove (84a).

The opposite of the approach of argument is the hatred of argument. And "no worse evil can happen to someone than to hate argument" (89d). Hatred of argument occurs when someone without skill in arguments has complete confidence in the truth of an argument and afterwards thinks it is false, and this happens again and again (90b). Such a man hates and reviles arguments the rest of his life and is deprived of the truth and knowledge of things (90d). The section of the dialogue concerned with hatred of argument is, in my view, of major significance. What I wish to point out here is that the two approaches to truth are somehow linked by the characterization of their opposites as "the greatest evil." These are strong statements from the man who says in his *Apology* that he does not know what human excellence is.

One thing is clear: for Socrates, death is not the greatest evil.[25] And in the *Apology* we find an equally strong statement of what he holds to be the greatest good for a man: " . . . and if I say that to talk every day about virtue and the other things about which you hear me talking and examining myself and others is the greatest good that can happen to a man, and that the unexamined life is not a life for man, you will believe me still less" (38a). The success or failure of Socrates's defense in the *Phaedo* also depends upon whether he is believed when he tells those present what the greatest evil is. The greatest evil, in both of the ways it is expressed by Socrates, involves some kind of deception.

This leads us to a second way in which the two approaches are linked. Both entail a rejection of what is given by the senses. The soul must "believe that there is no truth in that which it sees by other means [than nous] and which varies in varying conditions, since everything of that kind is visible and apprehended by the senses" (83a-b). And Socrates says of his turn to argument: "I was afraid my soul would be entirely blinded if I looked at things with my eyes and tried to grasp them with any of my senses" (99e). In the search for truth, the senses are not to be trusted. The eyes and ears and other senses are "full of deceit" (83a) in the description of the approach of sight. The senses are not said to be deceptive in his account of his turn from natural philosophy. He is afraid to examine things with his senses because it is dangerous for him: he is afraid that his soul would be blinded.

What is to be trusted in the approach of sight is the soul itself, collected and gathered within itself: "Philosophy . . . exhorts the soul to gather and collect itself within itself and to trust nothing except itself and its own thought of beings" (83a-b). The question of what is to be trusted in the approach of argument is one way of putting the question about the meaning of the whole dialogue.

If we consider the arguments of the *Phaedo* itself as illustrations of the approach of argument, we may be able to locate what is "trusted." This is especially clear in the final major argument for immortality. This is the argument that follows immediately after the story of Socrates's turn to argument and he says explicitly that he will show them what he means when he says: "I assume in each case some argument which I consider strongest, and whatever seems to me to agree with this, whether about cause or anything else, I hold as true, and whatever disagrees with it as untrue" (100a). Socrates's point of departure, his first assumption, in this argument is the existence of the "itselfs," such as beauty itself, good itself, greatness itself. He says: "If you grant me these and agree that these are, I hope to show the cause to you from these and to discover that the soul is immortal" (100b). They do agree that the "itselfs" exist and it is clear that Socrates expected this agreement. He refers here to the "itselfs" as the totally familiar: he is assuming "nothing new"; he is going back to what they have often discussed in the past (100b). He begins from what he knows they trust.

This is not the first time that Socrates has linked the existence of the "itselfs" to the immortality of the soul. At the end of the section concerning learning as recollection, Socrates asks Simmias: "Is it not necessary that just as these are, so our soul is before we are born and if these are not, our argument is spoken in vain? Is this the case, and is it equally necessary that these things are and our souls also are before we are born, and if these are not, neither did our souls exist?" Simmias asserts not only that there is "the same necessity," but also that there is "nothing so clear" to him as this, that the "itselfs" exist (76e-77a).

Now as Socrates himself shows in his refutation of Simmias's claim that the soul is a harmony, the starting point of an argument can be called into question if the argument leads to an unacceptable conclusion. In fact, one of these refutations is precisely directed to the point I am working toward. Socrates shows that the claim that the soul is a harmony leads to the conclusion that all souls are by nature equal (94a). Socrates asks Simmias, "Do you think that this is true and that our reasoning would have come to this end, if the hypothesis that the soul is a harmony were correct?" Simmias then rejects his hypothesis because the denial of the conclusion of the argument is more acceptable to him than the affirmation of his starting point.

If we consider again the argument for immortality that begins from the existence of the "itselfs," we have to ask if we are not in the same position. For as we saw earlier, this argument asserts the immortality of everything that lives. There is nothing distinctively human about the form "life." But the argument cannot distinguish among men's souls or among the souls of all animals and plants. If this is an unacceptable conclusion, then the starting point must be called into question. And Socrates himself, at the end of the argument, tells Simmias that "our first assumptions ought nevertheless to be more carefully examined, even if they are trusted by us" (107b).

The third argument for immortality, the argument that begins from the existence of the forms, works toward the conclusion that the soul is immortal because the forms are changeless. That is, if a thing has a quality that is essential to it, that quality cannot be changed without the thing's becoming something else. For example, snow must be cold. Its coldness cannot become warmness. This is based on the claim that an opposite can never become its own opposite. When approached by the opposite of one of its essential qualities, the thing must either perish or withdraw (103c-105e). Since life is the essential characteristic of the soul, the soul can never admit death (105e).

The changelessness of the forms is surely a good beginning for the attempt at proving that the soul is immortal. The context for this discussion is the investigation of the cause of *all* generation and destruction in order to see whether the soul is one of the things that can be affected by the cause of destruction. If the soul can be shown to "have" a form which cannot change, its own unchangeability can be based on that changeless form. But as this account of the argument shows, the soul's having the unchangeable form "life" as an essential quality does not necessarily mean that the soul is unchangeable. Snow cannot become warm and still remain snow; it becomes water. It is not unchangeable. It can lose its essential characteristics. This may not mean total destruction, or a complete disappearance, but it is destroyed as snow.[26]

One of the difficulties with the way the argument is presented in the dialogue, a difficulty reflected in my own account, is that no distinction is made among different kinds of "things." The discussion moves from one *kind* of thing to another as if they all existed in the same way. The cause of *all* generation and destruction is being investigated and all kinds of things are included as examples, but without apparent regard for the "level" of being of each.[27] The kinds of "things" mentioned are forms, bodily things, numbers, and souls. This is the second time in the dialogue that mathematical objects are discussed and the discussion is limited to numbers.

If we recall again the divided line of the *Republic* we find three of its segments mentioned. Images are not discussed in this argument. If the left side of the line divides up all being, then where does the soul belong? The most obvious place is "in" the visible bodies of living things. The right side of the line shows the human soul only, as it encounters all the levels of being. The neatness of the divided line points up the confusion concerning kinds and manners of being that pervades the argument in the *Phaedo*.[28]

Socrates is well aware that levels and kinds of being are not being kept straight. And this is one reason why the objection of the unidentified man is not trivial. It causes Socrates to separate out "opposites," "things," "having," and "being in" (103b). His answer to the objector really prepares the way for seeing that the changelessness of an opposite or form does not entail the changelessness of what the opposite is "in." And, as noted above, Socrates does not explore the objection as he might and even should. He clearly wants to pass over it.

The level of being of the soul is a special case among the examples: cold is said to be "in" snow, life is "in" soul, and soul is "in" body. There are three levels here. This is another clarification brought about by the objector: the argument based on the notion that "opposites come from opposites" does not make this explicit. And here we see what is troublesome about all these attempts to prove the immortality of the soul. The argument based on "opposites come from opposites" must refer to "being dead" as a kind of being. That is, it *assumes*, not proves, the existence of the "dead soul." And when we find ourselves forced to speak of "dead souls," we realize that the *term* 'dead' no longer has any meaning, as an opposite of 'life'. It can only mean "being separated from the body." And this is one of the first *assumptions* of the dialogue: "Death is the separation of the soul from the body" (64c).

It seems that only the second major proof for the immortality of the soul avoids both the difficulty of proving too much, that is, that everything living is immortal, and the difficulty of distorting the meaning of 'death' beyond recognition. This argument proceeds by connecting the soul with the uncompounded by way of the changeless and the forms. The uncompounded as least likely to disperse is the starting point. The uncompounded is most likely to be unchangeable and the soul is then associated with the unchanging by means of the forms which are unchangeable. The discussion of the "knowledge is recollection" thesis does the same thing. This argues only that the soul existed before birth: it cannot stand alone but must be combined with the argument based on "opposites come from opposites" to form a whole (77c-d).

By having the immortality of the soul hinge on knowing the forms (78e-79a), the second major argument appears to be able to address itself to the immortality of the human soul alone. But what we see from the mythical speech that follows the proof is that the argument may be proving too little. It may have to be taken to assert the immortality of only the philosophers. Or at most, it must be backed up by the mythical speech that has the "dead soul" enter into some other species depending upon its *moral* worth, not its ability to grasp the forms. And this last point confirms the overall impression being created by Socrates that the philosopher is morally virtuous: his "purification" is both intellectual and moral.

The purification of the philosopher can be both intellectual and moral at the same time if man is taken to be two, soul and body, and if the passions are all relegated to the body. Thus, soul is really identified with reason (*dianoias logismō*) (79a). (Then, of course, the problem becomes one of accounting for other animals and plants.) This leads to the second difficulty with this argument. As discussed above, the linking of the soul with the uncompounded may be contradicted by the Odysseus story. Socrates presents Odysseus as an instance of the rule of soul over body, but in order to do this he must speak of soul as if it were the reason alone. If the soul is reason alone, then the view that the soul is uncompounded is not contradicted. But if the soul is three, as in the *Republic*, then in ruling fear and anger the soul is ruling itself and, of course, has "parts." It therefore becomes much less easy to speak about the separation of soul and body.

The fear of death is itself evidence of the union of soul and body. Fear of death might be expressed as fear that the soul is not separable from the body. That we *feel* the fear at all is evidence that what we fear may be true; it is the vivid experience of the union of soul and body. So overcoming the fear is a kind of separation of soul and body. But we overcome fear by speech, persuasion, not by force. What the Odysseus story really shows, in spite of what it is *said* to show, is that the soul does not talk to the body but only to itself. This is also what Socrates is doing, and what we are given the briefest glimpse of, in the hatred of argument section.

The second and third arguments for the immortality of the soul both rest on the existence of the forms, but in different ways. The third argument, the one based on the claim that an opposite can never become its opposite, shows the soul as participating in the form "life" or as having the form "life." The argument linking the soul to the uncompounded shows the soul as knowing the forms and being invisible like the forms. The reason for the attraction of the forms as a starting point for arguments based on possession of the form is precisely what leads into difficulty.

The forms are attractive as a starting point because they are changeless. Starting points should be as firm, solid, and reliable as possible. And in this third argument for immortality Socrates constantly speaks about fear, danger, and safety. But the argument, when pushed to its limits, would have to imply that nothing ever really changes; all essential characteristics of things must remain unchanged. That is, they want an argument to show that the soul cannot perish, that it must always "have" life. The argument says that the soul must always have life because life is an essential characteristic of soul. (Dead souls, then, are really alive, and 'dead' no longer means what it was first taken to mean, that is, the opposite of life.) Again, the reason why the forms were taken as the starting point—their changelessness—is now what creates difficulties. In order to maintain that the soul does not perish, we have to be willing to agree that nothing every really changes. And this contradicts the first argument, based on "opposites come from opposites," just as the unnamed objector says. Indeed, Socrates himself says it (72b-c).

What we find at work on the ontological level of the dialogue is the argument between "all things are changing" and "all things are at rest."[29] Both views are presented by Socrates in terms of the arguments for the immortality of the soul. And he actually arrives at the same conclusion from starting points that are apparently contradictory. This, taken together with the insurmountable difficulties into which the arguments lead and which Socrates surely knows, makes it suddenly difficult to distinguish Socrates from the Sophists. We cannot help being suspicious about his manner of arguing and about the possibility that he is deliberately deceiving them.

This leads us to what I regard as the crucial section of the dialogue, the hatred of argument section. For here Socrates argues against the notion that "all things are changing" and at the same time allows us to see precisely how he differs from the Sophists. And it is here, in what seems to be a mere digression from the main plot, that the true action of the dialogue is displayed.

As noted above, the hatred of argument section is to be taken together with the final stage of Socrates's story of his turn away from natural philosophy to argument.[30] He makes that turn because he is in danger and afraid of being blinded. The hatred of argument discussion is introduced because Socrates realizes that they have reached a point in the conversation about immortality where they are threatened by misology. He has presented two major arguments for immortality, the argument based on "opposites come from opposites" and the argument linking the soul to the uncompounded. Then Simmias and Cebes come forward with their objections, Simmias comparing the soul to a harmony and Cebes comparing it to a weaver, both maintaining that the soul is destructible.

It is here that the brief exchange between Socrates and Phaedo occurs, and from which the dialogue gets its name. Socrates strokes the hair on Phaedo's neck, as he often did, and asks if Phaedo will cut off his hair the next day. When Phaedo says that he will, Socrates responds: "You will cut it off today, and I will cut mine, if our argument dies and we cannot bring it to life again. If I were you and the argument escaped me, I would take an oath, like the Argives, not to let my hair grow until I had fought over again and won a victory over the argument of Simmias and Cebes" (89b-c). Socrates and Phaedo then agree to help each other, like Heracles and Iolaus, "while there is still light."

But before he begins to fight back against the arguments of Simmias and Cebes, Socrates fights what is the true battle of the dialogue. He realizes that those present are deeply troubled by the objections, not only because his arguments have been called into question but also because they have begun to mistrust argument as such. This is the danger that he perceives and he begins his fight against it by saying that "no worse evil can happen to someone than to hate argument" (89d). Socrates is doing battle with the greatest evil. The battle against the fear of death is secondary.

Hatred of argument arises in the same way as hatred of men, from trusting completely and then being disappointed. When this happens again and again, the man hates everyone and trusts no one. But the misanthropist has only himself to blame. He has no knowledge of human nature; he expects too much of men. He does not realize that most men are "in-between" with respect to good and bad.

Socrates is careful to point out that arguments and men are *not* alike in being "in-between." He implies that arguments are indeed either true or false, not somewhere between the two extremes. The similarity between misology and misanthropy is this: "When someone without skill in arguments has put his trust in an argument as being true, and shortly afterwards believes that it is false—sometimes it is and sometimes it is not—and this happens again and again; then you know, those especially who spend their time in disputation come to believe that they are the wisest of men and that they alone have understood that there is nothing sound or sure in anything, whether argument or anything else, but all things twist up and down, just as in the Euripus, and nothing remains for any length of time" (90b-c).[31]

Those who spend their time in disputation come to believe that they are "the wisest of men." As we know from the *Apology*, Socrates is the "wisest of men." He is here comparing himself with the Sophists and associating the Sophists with the view that all things, including argument, are changing. The battle that Socrates is fighting here is to get those present to believe that the fault is in themselves, not in the nature of argument itself: "First, then, let us be on our guard against this, and let us not admit into the soul that there may be no soundness in argument at all. Let us far rather assume that we ourselves are not yet sound and that we must be manful and eager to be sound" (90d-e).

It is in this context that we *do* find pity in the dialogue. Socrates says to Phaedo: "Then, Phaedo, if there is any argument that is true and sure and can be understood, it would be pitiable if a man, because he has met with some such arguments which seem to be sometimes true and sometimes not, should then not blame himself or his own lack of skill but should end in his distress by throwing the blame gladly away from himself onto the arguments and should hate and revile them all the rest of his life, and be deprived of the truth and knowledge of things" (90c-d). Phaedo agrees that it would be pitiable. Again, the worst evil that can happen to a man is hatred of argument, not death.

The conclusion of the hatred of argument section allows us a brief glimpse of the otherwise hidden Socrates. Here he unmasks *himself*. He and Phaedo have just agreed that what is pitiable is hatred of argument, and thus deprivation of truth. It is within the context of not wanting to be pitiable that Socrates concludes:

> First, then, let us be on our guard against this, and let us not admit into the soul that there may be no soundness in arguments at all. Let us far rather assume that we ourselves are not yet sound and that we must be manful and eager to be sound, you and the others for the sake of your whole life still, and I because of death itself; for I am in danger just now of not being philosophical about this, but am contentious,[32] like those who are coarse. For when they argue about anything, they do not care how it [truly] is about the things they are discussing, but are eager only to make what they have put forward seem so to those present. And I seem to myself to differ from them just now only so far: I shall not be eager to make what I say seem true to those present except incidentally, but shall be most eager to make it seem so to myself. For I am calculating, my friend—see how selfishly—if what I say is true, it is fine to be persuaded; and if there be nothing after death, at least for this time before my death, I will be less unpleasant for those present by lamenting. And this ignorance of mine will not last, for that would be an evil, but will soon end. (90d-91b)

Socrates's revelation of himself is addressed directly to Phaedo. Now he turns back to Simmias and Cebes, bringing the "digression" to an end and preparing himself and them for battle: "So, Simmias and Cebes, I approach the argument prepared in this way. But you, if you are persuaded by me, will give little thought to Socrates but much more to the truth; and if you think what I say is true, agree to it, and if not, strive against it with every argument, that I may not in my eagerness deceive myself and you alike and go away, like a bee, leaving my sting in you" (91b-c).

The desire to be convinced that the soul does not change, that it does not die, prompts the discussion of immortality which is the "plot" of the dialogue. Now the notion that all things are changing is being fought on a deeper level, the level of argument itself. They must not admit into their souls the notion that there is no soundness in arguments at all. They must rather strive manfully to become sound themselves. Much of the language of this section is about battling, fighting, and striving. The courage that Socrates is trying to build in them is courage in the face of opposing arguments, not immediately in the face of death. But, given the setting of the dialogue and the asserted coincidence between philosophy and moral virtue, the two may not be ultimately different. The battle against hatred of argument is the "action" of the dialogue.

One of the initially puzzling things about Socrates's account of the manner in which hatred of argument arises is its very close resemblance to his own activity. That is, Socrates has spent his whole life weaving and unweaving arguments, constructing arguments that seem true and then showing them to be false. He is doing the same thing here in the *Phaedo* except that he is hiding the unweaving. It thus becomes very difficult to distinguish him from the "disputants" who think that they are the "wisest of men" and that they alone have discovered that there is nothing sure and sound in anything, including argument.

The distinction becomes even more difficult at the very point where Socrates reveals himself. He is *not* being philosophical; he wants to win. Those who simply want to win an argument do not care what the truth is in the matters they are discussing. They will say whatever they think can destroy the opposing argument. What Socrates is revealing here is his fear of death. In the *Apology*, the anti-philosophical erupted as anger. In the *Phaedo*, it is fear that forces itself to the surface as the manifestation of the irrational. There *is* a struggle within Socrates between reason and the spirited part of the soul.

When Socrates tells his hearers that they must not admit into their souls the notion that there is no soundness in arguments, he gives two reasons, one for them and one for himself. They must strive manfully for the sake of their future lives; he must do so because of his impending death. This is the only hint that Socrates does not regard this day as being the same as any other for him. And in the face of death, he is not being philosophical. As for the others, the admonition to strive manfully to become sound is addressed to Phaedo but includes all of them. To Simmias and Cebes, he addresses the request that in the battle to come they think about truth and not about sparing Socrates.

When we attempt to distinguish Socrates from the Sophists in this section of the dialogue, two questions seem especially pertinent. What does he mean by "skill" in argument, the kind of knowledge about argument that keeps one from hating arguments even when they suddenly appear false? And what is the "sound" condition that Phaedo should strive so manfully for?

If Socrates is to be distinguished from the Sophists, then this skill cannot be the skill of winning without regard to truth. The skill of simply winning is pursued if one does hate argument whereas the skill to which Socrates refers is one that prevents hatred of argument. The initial impression, on the basis of the comparison with misanthropy, is that the skill consists in not expecting too much of arguments. This is the misanthropist's mistake with respect to men. But Socrates denies that arguments are like men in this way. He implies that arguments *are* true and false. Nevertheless, the skill that prevents hatred of argument seems to involve having the proper expectations of arguments.

The opposites that dominate the arguments concerning immortality are life and death. The opposites that dominate the discussion about argument itself are true and false. On this level we might ask whether opposites come from opposites or whether an opposite can never become its opposite. The situation that Socrates describes as giving rise to hatred of argument is one in which an argument *seemed* true (and was therefore trusted) and then later turned out to be or at least to *seem* false. Has the argument changed? Or are true and false merely appearances?

An argument appears as true or false only in relation to some other argument. That is, an argument will appear true to me if it is consistent with other arguments that I accept as true. It will appear false if it is not. Or an argument that I accept and hold as true may be made to appear false if it is placed against another argument that is stronger. The point is that an initially plausible case can be made for the claim that arguments are relative with respect to true and false. Thus, true and false would not be essential predicates, merely accidental. Arguments would be included in the notion that "all things are relative," which is identified in the *Theaetetus* with "all things are changing."[33]

Socrates is fighting against hatred of argument and against the view that all things are changing. But his own "method," briefly described at the end of the story of his turn, seems to affirm the relativity of arguments. He begins with a *logos* that seems "strongest." Whatever agrees with it is taken as true and whatever disagrees with it as false. And if the starting point is put up against something stronger it, in its turn, will seem false. The philosopher, like Penelope weaving and unweaving, is engaged in an endless or futile task. But perhaps, like Penelope, the philosopher's true task is in fact accomplished. It is not a final victory but a holding-action.

At the beginning of the dialogue Socrates says that philosophy is the practice of death since it is the separation of soul and body. Here in the hatred of argument section he says that he is *not* being philosophical but is rather a lover of victory. It is not altogether clear whether he is referring to the state of his soul throughout the discussion or to this particular part of the discussion which directly concerns the life of argument as such. In any case, at the very moment when he looks most like the Sophists, he tells us how he is different: "For when they argue about anything, they do not care how it [truly] is about the things they are discussing, but are eager only to make what they have put forward *seem* so to those present. And I seem to myself to differ from them just now only so far: I shall not be eager to make what I say seem true to those present, except incidentally, but shall be most eager to make it seem so to myself" (90a-b). [Emphasis added.] The principal reason for the art of winning arguments is to make it possible for the winner to rule over others. To persuade is to rule, except under those regimes where rule is by force. Socrates is claiming here that he wants to rule himself, to rule his fear. He approaches the argument about immortality prepared in this way (91b-c).

We must ask two questions here: What does Socrates want to make himself believe and why does he want to convince himself? Our first impression, based on the "plot" of the dialogue, is that Socrates wants to convince himself that the soul is immortal. But I think that by now the discussion has caused this first impression to evaporate.[34] Socrates is carefully and deliberately, although secretly, unweaving the arguments for immortality. It seems that Socrates wants to convince himself of the soundness in argument, and that he must still strive manfully to become sound himself, even in the few hours that remain. *He, Socrates, is striving not to change.*

This striving to remain the same is manful and courageous because it is done with the full realization of the possibility of falsehood.[35] And this provides the answer to our second question. Socrates explains why he wishes to convince himself: "For I am calculating, my friend—see how selfishly—if what I say is true, it is fine to be persuaded; and if there be nothing after death, at least for this time before my death, I will be less unpleasant for those present by lamenting. And this ignorance of mine will not last, for that would be an evil, but will soon end" (91b). Socrates makes clear that the whole discussion is conducted in uncertainty. Much more needs to be said about this. But what I want to focus on now is the way in which the question of evil is raised in this passage.

Whether the arguments are true or false, the life of argument is good. It is at least a holding-action against the irrational, and at the same time, a holding-action against the fear of death. And Socrates is not altogether selfish. He does not make himself burdensome to his hearers by his lamentations. But he also does something else for them, for their "common good." In distinguishing himself from the Sophists, he says that he does not want to persuade his hearers except as a secondary matter. Even this task is accomplished in the *Phaedo*.

By remaining unchanged, by holding fast to the life of argument, Socrates brings about a change in those present. In Phaedo's words, he "cures" them; he makes them "sound" or "healthy." This, it seems to me, is the real meaning of Socrates's last words.

When Phaedo introduces the hatred of argument section, he describes to Echecrates their uneasiness upon hearing the objections of Simmias and Cebes: "Now all of us, as we told each other afterwards, were very uncomfortable when we heard what they said;[36] for we had been thoroughly convinced by the previous argument, and now they seemed to be confusing us again and to be bringing us into distrust, not only with respect to the past discussion but also with regard to what was going to be said, lest we be worthless judges or the things uncertain" (88b-c). The symptoms of the hatred of argument reveal that the question about the soul has *suddenly* become urgent and serious for them. For Socrates, it has always been urgent. Socrates cures them, recalls them from flight and defeat, and makes them face about and follow him and join in his examination of the argument (89a). The language of the section is both military and medicinal.[37]

The evidence that a cure has taken place is provided by Simmias at the end of the third argument: "I don't myself see how I can doubt, after what has been said; but on account of the greatness of what the arguments are about and my poor opinion of human weakness, I cannot help having some doubt still with myself about what has been said" (107a-b). There is doubt here, uncertainty about both the argument and human ability, but there is no more hatred of argument. Socrates has prepared them for the future. For surely when they remember and examine the arguments again, when Socrates is gone, they will see what is wrong with them.

What does Socrates's cure amount to? Phaedo said that they were uneasy about two things: that their judgment might be worthless and that the subject matter might be such that no certitude could be had. As we see from Simmias's remarks, the change that has occurred is *not* due to certitude about the immortality of the soul. And the subject of immortality seems to be one about which certitude is least likely to be had. In fact, this makes the arguments about immortality the perfect "plot" for displaying the "action" of the dialogue. Death is, at the same time, certain, inevitable, and common to all, and yet hidden, and mysterious. There can be no eye-witness, first-hand report about it. There can be no eye-witness report because, as the dialogue constantly reminds us, the soul is invisible.[38] The question concerning the immortality of the soul and the true nature of death illustrates the kind of question that occupies the philosopher, who in seeking to understand the most familiar is carried beyond the visible, ultimately to the forms. But as Socrates says in response to Simmias's expression of doubt: "Our first assumptions ought nevertheless to be more carefully examined, even if they are trusted by us" (107b). Simmias accepts the existence of the forms as more certain than anything else and the existence of the forms is the first assumption of the argument they have just completed. Socrates, then, is encouraging Simmias to start all over, to go back to the beginning. The matter cannot be regarded as settled once and for all.

It seems that Socrates's cure consists in his having restored their confidence in argument. But this is not the naive confidence that leads to hatred of argument. Simmias is convinced by the argument, he does not see now any way to doubt it, yet he does have some doubt. The confidence in argument that he has now is not the expectation of certitude. He will not lose heart if this argument is overturned. On the other hand, Socrates's hearers have not been pushed to the other extreme of complete relativity of arguments.

What Socrates says about arguments is that they are true and false, not that they are certain. Socrates's cure is accomplished by means of the distinction between truth and certitude. One of the characteristics of truth that first emerges in the process of making this distinction is that truth is compatible with uncertainty, with doubt. Truth must always go along with its opposite, the false, in the sense that the possibility of falsehood is always present. What saves this position from relativity is its grounding in the forms. And this is where we see Socrates most clearly distinguished from the Sophists. The forms are the firm foundation of discourse.

Socrates points to the firmness of the forms at the beginning of the third and final argument for immortality. The forms can be held onto in speech. They are firm and safe and reliable because they are unchangeable. In the second argument, connecting the soul to the uncompounded, Socrates refers to the place of the forms in discourse: "Is the being (*ousia*), which we call 'what is' in our questioning and answering, always the same or is it different at different times?" (78c-d). He is referring here to "the equal itself, the beautiful itself."[39] And in the discussion of the learning is recollection thesis, he also points to the manifestation of the forms in discourse: "For our present argument is no more concerned with the equal than with beauty itself and the good itself and the just and the holy and, as I say, with all those things which we stamp with the seal of 'that which is' in our process of questioning and answering" (75c-d).

I do not mean to imply that the forms are held to exist *only* in discourse. The manner of being of the forms is one of the "first asssumptions" that Simmias is encouraged to reexamine. The third argument for immortality shows the difficulties into which the unchangeability of the forms leads when the forms are regarded as "causes" (100c) of things.[40] The manner of being of the forms has to be distinguished, in the third argument especially, from the manner of being of bodies, numbers, and the soul. My point here is that, whatever else the forms may be, they are being held onto in the *Phaedo* as the ground of discourse.[41] Words, names, are not arbitrary, changeable conventions but have a foundation that is more-than-human.[42] The grounding of discourse in nature is Socrates's distinguishing himself from the Sophists.

That the meanings of words are not man-made is shown in the dialogue by the impossible distortions of the word 'death'. We are not free to have it mean what we want it to mean. We are bound by a meaning that is not even fully known to us. This, in one way, expresses the Socratic practice of philosophy: the grounding of speech in nature distinguishes Socrates from both the Sophists and the natural philosophers.

The story of Socrates's turn away from natural philosophy to argument is his response to Cebes's demand for a proof that the soul is indestructible and immortal. Socrates, in re-presenting Cebes's demand, has him say that this proof is needed "if the philosopher, who is about to die is confident and thinks that after death he will fare better there than if he had lived his life differently, is not to find his confidence foolish and vain" (95b-c). Cebes holds that the soul's entrance into the body is the beginning of its dissolution, a kind of disease, and that even if it lives many lives in many bodies, it finally perishes. His metaphor is that of the weaver who uses many cloaks but who himself must finally die. Socrates concludes his restatement of Cebes's objection: "Now it makes no difference, you say, whether [the soul] enters into a body once or many times, so far as the fear each of us feels is concerned; for it is proper to fear if someone is not a fool, when he does not know and cannot give an argument that the soul is immortal" (95d). In the first version of Cebes's demand, the need for a proof was linked to the philosopher's confidence in the face of death, based on the kind of life he has led. In this second version, the need for an argument (not proof) that the soul is deathless (not deathless and indestructible) is associated with the fear "each of us" feels. The philosopher is not distinguished from everyone else with respect to the fear of death.

Cebes's demand takes us back to the question of the relationship between theory and action: one can face death confidently only if one has a proof that the soul is immortal. As we have seen, the proof that Socrates offers after the story of his turn is based on the notion of the soul as the bearer of life. This makes it impossible to distinguish the human soul from any other and it certainly does not allow for any distinction between the philosopher and other men.

But, on another level, Socrates *is* revealing how the human soul is to be distinguished and how the soul of the philosopher in particular is to be located in nature. He does this in the story of his turn away from natural philosophy. For Socrates's dissatisfaction with natural philosophy is due to its inability to regard the soul as different from the body. Nature is bodies and so the soul is investigated in the same way as body. In this sense, Socrates's turn away from natural philosophy is a turn away from a version of the claim that "all things are the same." But his turn to argument is not a move to the opposite position that "all things are changing."

We must consider Socrates's story, then, not as simply the prelude to the argument for immortality but as a *display* of his soul, as a revealing of the soul's place in nature.[43] The story has to be taken on two levels, that of the content of his speech and that of his own actions and passions. Socrates tells this story as a way of talking about the search for the cause of all generation and decay. The implied question is that of the soul's place in nature. Is the soul no different from bodies? What is the manner of being of the soul?

Socrates begins the story not only by implying a distinction between man and the other animals but between the philosopher and all other men. When he was young, he was very eager for the kind of wisdom (*sophia*) called "the investigation of nature." He thought it was a glorious thing to know the causes of everything. The philosopher is "above" other men because he seems to them to be wise. And this wisdom is the knowledge of causes, the knowledge of why things come into being, exist, and perish. Socrates's initial position is the identification of wisdom and knowledge.

The questions that Socrates says he was first concerned with deal with animals and man in particular, proceeding from life to knowing. In each case he is seeking a bodily cause: even knowledge is held to be the result of some bodily state. He says in more general terms that he investigated heaven and earth and finally concluded that he was naturally unfit for this kind of investigation. The proof is that he was so completely blinded that he lost the knowledge that he and others thought he had. The search for knowledge brought about its opposite. From his glorious beginning he falls to a state of ignorance and blindness (96b-c).

The first example that Socrates gives of his unlearning is the cause of man's growth. He had thought that it was plain to everyone that man grows through eating and drinking: flesh is added to flesh and bone to bone. This example is, again, bodily. And the explanation cannot account for those aspects of *human* growth which have to do with learning and moral action. His second example has to do with size: he had thought that when he saw a tall man (or horse) standing by a short man (or horse) that one was larger than the other by a head. When he proceeds to his third example we see the pattern of his account: "and still clearer than those, I thought that ten were more than eight because two had been added to the eight and I thought a two-cubit rule was longer than a one-cubit rule because it exceeded it by half its length" (96e).

There is a progression in these examples from clear to more clear, from bodies to numbers and magnitudes. There is no mention of the soul. But, on another level, the soul *is* at work here, the soul of the investigator. The activity of the soul of the investigator is knowing: the emphasis in this segment of the story of the turn is on clarity and knowledge, the knowledge of causes which is identified with wisdom.

In one sense, it is surprising that Socrates should judge himself unsuited for this kind of study on the grounds that he came to unlearn what he thought he knew, for this sounds like a way of expressing the recognition of ignorance that characterizes his activity in the *Apology*. Perhaps we are meant to take this first segment as a prelude to the account given in the *Apology*: his initial response to the oracle is that he is not wise. What we see in the *Apology* is his coming to a different understanding of the word 'wisdom', an understanding that distinguishes human wisdom from more-than-human wisdom. That is, in the *Apology* we see a distinction being made between wisdom and knowledge. This distinction has to be contrasted with the initial identification of knowledge and wisdom in the story of his life given here in the *Phaedo*.

It should also be noted that, in denying that he is a natural philosopher in the *Apology*, Socrates never denies that such knowledge is possible for man: what is characterized as "more-than-human wisdom" is not held to be unattainable by man by nature. And here in the *Phaedo*, also, he does not deny the possibility of this kind of knowledge. He presents the story of his life as an account of his own particular experiences, an account which may be useful in some respects (96a), but which is not a model to be followed in every detail.

When Cebes asks Socrates what he thinks now about the various examples of his unlearning, Socrates identifies the causes that his initial pursuits had led him to. These causes are the opposites "addition" and "division," or uniting and separating. He illustrates his dissatisfaction with this notion of cause by speaking about the generation of two: "I wonder that when each of them was separate from the other, each was one and they were not then two, and when they were brought near each other this was the cause of their becoming two, the coming together and being placed closer to one another. And I cannot be persuaded that if one is divided, the division causes it to become two; for this is the opposite of the cause of becoming two in the former case" (97a-b). The difficulty with this notion of cause is that opposite causes produce the same effect: two is generated by both union and separation.

As in the argument for immortality that follows, so in the first segment of the story of the turn, there is no distinction made between the being of numbers and of bodies. Indeed, Socrates speaks about the generation of two as if the juxtaposition and separation in this case were spatial. The adding and dividing that effect the "generation" of two are accomplished by thought and do not occur in space. And the whole notion of the coming into being of numbers is highly questionable. Do we really want to claim that two is generated at all or that it comes into being when I add two ones or divide one one? The case of numbers is said to be "clearer" than the case of bodies but otherwise there is no distinction made between their respective modes of being.

Again, the soul is present in this part of the account, but only implicitly. The act of uniting or dividing that occurs in mathematics is accomplished by the soul through its reasoning faculty. And this leads us to ask whether the processes of growth and nutrition common to all animals and plants are not also attributable to the soul. Corpses do not eat and grow.[44]

Finally, there are two puzzling features of this account of Socrates's dissatisfaction, features that come to light when we consider what is going on and being said in the rest of the dialogue. For throughout the dialogue uniting and dividing are said to be causes. The uniting of soul and body causes life and the separation of soul and body is death. (Of course, if this cause of life is accepted, the final argument for immortality makes no sense since life is said to belong to the soul as such.) True, the uniting and dividing that is said to cause life and death do not represent the case of opposite causes producing the same effect: opposite causes are producing opposite effects. But what we see now is that this way of talking about soul and body, the way that dominates the dialogue, amounts to speaking about the soul as if it were a body. This spatial way of talking about the soul is never explicitly questioned. Yet it is constantly assumed in such expressions as the soul's being "in Hades" (70c) and "in the body" and "entering into the body." The manner of being of the soul, like the manner of being of numbers and of forms, has to be distinguished from the manner of being of bodies.[45]

There is another way in the dialogue in which juxtaposition and separation are apparently approved as causes. Socrates's own "method," as he describes it at the very end of the story of his turn, is a method of juxtaposition of arguments. And this juxtaposition or separation "generates" the true and the false. Again, this is not a case of opposite causes producing the same effect. But, again, we must raise the question of the manner of being of arguments. Arguments are not "things" alongside other "things." The manner of being of arguments comes more fully to light in the final segment of the turn story. There we should be able to get some clarity about Socrates's turn as he expresses it in the concluding lines of the first segment: "I no longer persuade myself that I know even how one comes to be, or, in a word, how anything comes to be or is destroyed or is by this method, and I no longer accept it, but I mix together another way of my own" (97b).[46]

The second stage of Socrates's turn centers around Anaxagoras and his claim that nous arranges and causes all things. Socrates is "pleased" by this notion of cause, that nous causes all things. He reasons that if this is so then each thing must be as it is best for it to be. Seeking the cause would mean finding out what is best: the good would be shown to be the cause of all things. He prized his hopes very highly and eagerly read the books of Anaxagoras as fast as he could. But he is sorely disappointed: "My glorious hope was swept away" (98b). Anaxagoras really made no use of nous at all. Rather, he spoke of such things as air, ether, and water as causes.

In order to better explain his disappointment with Anaxagoras, Socrates gives two examples of the deficiency of Anaxagoras's kind of account. Anaxagoras's way of talking about all things is like saying that Socrates does whatever he does by intelligence (nous) and then saying that the cause of his sitting in prison is that his body is composed of bones and sinews, and the bones are hard and have joints which divide them and that by relaxing and contracting the ligaments, he is able to sit with his legs bent. The second example is of giving voice, air, and hearing as the causes of their talking with each other. Socrates then gives "the true cause(s)": the Athenians decided that it was best to condemn him and therefore he has decided that it is best to sit in prison and undergo whatever penalty they order.

It seems clear that Socrates has here provided the cause, the true cause, of his sitting in prison. But it is not clear that he has answered the question raised by his second example. What is the true cause of their talking to each other? The two examples of what Anaxagoras's causes cannot account for are action and speech, both specifically human possibilities. Socrates's explanation of the true cause of his sitting in prison concerns action, as decision about what is good, and passion, that is, undergoing. He is, in the particular manner of his death, both actor and victim. Or rather, he himself is the instrument of the Athenians's will and the victim of their injustice.

What is at issue in this first example, what is presented as especially characteristic of human action, is the rule of soul over body. This becomes clear when he says: "For, by the Dog, I think these bones and sinews of mine would have been in Megara or among the Boeotians long ago, carried there by an opinion (*doxa*) of what was best, if I did not think that it was better and nobler to endure any penalty the city ordered rather than to escape and run away" (99a). Socrates keeps his bones and sinews in prison, in that particular place rather than some other place, because of an opinion about what is best. Here we see the soul ruling the body, the nonbodily forcing the body, in accordance with an "opinion."

With respect to the second example, the cause of their talking with each other, we are left to wonder. Perhaps the two examples are both about the rule of soul over body. That is, if the cause of their speaking with each other is their common fear of death, then by arguing about the immortality of the soul, they are, in that very act, controlling themselves. This is a control of the body if the passions are relegated to the body. Otherwise, it is the rule of the soul over itself by means of persuasion.

The fear of death is common to all men. At the beginning of the dialogue, Socrates explicitly excludes all others and limits their attention to themselves (64c and 63e). This is a private conversation with those friends who have been visiting him every day. So it is possible that the cause of their speaking with each other is friendship and that they are pursuing together their "common good" (63d). Friendship is what binds them together and their friendship is in their habitually being with each other.

These two possible meanings of 'cause' suggest themselves if we take Socrates's example to refer to the particular conversation they are having on that day or even to their customary association in dialogue. It may be possible, however, to take his example as referring to the cause of speech as such. If this is what he intends, then the most likely answer to the question about the true cause of speech is the forms, the unchangeable "itselfs" which serve as his starting point in the argument immediately following the story of his turn.

That Socrates may be referring to the cause of speech as such is suggested indirectly by the expression of his criticism of Anaxagoras. Here again we see the soul at work; we see it revealing itself in coming to terms with an account of "all things" that does not allow it any special place. Socrates has explained that Anaxagoras *says* that nous arranges and causes all things but then really makes use of such causes as air, ether, and water:

> But it is most absurd to call such things causes. If anyone were to say that I could not do what I decided if I did not have bones and sinews and other things that I have, he would speak the truth. But to say that I do what I do on account of those things and that I act by nous, but not by choice of what is best, would be an extremely careless way of talking. Whoever talks in that way is unable to make a distinction, that a cause is one thing, and the thing without which the cause could never be a cause is quite another thing. And so it seems to me that the many, when they give the name of cause to the latter, are groping in the dark, as it were, and are giving it a name that does not belong to it." (99a-b)

Socrates is critical of "a careless way of talking." This is perhaps meant to be contrasted with his own very careful, indeed almost ridiculously precise, way of talking in the argument that follows (see, for example, 102d). There has been a failure to distinguish and there has been an improper naming. Here we see revealed the action of the soul in speech. Careful speech is speech that distinguishes properly and attaches the right name to the right thing. Speech is a separating and uniting. The very act of naming always entails both separating and uniting: to name something is to separate it off from everything else and to join it with all the other things that have the same name. Assertion and denial are kinds of separating and uniting. The predicate is first separated out from the thing and then joined back to it in some kinds of affirmation. Denial is the separating of subject and predicate.[47]

Careful speech requires that the thing be given its name, the name that "belongs" to it. This insistence on the proper joining of name and thing, the insistence that things have names that "belong" to them, is also Socrates's answer to the partisans of "all things are changing," the haters of argument. Names are not man-made tags which can be moved around at will.

Now it is possible to see that natural philosophy and sophistry are in some sense complementary. If "nature" means bodies then everything else is man-made. Speech is mere convention. In affirming the essential connection between words and things, Socrates emerges and is presenting himself as a "third." He is distinguishing himself from both natural philosophers and Sophists. Words are not bodies, not "things" alongside other things. Nor are they mere tags, changeable at will. The relationship between words and things is addressed in the final stage of Socrates's turn.

Socrates speaks of his own "way" as a kind of second-best, a second "voyage" in search of the cause. The first-best has been denied him for the natural philosophers "do not think that the good and the fitting bind and hold all things together" (99c). Socrates was not able to discover the good of all things or to learn it from anyone else. He does not say that it is impossible for human beings to have this knowledge, but he (the wisest of men) does not have it.

This, of course, recalls the distinction in the *Apology* between human wisdom and more-than-human wisdom. A similar distinction is reflected in the *Phaedo* in Simmias's prelude to his claim that the soul is a harmony: "I think, Socrates, as perhaps you do yourself, that it is either impossible or very difficult to have sure knowledge about these matters in this life. To fail to test them in every way without desisting till one is utterly exhausted by examining them on every side, shows a very poor spirit. For it is necessary to do one of two things: either discover or learn about them, or if that is impossible, take the best and most irrefutable human account and, borne upon it as upon a raft, sail upon it through life in the midst of dangers, unless someone can sail upon some stronger vessel, some divine account, and make his voyage more safely and securely" (85c-d).

It is not clear from the context whether Socrates's reply, "Perhaps, my friend, you are right," is a reply to this or to Simmias's more specific claim that the immortality of the soul has not been proved. And we are not entitled to assume that, because Simmias thinks that this is Socrates's view, it really is what Socrates thinks. Nevertheless, whatever his own thoughts may be, Socrates presents his own "method" very much in the terms suggested by Simmias's raft metaphor: a voyage in the midst of danger.

The third segment of Socrates's story is about his second voyage in search of the cause:

> After this, then, since I had given up investigating things, it seemed to me that I must be careful not to suffer what happens to people who look at the sun and watch it during an eclipse. For some of them ruin their eyes unless they look at its image in water or something of the sort. I thought of that, and I was afraid my soul would be entirely blinded if I looked at things with my eyes and tried to grasp them with any of my senses. So I thought I must take refuge in arguments and examine in them the truth of things. Now perhaps my metaphor is not quite accurate, for I do not admit in the least that he who investigates things in words is looking at them in images more than he who investigates them in actions [works]. (99d-100a)[48]

As I noticed earlier, the tone of this segment suggests a kind of humbling. The first segment showed a confident Socrates who thought it a glorious thing to know the causes of everything. The Anaxagoras segment is characterized by his "wonderful hope." This final segment is dominated by fear and caution. With respect to this "humbling," we cannot help making a comparison between Socrates's caution in looking at an eclipse and the philosopher's looking at the sun in the allegory of the cave. And this comparison suggests that the sun in the eclipse metaphor *may* be meant to be taken as the good. This suggestion is given some support by the nature of his disappointment with the natural philosophers: "they do not think that the good and the fitting bind and hold all things together" (99c).

Socrates's turn to words, to argument, seems to imply a turn from eyes to ears. He had been "blinded" in the first segment. But even here there is a sense in which he begins from opinion: "Do heat and cold, by a sort of fermentation, bring about the organization of animals, *as some people say?*" [Emphasis added.] Yet the model of seeing is still preserved in the eclipse metaphor. And his initial blinding was not complete since here he is afraid that his soul would be blinded. In the second, Anaxagoras segment, the model of sight for knowing is used when Socrates refers to those who are "groping in the dark" (99b) when they give the name 'cause' to that without which the cause cannot be a cause.

With these observations in mind, we can now make an approach to the meaning of what has happened. There are, I think, three key terms that appear in this segment, terms around which the Socratic turn is to be more precisely fixed. These terms are 'soul', 'truth', and 'actions' or 'works'. I have in mind those passages where Socrates says that he was afraid his soul would be blinded, where he says he thought he should seek the truth of things in words, and where he says that seeking the truth in words is no more a seeking in images than seeking the truth in actions or works.

The term 'soul' does not appear in the entire turn story until the third segment, even though the context for the telling of the story is the attempt to determine whether the soul is indestructible. Socrates speaks of thinking (96c), of nous (97c, 97d), of knowing and not knowing (96a, 96c, 96e, 97b, 97d, 98b) as activities of the soul in the practice of natural philosophy. That is, only the rational part of the soul is presented. I understand his turn to "soul" to be an admitting of the "whole soul." What is emphasized is his fear. Indeed, it is fear that prompts his turn. The spirited part of the soul must now somehow be included in the account of the nature of philosophy.

The repeated use of such terms as 'knowing', of course, also has a bearing on the significance of the second key term, 'truth'. As with 'soul', so with 'truth': it is not used in the first two segments except to say that Anaxagoras's causes are not "true" causes. And the two examples that are intended to show the deficiency of Anaxagoras's account of nature both deal with specifically human matters, matters which have to do with the relationship between the *human* soul and body.

These two examples, the cause of his sitting in prison and the cause of their talking with each other, are taken into account in the third and final segment when Socrates adds the clarification that "actions" or "works" are also images of "things." This duality is one that runs throughout the dialogue: *logoi* and *erga*, argument and action (as the rule of soul over body).

Socrates's turn is a turn from "separated" intellect to the "whole soul," and from the search for knowledge to the search for truth. This marks a radical change in the understanding of philosophy as a divine activity. Again, Socrates's wisdom is human wisdom as distinguished from more-than-human wisdom. At the beginning of the story of his turn, Socrates shows us the identification of "wisdom" with knowledge, the knowledge sought in the investigation of nature (96a). We can, I think, infer that his turn is, in part, a rejection of that identification, at least for man. Making the distinction between human wisdom and knowledge is the work of careful speech.

But what could it mean to say that the Socratic practice of philosophy includes the "whole soul," and, in particular, the spirited part? Passion, after all, obscures the judgment, interferes with thinking, makes "objectivity" impossible. The search for truth seems to require the absence of the passions of the spirited part of the soul.

The requirement that the passions be put aside is, indeed, manifest in the beginnings of philosophy as natural philosophy. It might even be the case that philosophy *must* begin in this way. And it is also undeniable that being overcome by passion, being dominated by the spirited part, makes thought impossible. But there is perhaps a sense in which the spirited part of the soul actually makes philosophy possible at all.

In order to explain this claim, I would like to examine Socrates's eclipse metaphor more closely. As noted above, the eclipse metaphor preserves seeing as the model for the rational activity of the soul, even though the Socratic turn is to words. Further, this specific metaphor, the eclipse of the sun, invites comparison with the "sun" of the *Republic*, which the philosopher is able ultimately to look at directly.

In the *Republic*, the spirited part of the soul is explicitly distinguished as a "third" (439e, 441a). There, too, it is said to be the ally of reason (440e). In both the *Apology* and the *Phaedo*, the general impression is of the spirited part as the enemy of reason: anger in the *Apology* and fear in the *Phaedo* seem to be manifestations of the irrational and the anti-philosophical. And in the *Phaedo*, the "third" part of the soul is conspicuously absent. That is, the passions are relegated to the body and the soul is spoken of as one, namely as reason alone.

The use of the model of sight for the rational activity of the soul brings to mind another "third," also explicitly characterized as such in the *Republic* (507d-e). The sense of sight is said to be different from the other senses because it requires a "third thing." The third thing is, of course, light. Light allows the seer to see and the thing seen to be seen.

What I want to suggest is that, in the *Phaedo*, the conspicuously absent third part of the soul is the "light" that makes the Socratic practice of philosophy possible. The fear of death allows the question of the nature of the soul to come out of obscurity. The spirited part of the soul allows for the initial distinction between important and unimportant. (For those present with Socrates, the question about the soul has suddenly become urgent; hence, their "uneasiness," their tendency toward misology.) At the same time, if the spirited part rules, the practice of philosophy is impossible. Argument arises initially in the light of the passions but can only proceed if those passions are ruled. This two-sidedness is captured in the eclipse metaphor: the spirited part of the soul is a "mixture" of rational and irrational. It does not provide the blinding clarity of noon but is a kind of "half-light" where a struggle can take place.[49] The setting of the *Phaedo*, the dialogue of the soul in the shadow of imminent death, is precisely the setting that reveals most clearly the nature of the activity of philosophy: *philosophy always is done in the presence of death*.

The fear of death could surely paralyze, make all discussion and especially the discussion of death itself impossible. This would not be surprising. What we see in the *Phaedo* is a discussion prompted by the fear of death and a demonstration of the control of that fear by means of the very act of discussing. Argument requires the control of the very passion that gives rise to it.

The gods do not "practice dying," they do not engage in the activity of philosophy, because they do not die. That is, philosophy is not a possibility for them because they have no fear of death. Nothing can become truly *important* for them. The question of the immortality of the soul cannot be, for men, a "merely" theoretical question. A man cannot be a disinterested spectator of his own death or even of the death of another man.

This brings us back to our starting point and further in the discussion of the third key term '*erga*'. I have been taking this term to mean action and have been interpreting it as the ruling activity of the soul. If we accept the dialogue as an accurate report, we must face the gap that opens up between thought and action. That is, we must account for Socrates's control of fear on some other basis than any certitude that the soul is deathless. Indeed, insofar as philosophy is regarded as a human and not a divine activity, even that ground for the belief in immortality is eliminated.

Another way of expressing the gap between thought and action is to say that Socrates's certitude of action is not based on his holding beliefs about immortality which he regards as certain. In fact, if I am correct in saying that he is secretly and deliberately unweaving the arguments, then we cannot escape the conclusion that he is being deceptive. The possibility of deception is mentioned by Socrates at the very end of the hatred of argument section. He concludes his speech to Phaedo by saying that *no matter whether what he is saying is true or false*, their speaking is good (91b). Even if what he is saying about immortality is false, at least he is not being burdensome to his friends by his lamentations. Again, we see quite clearly that Socrates does not regard the arguments as certain. But he does regard the arguing itself as good.

But this is not for him, here and now, a theoretical matter. He is trying to *persuade* himself and his hearers.[50] He wants to persuade them so that they will act well. This is another aspect of his "cure." Socrates's last words refer both to his curing them of their mistrust of argument as such and to their controlling themselves when he tells them to after he has drunk the poison: "We were ashamed and controlled our tears" (117e).

When Socrates turns the conversation back to Simmias and Cebes at the end of the hatred of argument section, he begins by preparing them for the coming battle: "But you, if you are persuaded by me, will give little thought to Socrates but much more to the truth; and if you think what I say is true, agree to it, and if not, strive against it with every argument that I may not in my eagerness deceive myself and you and go away, like a bee, leaving my sting in you" (91c).

The bee is one of those "social and gentle species" into which the soul of the man who is virtuous without philosophy may enter (82b). We see here an important aspect of the Socratic practice of philosophy. Whether he is the gadfly among his fellow-citizens or a bee among his friends, the Socratic practice of philosophy is with other men. Philosophy as the separation of soul and body is also the separation from others. But the life of argument is with others. Socrates spends his last hours not in isolation, in silent contemplation of the good, but in conversation with friends, pursuing their "common good" (63c-d). He had been disappointed in Anaxagoras because he could not learn from him what the good of all things is. But in both the *Phaedo* and the *Apology* he shows himself pursuing a common good. In the *Phaedo*, their common good is accomplished: he "cures" them of hatred of argument *and* rules himself and them. Socrates does not rule Athens in the *Apology* and he apologizes for not having been the philosopher-king. But he does rule himself and his friends in the *Phaedo*. This rule entails deception.

At the end of the hatred of argument section, Socrates raises the possibility of both deception and self-deception. As we have seen, Socrates himself recognizes quite clearly the deficiencies of the arguments for immortality. But he does not point out these deficiencies to the others. Like Penelope, he secretly unweaves what he has openly woven. So we can accept the notion that he is deceiving the others, securing their "agreement," and uniting them in battle. On one level, this battle is against the fear of death. On another level, it is with the hatred of argument. And in the *Phaedo*, the plot displays the action. Hatred of argument is the worst evil that can happen to a man, and they must not admit into their souls the notion that there is no soundness in argument.

But what of the possibility of self-deception? Is there any sense in which Socrates could be deceiving himself, even deliberately? Immediately after the discussion of the thesis that learning is recollection and joining this to the first argument to form a proof, Socrates encourages them to pursue the question of immortality. He says to Cebes: "I think that you and Simmias would like to carry on this discussion still further. You have the childish fear that when the soul goes out from the body the wind will really blow it away and scatter it, especially if a man happens to die in a high wind and not in calm weather." Cebes laughs but half-jokingly admits to this fear: "Assume that we have that fear, Socrates, and try to convince us; or rather, do not assume that we are afraid, but perhaps there is a child in us, who has such fears. Let us try to persuade him not to fear death as if it were a hobgoblin" (77d-e).

"Persuasion" is also what Socrates says he wishes to accomplish for himself in the hatred of argument section. And this is *not* philosophical (91a-b). In response to Cebes's request to be persuaded, Socrates says of the child within: "You must sing charms to him every day until you charm away his fear." Cebes then characterizes Socrates as a good singer of such charms and Socrates does not deny this.

Persuasive speech is not philosophical speech; it is rhetorical speech. And rhetorical speech concerns the probable. There can be no "report" of death, so death is always a future event about which there must always be uncertainty concerning what follows it. Rhetorical speech deals with the future. There is here no *direct* link between the theoretical and the practical, between speculative thought and action. There may, however, be an indirect link. That is, the theoretical life has consequences for action. This is why Socrates must defend himself.

Socrates tells them that they must sing charms "every day." This may well be the significance of Socrates's other definition of philosophy. The definition that dominates the discussion in the *Phaedo* is of philosophy as the separation of soul and body. But the definition that is being acted out in the dialogue is of philosophy as "the greatest music" (61a). The two definitions correspond to the two approaches to truth presented in the dialogue, and to the two senses in which the soul is said to be divine (separating from body, ruling the body). And their complementary differences, the duality of the philosophical, reminds us of Penelope's "endless task": the soul of the philosopher separating from and uniting with the body "every day."

The task of weaving is the paradigmatic "work" (*ergon*). This is precisely the term that Socrates uses for Penelope's task. And *erga* are no less images of things than arguments are. But we must not forget that the true task of Penelope is deception, a deception to hold off the suitors while she waits for Odysseus. As Socrates says of the arguments, even if they are false, they "pass the time" until he dies.

The self-deception that is done by Socrates (that is, assuming the accuracy of the report) has to do with the requirements of action. Thought is never finished; it is an endless task. But action requires that a stand be taken. Since decision and action have to do with the probable and uncertain, and since speculation can never come to an end, the actor must pretend a certitude he does not have. He must act as if he knows what he does not know, all the while knowing that he does not know. The sureness of action that we see in Phaedo's report of Socrates's drinking the poison is like the decisiveness of the military commander who goes ahead as if he cannot fail, while knowing full well that he may lose everything. This is how Socrates recalls them from flight and defeat and makes them face about and follow him (89a). His action is the "proof," the real "demonstration" of the worth of the life of argument.

But there is a very obvious difficulty with this interpretation. If the definition of philosophy as the greatest music is taken to refer to the singing of charms, to the rule of reason over the spirited part and the body, then it seems impossible to distinguish it from rhetoric, from persuasive speech. And as we see from Socrates's description of his state of soul in the hatred of argument section, persuasion is "not philosophical."

Indeed, there is a sense in which the whole dialogue is not philosophical. Phaedo says at the beginning that he did not feel his customary pleasure in philosophy, even though the arguments or speeches were about philosophy (59a). And Socrates, in the very early discussion of the prohibition against suicide, sets the tone for the day's conversation: "I myself speak of these things [suicide, death, dying] only from hearsay [hearing]; but I do not mind telling what I have heard. And indeed it is perhaps especially fitting, as I am going there, to tell stories (*muthoi*) about the journey there and consider what we think about it; for what else could one do in the time until sunset?" (61d-e).

Myth is also associated with hearing at the end of the dialogue when Socrates tells the "story" about the earth and its regions. What he says at the end of the myth may really be intended to apply to the entire day's discussion: "Now it would not be fitting for a sensible man to insist that all this is just as I have described it . . . [but] he ought to repeat such things to himself as if they were charms,[51] which is the reason why I have been lengthening out the story so long" (114d). The myth had ended in the same way as the repeated descriptions of philosophy throughout the dialogue: "All who have sufficiently purified themselves by philosophy live henceforth altogether without bodies" (114c). Philosophy as the separation of soul and body is a myth, a "charm" to be sung to oneself every day, to charm away the fear of death.[52] (See also 67a-b).

What does this mean for my initial claim that the *Phaedo* is an apology? The crucial issue here is the identification of the *audience* for this apology.[53] Except for Phaedo himself and the unnamed objector (if he is different from Phaedo) Socrates's interlocutors are Simmias and Cebes. They are Pythagoreans and each at some point brings the discussion around to mathematics (73a-b and 92c-e). What they reveal at the very beginning of the discussion is a lack of clarity and precision about words. That is, they confuse poetry, philosophy, and rhetoric. It is made known that they have been speaking with Evenus (60d), that Evenus writes poems (60d-e), and, in the *Apology*, Evenus is identified as a Sophist. When Socrates asks if Evenus is a philosopher, Simmias replies: "It seems so to me" (61c).

Socrates's audience in the *Phaedo* is very different from his audience in the *Apology* or at least the angry majority. At his trial Socrates faces a hostile, and anti-philosophical audience, at the very least suspicious of philosophers and confused about the differences between natural philosophers and Sophists. In the *Phaedo* his audience is not hostile or anti-philosophical. We might characterize Simmias and Cebes as friends of philosophy, well-disposed to hear of the benefits it brings. Nevertheless, Simmias and Cebes are not themselves philosophers. They need to hear a defense of philosophy, they cannot really distinguish Socrates from Evenus, and their objections to Socrates's arguments take the form of metaphors about the soul.

It is not unheard of, even in our own day, that those who spend their lives in the mathematical sciences are sometimes confused about the various modes of speech and, in particular, are unable to distinguish philosophy from poetry. They may even look upon philosophy as "mere words." This is the tendency toward hatred of argument and it is conceivable that it could arise in those who are accustomed to the clarity, precision, and certitude of mathematical demonstration.[54]

What Socrates does for these friends of philosophy is to turn them away from this direction and lead them toward a respect for words. The failure to distinguish between philosophy and sophistry ultimately leads to the contempt for "mere words." In the case of Simmias and Cebes, Socrates accomplishes this by gently steering them away from the position that truth and certitude are identical and away from the position that truth can only be had in the mathematical sciences. Simmias and Cebes never articulate this position but it seems that Socrates finds them to be making this assumption.

Socrates's first description of philosophy as the separation of soul and body is perfectly acceptable to them. This is what I have called the approach of sight to truth, "sight" meaning a kind of "sight" of the mind. One such discussion occurs very early in the dialogue where Socrates speaks about the philosopher's disregard, if not contempt, for the body and the need to separate the soul from the body in order to have knowledge. The term that dominates here is 'dianoia' (65e 4, 8, 9). There is no distinction made between the "lovers of wisdom" (66b 3) and the "lovers of knowledge" (67b). Socrates concludes this long speech on the need for purification by hinting at the speech's charm-like character: "I think, Simmias, that all who are rightly lovers of knowledge must say such things to each other and must believe such things. Do you agree?" And Simmias assents enthusiastically (67b).[55]

Socrates's description of his "method," the method of hypothesis, seems designed to appeal to mathematicians and, in this respect, brings to mind the divided line of the *Republic* (509d-511e).[56] There the level of *pistis* (of trust or certitude) is precisely the level which must be transcended since it is the level of opinion. The next level, where mathematical objects are located, is the level of *dianoia*. Dialectic, of course, is the highest level, and dialectic is the art of discourse, of asking questions and giving answers.[57]

By the end of the dialogue, Socrates has introduced the approach of argument to truth, specifically in the story of his turn to words. What he accomplishes is to bring about in his audience a recognition of the importance of careful speech and a willingness to engage in dialectic without slipping into hatred of argument, into contempt for "mere words." Simmias and Cebes are led to respect the precision of words. We see this, for example, toward the beginning of the third argument for immortality. Socrates is here distinguishing philosophy from disputation: "You would not mix things up as disputants do, in talking about the starting point and its consequences, if you wished to discover anything of things; for perhaps not one of them thinks or cares in the least about these things. Their cleverness enables them to be pleased with themselves even when they mix everything up; but if you are a philosopher, I think you will do as I have said." Simmias and Cebes reply together: "What you say is most true" (101e-102a).

Socrates's defense of philosophy before the court of the friends of philosophy does not amount to making them into philosophers. Rather, Socrates brings them to a recognition of the need for careful speech, away from a tendency toward contempt for "mere words." This contempt arises from the failure to carefully distinguish between philosophy and disputation. (And this distinction requires that philosophy as practiced by Socrates be distinguished from natural philosophy.) But what really convinces them that philosophy is not "mere words," what "proves" or demonstrates the importance of words to this audience, is the manner in which Socrates dies.[58] That is to say, the defense of philosophy to the nonphilosopher must be in terms of its effects on action.[59] The term used by Phaedo at the end of the dialogue to describe Socrates is not *sophia* (90c) but *phronēsis* (118). This is consistent with the tendency throughout the dialogue to blur the distinction between theoretical and practical wisdom: '*sophos*' or '*sophia*' is used, I think, only twice, once in reference to the Sophists or disputants (90c) and once in reference to natural philosophy, to that "kind of wisdom" (96a). And Socrates distinguishes himself from both. The term used throughout the dialogue is *phronēsis*.

The defense of philosophy to the friends of philosophy is accomplished by the failure to distinguish between wisdom and prudence, or by letting the ambiguity of the term 'wisdom' go unexamined. Theoretical excellence and moral excellence appear to be inseparable. Yet, as we have seen, there is a gap between theory and action in the *Phaedo*: Socrates does not act as he does on account of any certitude that the soul is immortal. Philosophy does not provide him with principles in terms of which he can act. The closest he comes to accounting for his actions is in the Anaxagoras segment of the story of his turn: he is sitting in prison because of an "opinion about what is best."[60] Here he points to the particularity of action. Given the fact that the Athenians have decided to condemn him, he has decided to remain and accept the penalty.

At the end of the dialogue, after having just described Socrates's drinking the poison without trembling or turning pale, Phaedo eulogizes him as "the best, the wisest [*phronēsis*], and the most just man" of all those they have known. He does not call Socrates courageous or even self-restrained. This is consistent with his very early description of his own feelings: he did not feel pity because Socrates was so cheerful. There is no visible struggle which would call forth their pity. But there is reason to think that Socrates's sureness of action is a deception and a self-deception. He has gone away like a bee, leaving his sting in them.

Phaedo

This takes us back to the unavoidable suspicion that Phaedo is not simply presenting an accurate eye-witness account. He has, perhaps, constructed "the myth of Socrates." What is being called into question at this level is the identification of truth with accuracy of reporting, or the taking of sight as the model for approaching truth. In many ways Phaedo's conversation or rather his sequence of brief exchanges with Echecrates mirrors what happens in the conversation between Socrates and those present in the prison.

Echecrates, like Simmias and Cebes, is a Pythagorean.[61] This does not entitle us to identify his views with theirs in every respect, but there are times in the discussion when he agrees with what one of them has said. Echecrates's first words in the dialogue (and these are the very first words of the whole dialogue) are to inquire of Phaedo whether he was actually there with Socrates when Socrates drank the poison and died. Or, he wants to know, was Phaedo absent and has he heard about it from someone else?

We have the initial impression that Echecrates is revealing a preference for an eye-witness account over an account from hearsay, a preference for sight over hearing. When Phaedo indicates that he was actually there with Socrates, Echecrates twice questions him about what Socrates said and did (57a, 58c). And twice he specifies that he wants Phaedo to be as accurate as possible: "Be so good as to tell us as *exactly* as you can about all these things, if you are not too busy" (58d) and "Try to tell us everything as *accurately* as you can" (58d). [Emphasis added.] Echecrates wants to know every detail, as only an eye-witness could supply. And Phaedo responds that he will try to tell them "everything from the beginning" (59c).

What we are presented with at this level of the dialogue is a change that takes place in Echecrates, a change brought about by Phaedo's narration and which mirrors the change in Simmias and Cebes brought about by Socrates. There are two places in the dialogue where Phaedo's narrative is interrupted for a brief exchange with Echecrates. The first occurs immediately after the objections of Simmias and Cebes and before the "digression" on hatred of argument. Phaedo reports that all of those present had been made very uneasy by the objections of Simmias and Cebes: they had been thoroughly convinced by Socrates's argument and now they were confused again. They had begun to mistrust argument as such.

Echecrates breaks in here to say that he is "with" Phaedo and the others. He feels as they did: "For I myself, after hearing you now, find myself asking myself: 'What argument shall we trust? For the argument of Socrates was perfectly convincing, and now it has fallen into distrust.'" Then Echecrates specifically identifies his view of the soul with the one expressed by Simmias: "For the argument that the soul is a kind of harmony has always had, and has now, a wonderful hold upon me, and your mention of it reminded me that I had myself believed in it before." Echecrates had at one time held this view of the soul and now when he hears it stated he believes it again. Echecrates had literally forgotten about the soul. He has to be reminded of what he had once believed. The change that we begin to see here is two-fold and has to do with his having forgotten about the soul and with his mistrust of argument: "Now I am in need again, as if from the beginning, of another argument to convince me that when a man dies his soul does not perish with him." Echecrates is becoming eager for argument. Now he not only wants to hear Phaedo's report but also to be persuaded by Socrates: "So, for heaven's sake, tell how Socrates pursued the argument, and whether he also, as you say the rest of you did, showed any uneasiness, or calmly defended his argument. And did he defend it successfully or not? Tell us everything as accurately as you can" (88c-e).

Echecrates is moving away from the tendency toward contempt for argument. He has been drawn into the presence of Socrates and cannot regard arguments as "mere words." Yet he too wants to know how Socrates acted, not only what he said. Socrates's actions are the real "demonstration" of what he thinks. So Phaedo begins his reply by expressing his wonder at the way Socrates behaved: "Echecrates, I have often wondered at Socrates, but never did I admire him more than then. That he had an answer ready was perhaps not strange; but what astonished me most about him was, first, the pleasant, gentle, and respectful manner in which he listened to the young men's argument, his quick sense of the effect their words had upon us, and then, the skill with which he cured us and, as it were, recalled us from our flight and defeat and made us face about and follow him and join in his examination of the argument" (88e-89a). It is Socrates, not the argument for immortality, who remains unshaken. He holds fast to the belief that there is soundness in argument.

The third and final time that we hear Echecrates, he interrupts the narrative in order to agree with Simmias and Cebes who have just been reported to have agreed with Socrates. This is at the point where Socrates has said that the philosopher does not "mix things up, as disputants do" (101e-102a). When Simmias and Cebes say together that this is "most true," Echecrates is again drawn into the flow of the dialogue: "By Zeus, Phaedo, they were right. It seems to me that he made these things wonderfully clear to anyone with even a little intelligence" (102a). Echecrates is referring to the forms and their place as causes in things and in speech. Echecrates can now admit the clarity and precision of speech.

And when Phaedo answers that those who were present at the time also thought that Socrates had made these things clear, Echecrates shows that he has come to regard hearing as something more than mere "hearsay." He speaks for the last time: "And so do we who were not present but are hearing about it now. But what was said after that?" (102a). Echecrates has moved away from his initially sharp distinction between hearing and truth.

As for Phaedo himself, if I am correct in identifying him with the man whose identity is not revealed, then we may infer that he does not regard his task as that of a reporter, a spectator who later tells what he saw and heard. He has become the ally of Socrates, preserving agreement, and bringing about in his hearers what he understood Socrates to have done in those who were with him.[62] At the beginning of the dialogue, when Echecrates asks him to tell them "as exactly as you can about all these things, if you are not too busy," Phaedo's answer reveals his own turn to words: "I am not too busy and I will try to tell you. It is always my greatest pleasure to be reminded of Socrates whether speaking himself or listening to someone else." Socrates is present through speech.

This enduring presence in speech, the "endless task" of argument, is the "immortality" that is revealed in the dialogue.[63] There is a joke at the beginning that goes unnoticed. When Simmias asks Socrates to share his thoughts with them for their common good and in his own defense, Socrates pauses to let Crito speak. Crito says: "The man who is to administer the poison to you has been telling me for some time to warn you to talk as little as possible. He says people get warm when they talk, and heat has a bad effect on the action of the poison; so sometimes he has to make those who talk too much drink twice or even three times." Socrates answers: "Never mind him. Just let him do his part and prepare to give it twice or even, if necessary, three times" (63d-e). Surely this merits at least an ironic smile, if not the untroubled laughter of the gods.

At the end it is Crito who asks Socrates how they should bury him. Socrates's reply is reminiscent of the bee metaphor: "However you please, if you can catch me and I do not get away from you." Then he laughs gently and looks toward the others and says: "I do not persuade Crito, my friends, that I am this Socrates who is now talking to you and ordering each of the things I say; he thinks I am the thing he will soon see as a corpse, and so he asks how to bury me. I have been saying for some time and at great length that after I drink the poison I shall no longer be with you, but shall go away to the joys of the blessed, but it seems that this was *idle talk* to encourage you and myself." Crito, apparently, has not yet been cured. Socrates asks the others to help Crito bear more easily what is to come so that Crito will not be troubled when he sees the body being burned or buried and so that Crito will not *say* at the funeral that he is laying out Socrates or following him to the grave or burying him. This would indeed be a careless way of talking, a failure to distinguish, a joining of a name to something to which it does not belong. And such talk would not be idle, it would be harmful. Socrates addresses himself again to Crito: "For, dear Crito, you may be sure that to speak badly is not only erring in itself, but also causes evil in the soul. No, you must be of good courage, and say that you bury my body" (115c-116a). [Emphasis added.] Socrates *is* in his "talking and ordering each of the things" he says. Concerning the burial of the body, Phaedo is appropriately silent.

Plato

The ironic Socrates and the half-hidden Phaedo point to the third level of the dialogue, that of Plato who is almost completely hidden. Plato mentions himself in only two of the Platonic dialogues. In the *Apology*, he is pointed to by Socrates as one of those who have expressed willingness to pay a fine for him (38b). In the *Phaedo*, Echecrates asks who were those present in the prison when Socrates died. Phaedo begins with a list of the Athenians who were there and ends with a somewhat vague reference to Plato: "But Plato, I think, was ill" (59b). Plato is the only Athenian who is specified as not having been there and the fact that Phaedo mentions him at all, then, shows that he would have been expected to be there.

The references to Plato himself, in the *Apology* and in the *Phaedo*, point to his presence and absence respectively. Here we are at the third level on which the questions of truth and of being are displayed in the dialogue.[64] What do these glimpses of Plato allow us to say about him in relation to what has happened at the other two levels? It seems to me that we are entitled to say very little and to claim no certitude in this matter. We can, at best, suggest some possible meanings for these contrasting but complementary references.

Even Phaedo does not seem certain about why Plato was absent. He thinks that Plato was ill. If illness is the cause of Plato's absence, then perhaps, by presenting himself as ill, he is associating himself with the view that "all things are changing." This is the "illness" that Socrates cures and this cure is the significance of his last words. We have to wonder whether Plato puts these last words into Socrates's mouth as an expression of thought about Plato. And if Plato's illness means he is associating himself with the notion that "all things are changing," we have to wonder whether he was indeed "cured" or whether he is dissociating himself from Socrates's battle and also from Phaedo who becomes the ally of Socrates in fighting this notion.

Or, Plato's presence at the trial may indicate at least an initial willingness to associate himself with the defense of philosophy before the city. Perhaps he approves of Socrates's manner of defending himself, perhaps not.[65] His absence from the *Phaedo* may indicate an unwillingness to associate himself with this defense of philosophy. Or it may suggest that Plato disagrees with Socrates's opinion that he should remain in prison and accept the penalty. This last suggestion is supported by his action in the *Apology*: it is Plato whom Socrates first mentions as telling him to propose a fine as his penalty. And it is also possible that disagreement with Socrates's decision to die and dissociation from his defense of philosophy in the *Phaedo* are inseparable.

In the end, Plato may be distancing himself from the Socratic practice of philosophy. But, then, it is Plato who allows us the pleasure of "remembering Socrates whether speaking himself or listening to another." Within the dialogue he presents himself as being a hearer, as absent. As writer, it is he who makes Socrates present for us. Just as he has Socrates give an account of his activity by distinguishing it from that of the Sophists and the natural philosophers, so Plato's account of himself may be in terms of his own distinctness from Socrates. If this is so, then Plato himself makes no public apology.

Transition: From Philosophical Courage to Christian Hope

The apology for the philosophical life which Plato has Socrates present and act out in the *Phaedo* displays the dependence of philosophy on rhetoric in its task of preparing for death. The manner in which Socrates faces death is not due to any certitude about the immortality of the soul: there are no purely philosophical grounds for hope. In spite of Phaedo's silence about it in his eulogy at the very end of the dialogue, courage may, after all, be the virtue of the philosopher.

When we turn now to St. Augustine we are given grounds for hope. But these are not philosophical grounds. The notion of a divine part of the human soul, upon which the philosopher's pretensions to immortality rest, is rejected as the sin of pride, the original sin. Augustine's hope rests not on the divine status of philosophy but on the divine compassion. Our mortality is the evidence that God resists the proud; the divine compassion is perfectly manifested in the death of Christ who humbled himself.

CHAPTER II

St. Augustine: The Look of Pity

Confession and Apology

There is a sense in which confession and apology strike us, at least at first, as opposites. And there is some truth in this initial impression. An apology is above all an account aimed at showing and explaining how an action or way of acting is good. Confession, on the other hand, is primarily an admission of some wrong and entails feelings of shame. Of course, 'confession' does have a meaning that is now hardly recognized, that of "confessing the faith." This refers to the public statement of the content of the faith and not to any admission of one's own sins. While Augustine's *Confessions* can surely be said to express the content of the faith, confession in the first sense comes closer to describing the tone of the work.

The initial impression of apology and confession as opposites, however, needs to be modified, not so as to destroy their differences of emphasis but to allow both to be concerned with both good and bad. It is difficult to imagine how an apology could be made or even why one would be needed without some reference to an accusation. Confession, as admitting to something bad, does not make sense without at least implicit reference to what would have been good to do. Where human action is concerned, there seems to be no way to talk about good without also at least implying something about evil, and no way to confess evil without pointing to good.

Augustine's *Confessions*, then, is not an unrelieved outpouring of self-condemnation. It is as much a showing forth of God's goodness as it is an admission of Augustine's own sins.[1] This two-sidedness is manifest in Augustine's discussion of the nature of confession: "For when I am wicked, confession to you is the same thing as being displeased with

85

myself; when I am good, confession to you is the same thing as not attributing my goodness to myself" (X.2). Here, of course, he is addressing God, "to whose eyes the very depths of man's conscience are exposed." God does not need to hear Augustine's confession in order to know: God's knowledge is not improved by what Augustine says to him. Rather, in the act of confessing, something is revealed to Augustine: "And there is nothing in me that I could keep secret from you, even if I did not want to confess it. I should not be hiding myself from you, but you from myself."

The Confessions is addressed to God, but not as a speech made to God to inform or persuade him. On the contrary, it is God who is made known in the act of addressing him. And this means that God is a being who is known not by being examined as an "object" but in being addressed, in the kind of speech that is called prayer. We begin to see here what is perhaps the essential difference between apology and confession.

Socrates's apology is addressed to other men.[2] It is meant to reveal the truth about himself to those who have been deceived by his accusers. And it is made in the hope that his hearers, who are his judges, will make a just judgment of him on the basis of the truth they have learned. Their judgment entails an action, the vote for acquittal or condemnation, which will have the gravest consequences for him. Thus, Socrates's speech to the city is persuasive speech. It is not simply for the sake of revealing himself: his self-revelation is undertaken so that his fellow citizens will act toward him in the way he deserves.

Augustine's speech, insofar as it is addressed to God, is in no way persuasive. It represents no effort on his part to have God form a better opinion of him. Confessing is placing oneself in the presence of God. And in this presence one knows oneself to be completely known. Nor is this prayer an attempt to persuade God to do something or to act in a certain way toward him. Even the so-called "prayer of petition" cannot be understood as a way of convincing God to do one's will. To persuade in this sense is to rule and it is unthinkable that a man should rule God, by speech or in any other way. Further, God has no interests that could possibly conflict with man's and there is no good for which he depends upon man. It makes no sense to try to persuade such a God to do one's will and there is no need to persuade him to do what is best.

The only way in which Augustine's speech might be rhetorical is in its publicness.[3] It is customary for the self-examination that is part of confession to be hidden from other men. But Augustine's confession is public. He addresses himself to God, but other men can hear: "I make my confession not only in front of you . . . but also in the ears of the believing sons of men, companions in my joy and sharers in my mortality, my fellow citizens and fellow pilgrims" (X.4); and ". . . Lord, I make my confession to you in such a way that men may hear it" (X.3).

The public character of Augustine's *Confessions* needs to be accounted for: that he should write down what is addressed to God reveals a purpose at work with respect to other men. One of the reasons that Augustine gives is the prevention of despair: "You have forgiven and covered up my past sins. . . . Yet when the confessions of these past sins are read and heard, they rouse up the heart lest it sink into the sleep of despair and say 'I cannot'"(X.3). Augustine will uncover what God has covered so that others may see what God has done. This is the decisive claim: God has done these good things, brought about these great changes in Augustine. Augustine himself did not and could not. The reader and hearer of these confessions will not be encouraged to trust himself, to be self-confident. On the contrary, he will become conscious of his own weakness so that his trust can be put where it belongs, in God's grace and mercy. Augustine is not presenting himself as a model of what a man can do for himself. The persuasiveness of *The Confessions* has to do not with a recital of human action but with the uncovering of God's action. So, on the level of publicness also, *The Confessions* is a revelation of God and not primarily a revelation of Augustine himself.

In its being addressed to God and in its being written for other men, *The Confessions* is primarily intended as a way of discovering truth: "For see, you love the truth, and he that *doth the truth*, *cometh to the light*. This is what I want to do in my heart, in front of you, in my confession, and in my writing before many witnesses" (X.1). Confessing is a "doing" (*facere*) of the truth. But even this doing is not Augustine's alone: it is done "in front of" God. That the doing of truth is in the presence of God and is an addressing of oneself to God is of the greatest significance for understanding what truth is.[4] There is no irony in Augustine's speech to God.

Laughter, Tears, Trembling, and Wonder

There is no trembling in the *Phaedo*. We are told this explicitly: Socrates took the cup without trembling or turning pale. This is consistent with and a manifestation of the philosopher's separating of soul and body. It strikes us as inhuman and indeed it is: the separation of soul and body in this way is "divine." Looked at in another way, Socrates's not trembling or turning pale is a manifestation of the rule of soul over body, the other sense in which the soul is said to be "divine."

Of course, a good deal of my analysis of the *Phaedo* pointed to the questionableness of both these possibilities. The presence in the dialogue of the spirited part of the soul as a "third," inserting itself between body and "disembodied mind," was seen to have a moderating, "humanizing" effect. Nevertheless, the notion of philosophy as separation of soul and body is powerfully conveyed throughout the dialogue and is clearly intended to be the first and strongest and most lingering impression of the character of the philosophical life. The suspicion that this is a distortion arises only on reflection along with the suspicion that Phaedo is more or less than a reporter. Certainly, Simmias and Cebes are ready to accept this description of philosophy. And it seems to be Augustine's own perception of the Socratic practice of philosophy.

In discussing Socrates as "the first to turn the whole of philosophy towards the improvement and regulation of morality," Augustine finds it impossible to decide with certitude why Socrates made this "turn." The first possibility is that he was bored by the obscurity and inconclusiveness of natural science or physics. The second is that "he did not wish men's minds to seek to invade the sphere of the divine, when they were polluted by earthly passions." It is in connection with this second possible reason for the Socratic turn that Augustine emphasizes the notion of purification: "Socrates saw that man had been trying to discover the causes of the universe, and he believed that the universe had its first and supreme cause in nothing but the will of the one supreme God; hence he thought that the causation of the universe could be grasped only by a purified intelligence. That is why he thought it essential to insist on the need to cleanse one's life by accepting a high moral standard, so that the soul should be relieved of the weight of the lust that held it down, and then by its natural vigor should rise up to the sphere of the eternal and behold, thanks to its pure intelligence, the essence of the immaterial and unchangeable light where dwell the causes of all created things in undisturbed stability" (*City of God* VIII.3).

I would not want to infer from this passage that Augustine's view of Socrates derived from any direct acquaintance with the *Phaedo*.[5] I wish only to show that Augustine's understanding of the Socratic practice of philosophy is very similar to the account presented by Socrates in the *Phaedo* when he speaks of philosophy as the separation of soul and body or of the purification of the philosopher.

The notion that the philosopher is a kind of "purified intelligence" is, as I have argued above, consistent with Phaedo's claim that Socrates did not tremble. We can add to this the fact that Socrates is said sometimes to have laughed, even on the day of his death, but never to have wept, even on the day of his death. Socrates's bearing on that day is such that Phaedo felt no pity for him and, at the very end, does not even credit him with courage.

Socrates's laughter in the face of death has the effect of making him seem to be the disinterested spectator of his own death. The one who laughs distances himself from what he laughs at, as if it cannot touch him. The occasions for Socrates's laughter in the *Phaedo* are those in which Simmias, Cebes, or Crito has shown some lack of understanding of Socrates, especially with respect to his attitude toward death. In particular, he laughs when one or another of those present implies that their talk has been "idle," that there is no real connection between what has been said and the way Socrates should be expected to act. Socrates's laughter is in a sense the laughter of ridicule but it is not intended to distance him from those present. It is friendly and meant to help them to understand. It is mildly reproachful but the reproach that might have pushed them away is tempered by a kind of laughter that unites them. Socrates tries to draw them into his laughter, to get them on his side, to unite them in a kind of laughter of complicity. The laughter that distances him from death is the laughter that unites him with his friends.

In comparing Augustine with Socrates I am not implying that Augustine intended such a comparison and I know of nothing that would suggest that intention. My comparison rests on the notion that laughter, tears, and trembling, or their absence, reveal something about beliefs concerning man's nature, his place with respect to other things that are seen as either having or not having the power to affect him, and his place among other men. I am taking laughter, tears, and trembling as spontaneous, uncalculated manifestations of beliefs, and these beliefs may be either examined or unexamined. Beliefs are, in good part, the material for the activity of philosophy; they are among the first occasions for wonder.

If we consider Augustine's *Confessions* as a whole, we see that laughter, tears and trembling reveal the radical changes that take place in his life. When he was a boy, he laughed with his friends about their theft of some pears. Now, as he writes his *Confessions* with the understanding of what that theft and laughter really were he is ashamed of both. The change that has taken place in him makes him see the laughter and tears of his past in a very different light.

There are several kinds of laughter presented throughout *The Confessions*. In a few cases, the laughter is like that of Socrates, described above. This is the friendly laughter of mild reproach, rooted in charity and occasioned by nothing evil (see for example, I.6; V.10). But for the most part, the laughter of *The Confessions* is mocking. The story of the theft of the pears provides an instance of this: "We laughed heartily, as though our hearts were tickled at the thought that we were deceiving people who had no idea what we were doing and who would have strongly disapproved of it" (II.9). They laugh at the people who are being deceived by them because these people appear foolish for being deceived. Mocking laughter is often occasioned by the sight of someone's being deceived. In the case of the comic character, the deception is usually a self-deception.

Another characteristic of mocking laughter is noted by Augustine in connection with this same story: "Why, then, was my pleasure of such a kind that still I did not do the act myself? Was it because people do not generally laugh by themselves? Generally they do not; but nevertheless there are times when, if something really ridiculous occurs to the mind or is presented to the senses, people, even quite alone by themselves, will be overcome by laughter. But I would not have done that alone; no certainly, I would not" (II.9). Mocking laughter is often pleasant and often shared. Part of the pleasure of this kind of laughter is due to the fact that those who have done the deceiving feel themselves to be in a superior position to those who are deceived. So the shared pleasure of this mocking laughter can now be more precisely located: there is, on the one hand, pleasure in the truth and, on the other hand, pleasure in the deceiving. Those who are "in on" the truth are united by their shared knowledge and find pleasure precisely in the fact that the others are ignorant of what they themselves are undergoing. This pleasure is usually had in the company of others and not alone: the ignorance of those being deceived is somehow played off against the knowledge that the deceivers keep revealing to each other. This is the "tickling" which the deceivers do to each other: it is a mixture of hiding and revealing that pleases. At least part of this pleasure is due to the deceivers' recognizing each other's superiority over the deceived. This particular kind of superiority must be shared because without the sharing of truth there could be no recognition.

Mocking laughter of the kind presented in the story of the theft is malicious. This is not what we might call "innocent" laughter: it is wrong to take pleasure in another's being deceived. For Augustine, laughter is not morally neutral because deception is not morally neutral. But this is not to say that all laughter is bad. There is the friendly laughter of reproach which springs from charity and fellowship. And there is even a kind of mocking laughter, not friendly, but that can be said to spring from charity.

This kind of mocking is shown in Book Seven in Augustine's discussion of the astrologers. Augustine himself had not always been an enemy of astrology. In fact, the story that finally convinces him that astrology is not an art is told to him by Firminus who has come to him to consult about his "constellations." When he has heard Firminus's story he becomes certain that whatever is correctly foretold by the astrologers is spoken only by chance. Now he regards the astrologers as fools, or even madmen (*deliri*), and he wants to confute them with derision, to make laughingstocks of them. There is no hiding in this mockery. It is completely open so that the lies of the astrologers will be exposed to all, their beliefs and practices discredited. And it is not hidden from the astrologers themselves. In this instance, the objects of mocking laughter are the deceivers whose deceits are to be uncovered. Such laughter is intended to combat dangerous lies by making them appear worthy of ridicule and contempt.

What is at least initially surprising is that God is presented as mocking in *The Confessions*. Augustine is speaking of the time he was taken up with the teachings of the Manichees. In light of these teachings he misjudged what is said in the Scriptures about the prophets: "I was ignorant of this and so I used to mock at those holy servants and prophets of yours. And all my mocking of them meant nothing except that I myself was being mocked by you" (III.10).[6] And later, of the time not long before his conversion, he writes: "I panted after honors, money, and marriage, and you were laughing at me" (VI.6). The same kind of divine laughter occurs when Augustine and his friends make plans to form a community based on the principle of common property, for the sake of retiring from the business of daily life in order to live in peace. But God has other plans: "And out of [your] counsel you laughed ours to scorn, and you were preparing for us your own things" (VI.14).

God's laughter, even his mocking laughter, is the laughter of one who knows the truth, a truth which is hidden from the one being laughed at. Augustine is going his way, planning and striving as if he had power over the future. God, who knows what that future will really be, is laughing at all this futile motion. But God is not a deceiver; he is not causing Augustine's foolishness and he is not ultimately a mocker: "Yet nevertheless allow me to speak in front of your mercy. I am only dust and ashes, but allow me to speak, since, see, it is to your mercy that I am speaking and not to man, my mocker. You too may smile at me, but you will turn and have compassion on me" (I.6).

Ridicule and compassion are, at least in several ways, opposites. The one who mocks puts a distance between himself and the object of his mockery: he places himself above the other, looks down upon him in the confidence that he himself could never be like the one he ridicules. Compassion, on the other hand, is a kind of uniting with the one who suffers. It is not completely incompatible with a position of superiority because the one who pities is better off in some respects than the one he pities. But compassion also entails the realization on the part of the one who pities that he too could be in this pitiable condition: he is not certain that at some time in the future he might not have to undergo the same thing that he now witnesses.

When Augustine says, then, that God "will turn and have compassion" he cannot be taken to mean precisely what is ordinarily meant by 'compassion'. God can never be in a pitiable condition for God never changes, never "turns." Yet it is not *false* to say that God has compassion for us. We do not want to deny God's compassion, the compassion of a God who delivers up his only son for us. So we must distinguish God's compassion from human compassion. It seems to me that the crucial difference is located in God's unchangeableness: his compassion has no ingredient of fear, no uncertainty about the future, no possibility that he may someday be in the condition of the one who is pitied.

Throughout *The Confessions* God is said to have compassion for man but he is never said to weep. He laughs, is angry (VII.8), mocks, is gentle and compassionate but he never cries. Jesus, as we know from the Scriptures, does weep, two or three times. He weeps for Jerusalem (Luke 19:41) and he weeps for Lazarus (John 11:35). St. Paul leaves it uncertain as to whether he wept a third time, perhaps in the garden before his passion (Hebrews 5:7). Nowhere does it say that Jesus laughed. Augustine, in discussing what his views on the Incarnation had been, refers to Jesus's sadness, not explicitly to his tears: "All that I had gathered from the written tradition about him (accounts of how he ate, drank, slept, walked, was glad, was sad, preached) led me to believe that his flesh had only become united with your Word by means of a human soul and a human mind. This must be known to everyone who knows the immutability of your Word" (VI.19).

The distance between God and man, a distance put there by man, is bridged by Christ. And the central fact of Christ's humanness is his mortality: "But the true mediator whom in your secret mercy you have shown to men and have sent him so that they, by his example, might learn humility, that *Mediator between God and man, the Man Christ Jesus,* appeared between mortal sinners and the immortal Just One: mortal with men, just with God; so that, because the wages of justice is life and peace, he might, by a justice conjoined with God, make void the death of those sinners who were justified by him; for he was willing to let that death be common both to him and to them" (X.43). What must be especially noticed here is that Christ *willingly* takes on our mortality: he *lets* death be common to him and to us. There is no compulsion of any kind at work. The Incarnation, like creation, is absolutely free. And the Incarnation is the unsurpassable manifestation of God's compassion for men. Again, this divine compassion has no element of fear or uncertainty as human compassion must.

Augustine discusses compassion within the context of the feelings connected with tragedies performed in the theater. At Carthage, he was carried away by these plays. Now, as he writes, he wonders that people want to feel sad at tragic happenings which they would not want to suffer themselves. He wonders at the pleasure which arises from being a spectator of such tragic events: "Yet as spectators they do want to suffer the sadness and indeed their whole pleasure is just in this" (III.2). Augustine is not suggesting that compassion is a bad thing. But it should be properly directed, that is, directed toward the proper objects: "But now I feel more pity for someone who rejoices in his wickedness than for someone who is supposed to be suffering great hardships because of the lack of some harmful pleasure or the loss of some miserable felicity." Compassion is indeed a sign of charity but it is not suffering simply that should evoke it: a man who is joyful but wicked is in a far more pitiable state than one who is suffering because he cannot have something that he should not have. Tragedies on stage often present us with the latter, and we feel sad over things that do not merit our pity.

But it seems that, for Augustine, the real difficulty lies with the fact that the spectator is merely a spectator: "There can be no real compassion for fictions on the stage. A man listening to a play is not called upon to help the sufferer; he is merely invited to feel sad." The spectator loves his sadness, finds pleasure in it. Again, divine compassion must be distinguished from this. God feels no sorrow and takes no pleasure in sorrow, yet he is compassionate: "You are wounded by no sorrow, yet you love souls far more deeply than we can, and your compassion is more lasting and indestructible than ours" (III.2). It would be monstrous to think that God in any way enjoys the sufferings of men: he is not in the position of the spectator at a tragedy; he does not create objects of compassion so as to enjoy his sadness.

Indeed, it would have to be said that there can be no Christian

tragedy. This does not mean that the good prosper and the bad do not, or
that tears have no rightful place in the life of the believer. It means that
ultimately there is justice: "And what a light of beauty is that, when we
shall see him as he is, and those tears be passed away, which have been my
meat day and night, whilst they daily say unto me, Where is now thy
God?" (XIII.13). God's judgments are just even if they are incomprehensible to us (VII.6).

There is another aspect of classical tragedy which can ultimately
have no place in the Christian understanding of man. The character in a
tragedy does not know what he is doing. He thinks he knows quite well
but in fact he is bringing about the opposite of what he intends. Oedipus
is, of course, a remarkably clear case of this. He does indeed bring about
his own ruin and he does it by means of his own admirable qualities.[7] Yet
we cannot blame him for he does not deserve what happens to him.
Tragedy presents us with the inescapability of the irrational in human life.
It confronts us with our powerlessness as we witness evil coming out of
good.

What we see in Augustine's *Confessions* is his rushing to his ruin,
working and planning toward his own destruction all the while trying to
be happy. But what is really happening is that God is bringing good out of
evil: "I panted for honors, for money, for marriage, and you were laughing at me. I found bitterness and difficulty in following these desires, and
your graciousness to me was shown in the way you would not allow me to
find anything sweet which was not you" (VI.6). While Augustine is relentlessly pursuing his ruin, God is relentlessly working out the opposite. So,
again, Augustine's purpose in making his confession public: "When the
confessions of these past sins are read and heard, they rouse up the heart
lest it sink into the sleep of despair and say 'I cannot'" (X.3). It is God,
not Augustine, who brings good even out of evil, the very evil that
Augustine has worked so hard at doing.

But God's action does not diminish human action and the need for
human striving. Nor does God's bringing good out of evil mean that tears
have no place in human life. The life of Jesus shows this and so also does
Augustine's life. There is no joyful, innocent laughter in Augustine's
Confessions. There are tears of many kinds from many causes. He weeps
over the death of his friend whom he "had loved as though he would
never die" (IV.6) and he finds solace in weeping for his mother after her
death (IX.12). But the tears that should be shed, the tears that are proper
to man, are tears of contrition, the tears that beg for mercy. After recounting the good things about his mother that caused him to weep for her and

for himself at losing her, he says that now he pours forth "tears of a very different sort" for her, "tears that well up from a spirit shaken by the thoughts of the dangers that threaten every soul *that dieth in Adam*" (IX.13). He begs God's mercy for his mother's sins.

This is true compassion and it is the pity that he has for his own self. His pity is no longer wasted on fictions: "What indeed can be more pitiful than a wretch with no pity for himself, weeping at the death of Dido, which was caused by love for Aeneas, and not weeping at his own death, caused by lack of love for you" (I.13). The spectator at a tragic play is not called upon to do anything about the sufferings of the actors. There is, then, even in tragedy, something not serious. But there is nothing playful about *The Confessions*: the tears that will be wiped away are the tears "which have been my meat day and night" (XIII.13).

It is precisely with respect to the place of tears, or their absence, that we can begin to see where Augustine stands on the question of the nature and worth of philosophy. The tears of the spectator at a tragedy are somehow pleasant, and the compassion of the spectator is "not true," but the feeling of grief at another's misery does have its source in friendship (III.2). The compassion, the tears and pity, and even fear evoked by the tragic spectacle, come from an implicit recognition of our common lot, of our fundamental equality in the face of the dreadful, of our equal powerlessness to escape the irrational. But the books of the Platonists have "no look of pity, no tears of confession" (VII.21). Having read the books of the Platonists, "I began to desire to seem wise; full of my own punishment, yet could not weep for it, but became more and more puffed up with my knowledge. For where was that charity that should build me up from that foundation of humility which is in Christ Jesus?" (VII.20). The wisdom that he finds in the books of the Platonists is the kind of wisdom that raises one above what is common, above the human.

Even though the Platonists are the occasion for the beginnings of the radical change in his life and even though "in the Platonists, God and his Word are everywhere implied" (VIII.2), the differences between Augustine and the Platonists are as important and even more important than any similarities.[8] That Augustine learned a great deal from the Platonists, that he respected their writings, cannot be denied. But there can be no easy harmony between Platonism and Christianity, no simple fusion of the books of the Platonists and the Bible. For what stands out in Augustine's encounter with the Platonists, what Augustine was most clearly shown is "the difference between presumption and confession" (VII.20). It was because God wished to show him how he "resists the proud and gives grace to the humble" that he provides for Augustine's coming into contact with these books.

The absence of tears and of pity from the books of the Platonists is due to pride, the presumption that has to be compared with confession. And this absence also reveals why the Incarnation is inconceivable to them, even though "God and his Word are everywhere implied" in their works. Their pride must blind them to the compassion of God. In the words of St. Paul: "For Jews demand signs and Greeks seek wisdom, but we preach Christ crucified, a stumbling block to Jews and folly to Greeks" (1 Cor. 1.23).

This difference between the Platonists and Christian teaching is not such that they can be harmonized simply by adding on the doctrines of the Incarnation and Redemption to the teachings of the Platonists about God and the Word. That is, the books of the Platonists are not simply a kind of "first part" of Christian theology which can then be completed by adding on the New Testament teachings concerning Christ as a "second part." This may be the impression created at first by Augustine's discussion of the Platonists in Book Seven, Chapter Nine. There he goes through the Prologue of the Gospel according to John identifying what is in the books of the Platonists and what is not. The first part of the Prologue is found in the Platonic books but the Incarnation, Redemption, and the notion of grace are clearly not found there. From this account, it might seem that a whole could be patched together of the Platonic books and a few other teachings.

Without in any way denying that Augustine does claim to find God and his Word in the books of the Platonists, it is still the case that the differences between Augustine and the Platonists are essential differences. The presumption of the Platonists is not an ultimately extraneous consideration. What is distinctively Augustinian shows itself in the manner in which he distinguishes himself from the Platonists, not in any blending of Platonism and the Bible. That is to say, Augustine's turning point is better described and understood as a turn away from, and not as a turn to, Platonism. Of course, the turning away presupposes not necessarily a prior accceptance but at least a serious engagement. As Socrates defines himself in terms of his distinction from the natural philosophers, so Augustine defines himself primarily in terms of his distinctness from the Platonists.

The absence of tears and of pity from the Platonic books is a manifestation of these differences. So also is the presence in Augustine's *Confessions* of trembling. One of the most striking instances of this trembling is presented in Book Seven, Chapter Ten, immediately after his encounter with the Platonic books. But this trembling is not brought about by what he reads in these books, even though what he reads sets him on the inward course of Chapter Ten. He is only able to "enter within" because God is now his Helper. And when he enters within, he sees "above" his mind the unchangeable light which made him. "And I trembled with love and terror: and I found myself to be far off from you in a region of total unlikeness" (VII.10). The trembling is with both love and terror (*horrore*)—love drawing him to union, and terror pulling him away to preserve himself. Yet the terror or horror is caused by his recognition of his unlikeness to God. Like the recognition that occurs in tragedy, Augustine's sudden coming upon the gulf that separates him from God horrifies and terrifies him. At the same time, the realization that there is such a distance means that he has understood something about God and about himself, something he did not understand before. The manifestation of this recognition is his trembling.

The second reference to trembling in Book Seven occurs in Chapter Seventeen, and this chapter is a kind of redoing of Chapter Ten. That is, in Chapter Seventeen he takes us, more slowly, through the steps that lead "within" until "in the flash of a trembling glance" his understanding arrives at "that which is." The account of this movement from bodies to soul to "that which is" seems quite similar to what I called "the approach of sight" to truth in the *Phaedo*. But again, what must be insisted upon is the fundamental difference: disembodied minds do not tremble. Augustine's trembling glance is not identical with the "pure" sight of the philosopher's separated soul.[9] This is revealed at the very beginning of Chapter Seventeen: "And I wondered that now I loved you and not a phantasm instead of you."

The two other instances of trembling recorded in Book Seven both have to do with his reading of St. Paul. He finds that Paul does not contradict himself and that he does indeed agree with the testimony of the Law and the Prophets: "And there appeared to me but one face in that chaste eloquence; and I learned *to rejoice with trembling*" (VII.21). This rejoicing with trembling is the counterpart of his trembling with terror. Not only do the Platonic writings show no face of pity and no tears of confession, they offer no salvation, no redemption: "No one sings there, *Shall not my soul be submitted unto God? For of Him cometh my salvation? For he is my God, and my Salvation, my guardian, I shall no more be moved*" (VII.21).

It is after a long sequence of contrasts between St. Paul and the

Platonists that Augustine concludes this final chapter of Book Seven: "These things did by wonderful means sink into my very bowels (*mihi inviscerabantur*), when I read that *least of thy Apostles*, and had considered your works and trembled."[10] The imagery of sinking into the bowels is not meant to suggest the separation of soul and body. And the trembling which is caused by considering God's works is not consistent with the kind of rule of soul over body that presupposes their separability. Rule of soul over body is indeed associated with man's being in the image of God: "And this was the due proportion and the middle region of my salvation, that I might remain in your image, and, serving you, have dominion over my body" (VII.7). But this rule does not rest on the "purification" of the soul: "You are not of any bodily form, yet you made man 'after your own image' and, see, man is in space from head to foot" (VI.3).

When Augustine writes: "And I wondered that now I loved you and not a phantasm instead of you" (VII.17), he is expressing one of the radical changes that has occurred in Book Seven. At the beginning, he had shown himself as unable to think of anything except the kind of thing that can be seen, the kind of substance that he was accustomed to see with his eyes. He is constrained, then, to think of God as a corporeal substance taking up space: he thought that anything not stretched out in space was "nothing." Now as he is about to recount the steps leading "within" to "that which is," we see that he no longer loves a "phantasm." In part because of his reading the books of the Platonists, he is now able to think of incorporeal substance.

The other radical change that has taken place in Book Seven is also expressed in "And I wondered that now I loved you and not a phantasm instead of you," although less obviously. This change has to do with the question of the origin of evil. That Augustine can say that he loves God and not a phantasm indicates that the dreadful suspicion that God must be the ultimate cause of evil has disappeared along with the phantasm.

Finally, "And I wondered that now I loved you and not a phantasm" locates the cause of Augustine's wonder and the focus of the whole of *The Confessions*: God and the soul.[11] There is an important sense in which "the world," as it might be the object of wonder for the natural philosopher, is not the cause of Augustine's wonder. This is not to say that Augustine is not at all concerned with the kind of account that can be given of nature as "corporeal nature." Insofar as *The Confessions* is about Genesis, and it is about Genesis from beginning to end, the whole created world is never far from his thoughts. The whole of creation is always the background for his attending to the soul: "And man wants to praise you, man who is only a small portion of what you have created. . . . Yet still man, this small portion of creation, wants to praise you" (I.1).

To say that the focus of Augustine's concern is God and the soul now begins to look like a distortion; it is man, not soul alone, who is created by God. Man is body and soul, and man, created in God's image, "is in space from head to foot." To speak of God and the soul instead of man and God may be potentially distorting if it is taken to suggest any contempt for the body on Augustine's part. This, at least, must be insisted upon from the outset: there is no contempt for the body in Augustine. The two overriding issues of Book Seven, the overcoming of the constraint to think of God as material substance and the question of the origin of evil, may, in their linking, be taken to suggest contempt for the body. But matter as the cause of evil is precisely the view that Augustine rejects. There is no contempt for the body, either "conscious" or "unconscious," in Augustine.[12]

The claim that the primary focus of *The Confessions* is God and the soul need not hint at any distortion if it is understood that "soul" is not "disembodied mind" or even "separated soul." It is always the soul "in" a body. As troublesome as the emphasis on interiority may be in other respects, it has the advantage of always calling us back to the whole man: "And I turned my attention on myself and said to myself: 'And you, who are you?' And I replied: 'A man.' Now I find evidently in myself a body and a soul, the one exterior, the other interior" (X.6). So, too, Augustine's trembling in the presence of and distance from God is not the "trembling" of a disembodied mind.

Augustine's focus on the soul is not, then, due to hatred of the body or to contempt for the whole man. His turn to the soul is undertaken not only because the interior part is the better part (X.6) but also because the soul is far more mysterious and wonderful than the body. We see this in his own investigation of the memory as mind: "For me, Lord, certainly this is hard labor, hard labor inside myself, and I have become to myself a piece of difficult ground, not to be worked over without much sweat. For we are not now examining the regions of the heaven or measuring the distances of the stars or inquiring into how the earth is balanced in space. It is I myself who remember, I, the mind. There is nothing remarkable in the fact that something other than myself is far away from me; but what can be nearer to me than my own self? Yet this force of my memory is incomprehensible to me, even though, without it, I should not be able to call myself myself" (X.16). What is closest to him, what is indeed in some sense identical with him, is most mysterious.

What, then, is Augustine's position with respect to natural philosophy? His discussion of the natural philosophers occurs, for the most part, as a comparison of the teachings of the philosophers with those of the Manichees. Against the measuring, predicting, and reasoning of the philosophers, the teachings of the Manichees concerning the heavens show up as "fables" and "fantasy." The philosophers say much that is "true" about the created world. They predict eclipses of the sun and moon and everything happens as they foretell. Their rules have been set down in writing, and on the basis of these rules accurate predictions can be made by others. Their calculations have been proved correct. When Augustine compares the philosophers with the Manichees, he finds that the philosophers' calculations are "reasons" whereas Manes gives no "reasons" for the solstices, equinoxes, and eclipses. He was told to believe in the views of Manes, but these views do not correspond with what had been established "by mathematics and my own eyesight" (V.3).

Augustine does find *truth* in the teachings of the natural philosophers. They do indeed give reasons for what can be seen in the heavens. Mathematics and eyesight are the means whereby truth about these things is attained. Wonder, then, is replaced by knowledge. There is no cause for wonder anymore: "And everything will take place as predicted. And men who are ignorant of the subject are full of astonishment and admiration, while those who know will boast of their knowledge and will be praised for it, thus turning away from you in their evil pride and losing the light that comes to them from you" (V.3). Again, the activity of philosophy is associated with pride.

The natural philosophers say many true things about what is created but they do not seek for the truth which is the creator. "They can see an eclipse of the sun long before it happens, but cannot see their own eclipse when it is actually taking place. For they do not approach the matter in a religious spirit and ask what is the source of the intelligence which they use to inquire into all this" (V.3). The natural philosophers do not turn "within." The Platonists admonish him to enter within himself (VII.10). But both the natural philosophers and the Platonists are proud and therefore cannot seek the Truth, even while they say many true things: "The proud cannot find you, however deep and curious their knowledge, not even if they could count the stars and the grains of sand, or measure the constellations in the sky and track down the paths of the stars" (V.3). And those philosophers who do find God do not honor him and give him thanks: "Instead they become vain in their imaginations and consider themselves to be wise; they attribute to themselves what is yours, and in this way, such is the perversity of their blindness, they actually attribute their own qualities to you, making you, who are Truth, responsible for their own falsehoods" (V.3). The philosophers who do find God do not worship him. Rather they change the truth into a lie "and worship and serve the creature more than the Creator" (V.3 *and* VII.9).

It is not Augustine, then, who manifests any contempt for the human, for the whole man. Rather, the philosophers cannot be content to be mere men. There is no face or look of pity in the Platonic books. There is no human pity because there is a philosophical contempt for the equality of the body, the human equality in the face of the irrational. The absence of pity is due to the absence of any notion of God's compassion for man: "that *Thou sparedst not Thine only Son, but deliveredst Him for us all*, is not there" (VII.9).

The books of the Platonists are full of God and his Word, but the Platonists attribute to themselves what is God's: the philosophers think themselves to be somehow divine.[13] They fail to make the distinction that is absolutely first. This is the distinction that makes Augustine tremble.

And for Augustine, trembling and wonder are inseparable. There is no wonder without there having first been trembling. The wonder that Augustine feels, then, must be distinguished from specifically philosophical wonder. Augustine's wonder does not coincide with his assuming the posture of the disinterested spectator with respect to God or to the works of God—to nature. Indeed, he wonders only after having abandoned the attempt to assume this posture. On the other hand, Augustine's perspective on nature does, in some sense, prepare for the Cartesian elimination of wonder from philosophy.

Actor or Spectator

When Augustine considers God's works after having learned the difference between presumption and confession, he trembles. This is not the stance of the disinterested spectator, the stance which the philosopher takes to be the divine stance. Yet there is a sense in which Augustine does present himself as a spectator of God's works and as somehow seeing them from the divine perspective. After his turn within, which is prompted by his reading of the Platonists, his perspective on the "other things" created by God is radically changed. Whereas he had been in anguish seeking the cause of evil in these things, he now sees that they are good:

"So I saw and it was made plain to me that you have made all things good nor are there any substances at all which you have not made. And because you did not make all things equal, therefore they each and all have their existence; because they are good individually, and at the same time they are altogether very good, because our God *made all things very good*" (VII.12). Augustine's judgment now coincides with God's own judgment as recounted in Genesis (1:31).

The emphasis in these chapters (11, 13, and 15 especially) is on the "other things" that God has made. That is, his perspective here is on things other than man. This is not to say that God did not make man good. But Augustine's perspective on the human and on the divine itself is not the same as his perspective on these other things. These other things are "below" him: he sees them from a superior position and they cause no wonder in him.

Yet even his stance with respect to these other things is not disinterested: "Since . . . [all these] *praise thy name*, . . . I no longer *desired* better things. I had envisaged all things in their totality, and, with a sounder judgment, I realized that, while higher things are certainly better than lower things, all things together are better than the higher things by themselves" (VII.13). [Emphasis added.] Augustine's judgment, which now coincides with God's, is as much a matter of desire as of intellect. He now desires what is. He sees that inequality lets things be what they are: "*because* you did not make all things equal, therefore they each and all have their existence." But this judgment is not "purely" intellectual. His desire is that each thing should be what it is. At bottom, this is an acceptance of his *own* inequality: he is not divine and he now does not desire to be divine.

The disinterested spectator is indifferent to the praise of God, to the glory of God which nature manifests. The disinterested spectator is not indifferent to his own pleasure in knowing. Augustine discusses such "empty curiosity" in terms of the temptation which he calls "the lust of the eyes." This is the appetite for knowing and, because the eyes are the primary sense for acquiring knowledge, it is called "the lust of the eyes." Augustine places the investigation of the workings of nature in the same category with the display of monsters in the theater and with magic. The investigation of nature is concerned with "things which it does no good to know and which men only want to know for the sake of knowing" (X.35). In claiming that it is in some way essentially the same as the display of monsters and as magic, he is pointing to the experience of wonder, of delight in the unusual, but a wonder and delight that are ultimately sterile and "do no good."

What causes Augustine to wonder is that now he loves God and not a phantasm instead of God. This is not the wonder of the disinterested spectator. It follows upon the torment of his soul as he seeks the origin of evil and fights back the phantasms which come in swarms before the eye of his mind (VII.1). The primary cause of Augustine's torment in Book Seven is his search for the origin of evil. But this question is linked throughout with the other question that dominates Book Seven, that of the manner of being of God and the manner of his presence to the world.

We see these two questions come together in Chapter Five. Here he shows us how he goes about seeking the origin of evil: "I put the whole creation in front of the eyes of my spirit, both whatever we can discern in it . . . and whatever we do not see in it . . . like . . . all the angels . . . but even these spiritual beings I conceived of as bodies arranged in different places, according to my imagination." He orders and arranges the whole of creation as he pleases, in accordance with his imagination, and pretending bodies for beings that have no bodies. Then he fits God into this construction: "But you, Lord, I imagined on every part surrounding and penetrating it, though every way infinite." His analogy is that of the sponge in the sea. The sea is infinite and both fills and surrounds the sponge (VII.5). Earlier, he had thought of God's presence in the world as analogous to the way in which light fills the air (VII.1).

Having constituted the world and God in this way, he now proceeds to look in this construction for the seed of evil: "Where, then, did evil come from? Was there some evil element in the material of creation, and did God shape and form it, yet still leave in it something which he did not change into good?" Augustine is seeking the origin of evil in matter. This is inevitable because he can think of no other kind of substance. He goes through a whole series of questions about God's making things, about God's omnipotence and the impossibility of his being limited by some evil matter. He does not want to believe that God is the ultimate cause of evil but the logic of his questions forces him in that direction.

The question of the origin of evil is clearly not a "purely" theoretical question for Augustine. At the end of his long series of questions about God's creating and the origin of evil, he tells us: "Such were the thoughts I turned over and over in my wretched heart, a heart overburdened with biting cares, that came from the fear of death and not finding out the truth" (VII.5). The same torment is expressed in Chapter Seven: "I inquired whence came evil, but found no way out of my question. . . . I sought with fierce agitation whence evil might come. What agonies I suffered, what groans, my God, came from my heart in its labor!" The question of the origin of evil torments him so because he is afraid of evil.

It is, then, the fear of death that causes Augustine's torment, that goads him on in his search for the origin of evil. He is not and cannot be the disinterested spectator with respect to this question. The fear of death, or the desire for immortality, had earlier attracted Augustine to philosophy. But the absence of the name of Christ from Cicero's *Hortensius* holds him back from wholeheartedly embracing the philosophical life (III.4).

The faith that holds him back, however, has not itself eliminated his fear of death. For it is precisely this faith, by which he believes that God is creator, that he is seeking to understand in his torment. It is by faith that he knows himself to be created from nothing, to have nothing of his own. Belief in the immortality of the soul does not simply eliminate the fear of death as the greatest evil.

The "way out" of his question begins with the realization that there is something radically wrong with the inquiry itself. This is not to say that it is wrong to inquire about these matters simply. The manner of his questioning is wrong. And this is not only intellectual error, it is morally wrong: "And I sought whence evil should be, and I sought in an evil way, and I did not see that evil which was in this very inquiry of mine" (VII.5).[14]

Augustine's first mistake is to think of God as a body. But even this mistake has a moral aspect: he is constrained to think that what is not in space is nothing because he is "gross-hearted" (VII.1). The evil in thinking of God as a body is *not* due to any evil in matter as such. Augustine's second mistake is revealed in the sequence of questions about God's creating. What we see in these questions is that Augustine fails to distinguish God's activity in creating from the activity of making of the human craftsman.

We must consider, then, why Augustine's inquiry is fundamentally mistaken, both intellectually and morally. And we can begin to do this by seeing what it is that changes between the first and second halves of Book Seven, the change expressed when he writes: "And I wondered that now I loved you and not a phantasm instead of you" (VII.17). The phantasm that has disappeared was not merely a mistaken way of thinking, a failure of the mind which could not justly be thought of as blameworthy. The phantasm was an idol, an image that he had made and worshipped. "I am the Lord thy God. Thou shalt not have strange gods before me." Augustine's imagination is not innocent. The idol is constructed and set up *against* God: "My soul . . . had made for itself a god to fill the infinite distances of all space, and it had thought this God to be you and had placed it in its own heart, thus again becoming the temple of its own idol, a temple abominable to you" (VII.14).

The change that takes place in Augustine is that now he sees God to be infinite but in another way, not infinite in space (VII.14). And he sees also that all finite things are "in" God, but not as in space. Rather he contains all things in his truth (VII.15). God's presence to the world and "in" the world is not spatial, not the presence of one body to another. This is, of course, reflected in what he now knows about creation. God is not like the craftsman: "And that you, who only are eternal, did not begin to work after [the passage of] innumerable spaces of time, for all spaces of times, both those which are passed already and those which are to pass hereafter, may neither come nor go, but by you, who are still working and still remaining" (VII.15).

The change that has taken place in Augustine is not such that he can now answer the series of questions of Chapter Five, the series based on his "constitution" of the world and God. Rather, it shows this constituting to be radically mistaken and in itself evil. The phantasm, the idol, which owes its being to the human imagination is an attempt to manipulate God. The "spectator" of Chapter Five is not merely a spectator: he arranges, places, disposes. He takes up a position "outside" the whole creation and even "outside" of God and then arranges God and the world in relation to each other, spatially. The "seeker" of Chapter Five is attempting to seize what he takes to be the divine position and in so doing to subordinate God to himself.

Augustine's torment is due to the fear of death (VII.5), the fear that death is evil. But it is this very fear that causes him to search for the origin of evil in an evil way. That is, the attempt to assume the divine position, to subordinate God, manipulate and control him, is ultimately the attempt to escape death. Augustine wants some power of his own against death. In this attempt, we see a kind of foreshadowing of the project that Descartes presents in the *Discourse on Method*: the mastery and possession of nature is for the sake of overcoming death. From Augustine's point of view, the stance of "distinterested" spectator may be inseparable from the desire to assert one's own power. It is only when he abandons this effort that he finds truth.

Augustine's turn away from phantasms to the true God does not *begin* with his reading of the Platonists, even though the Platonic books do play an important role in the change that takes place. His turn begins in Chapter Seven, but at the time it was happening he did not know it: "I sought with fierce agitation whence evil might come. What agonies I suffered, what groans, my God, came from my heart in its labor! Yet your ears were open, though I knew it not. And when in silence I so vehemently sought after it, the silent contritions of my soul were great cries for your mercy" (VII.7). God *takes* his groans as cries for mercy, takes his silent vehemence as contrition.[15] Augustine did not intend to cry for mercy and he did not know that God's ears were open to his groaning. If God *takes* his silent inquiry as a cry for mercy, then this is what his silence truly *is*.

Now, Augustine is no longer a spectator and a manipulator. He is not investigating God as an "object" or controlling him in an image. He is, even though he does not know it, addressing himself to God. He is asking for mercy. And it is only now that he can begin to know and understand. The second decisive aspect of this turn is that Augustine himself does not know at the time it is happening that his silent vehemence is being taken as contrition and as the cry of his soul for mercy. This points to a change of the greatest significance concerning what is thought to be the nature of the divine.[16] Augustine's own turn from spectator to speaker in prayer is the corollary of this manifestation of the divine.

In hearing Augustine's groans and taking his silent inquiry as a cry for mercy, even though Augustine does not intend this or know it, God shows himself to be, not the disinterested spectator of the world and of men in particular, but an actor in men's lives. The notion of the divine that served as the goal of philosophy and the model for the philosopher as the disinterested spectator is now radically altered. The God of Augustine's *Confessions* is a God who can be addressed by men and who acts at every moment in human life. Nor is this God the spectator of the world, of nature. He not only brought it into being but he is "still working" (VII.15).

The story of Augustine's life as told in the first nine books of *The Confessions* is really an account, necessarily fragmentary, of God's action in his life. In Book Five, for example, we see that it was God who brought about his move from Carthage to Rome: "You acted upon me in such a way that I was persuaded to set out for Rome to teach there the same subjects as I had been teaching in Carthage. How it was that I came to be persuaded to do this must not be passed over in my confession to you; here too I must ponder over and openly declare the *deep secrecy* of your ways and your mercy which is always so close to us" (V.8). [Emphasis added.] Augustine wanted to go to Rome because the salaries were better, the chances for a greater reputation were better, but mostly because the students were said to be better disciplined than the students at Carthage. These are the reasons for Augustine's decision and they account for his action. He wants to bring something about and he takes the necessary action.

Without in any way denying Augustine's agency or the reality and efficaciousness of his intentions, he can say that what happens is at the same time brought about by God: "In Carthage you prepared goads for me, so that I should be driven from the place, and at Rome you provided attractions which would draw me there" (V.8). God does this for reasons very different from Augustine's reasons. What God is bringing about is the salvation of Augustine's soul. Divine action does not destroy human action, does not reduce it to a mere illusion. Of this Augustine is certain: "I knew as well that I had a will, as that I had a life. So when I willed to do or not to do something, I was perfectly certain that the act of willing was mine and not anybody else's, and I was now getting near to discovering that there was the cause of my sin" (VII.3). God accomplishes what he intends without in any way compelling the will. Of course, it is not clear in every instance, even from the perspective of memory, what God is doing. For the most part, God's intentions and his means are held in "deep secrecy."

It is impossible, then, for man to have the divine perspective on his own life or on other men. Augustine can "see" the "other things" that God has made so that his judgment of them coincides with God's own judgment that they are good. But of the action of God in his own life he has only glimpses, and of God's judgments of men he simply does not know. It is the human soul in its relation to God that is mysterious and wonderful.

The radical change in the notion of the divine, from spectator to actor, is strikingly clear in Augustine's account of his turn from astrology. The astrologers are "the mathematicians" whose task is to predict the future.[17] Mathematics is the realm of certitude, and the astrologers attempt to provide certitude about the future so as to eliminate chance from the lives of those who consult them. The belief that this can be done by measuring the positions of the stars reflects a view concerning men's place within the whole of nature. And if the philosophers can, by means of their calculations, make precise predictions about the time and extent of an eclipse, mathematics seems to offer itself as the means for overcoming human uncertainty about the future. The ultimate end of the art of astrology is to give men control over the future by making it possible for them to plan. Human action, then, instead of being initiated in what is at best half-light, can be done in full daylight.

Augustine's account of his turn from astrology is given on two levels, consistent with the way in which the turn is brought about. He tells us the story of Firminus's conversation with him and he allows us to see what God accomplishes and how he accomplishes it. Firminus is Augustine's friend and comes to him for advice concerning his hopes and plans; he wants to know what Augustine sees in his constellations. In response to Augustine's expressions of doubt about the worth of astrology, Firminus tells him the story of his father's experiment. The result of the experiment is that the same predictions would have had to be made for Firminus himself and a slave who were born at the same moment. And since Firminus and the slave had in fact very different lives, the same predictions would have been false in at least one case. Or if true, they would have to have been different predictions made on the basis of precisely the same observations. Augustine is now persuaded that astrology is not an art, that anything truly said is said by chance. He had been leaning toward this view already, thanks to the arguments of his friends Nebridius and Vindicianus, and he is now completely convinced. On one level, this is the story told in Chapter Six, the story of how Augustine came to reject the foolishness of astrology with the help of his friends.

On another level, this is a story of God's action. Augustine begins Chapter Six by addressing God as the ruler of the world, even to the fluttering of the leaves of the trees. God's working in nature, his rule of the world is so complete, so thorough and pervasive, that it includes the most fleeting motions. The fluttering of the leaves of the trees is, in its rapidity and manyness, hardly observable and certainly immeasurable by any human calculations. The presence of God by his rule is not spatial, yet it manifests itself even in the slightest movement of the most fragile things, just as surely as it does in the great motions of the stars. God's action with respect to nonhuman nature is not complete with creation but continues at every moment in every place.

How does this God who rules the world, even to the fluttering of the leaves of the trees, exercise his rule over men, who rule themselves? In the case of Augustine's turn away from astrology, God "procures" for him the arguments of Nebridius and Vindicianus that begin to wear down his obstinacy. Then he "procures" for him a friend, Firminus, who is a follower of the astrologers and who tells Augustine the story that finally convinces him. At the same time that Firminus is carefully and deliberately pursuing his own ends, he is serving as the instrument of God, who is turning Augustine away from astrology. The pretensions of astrology are completely undercut by the realization that the future being talked about by the astrologer is really being provided for at an entirely different level, the level of divine action, at precisely that moment.

Augustine concludes Chapter Six by addressing himself again to God as ruler of the universe, and now with specific reference to his rule over men: "For you Lord, the most just ruler of the universe, act in your own secret way so that, while neither he who consults nor he who is consulted knows what is being done, still when a man consults he is told out of the abyss of your just judgment what, in accordance with the secret deservings of souls, he ought to be told" (VII.6). The workings of nature, insofar as they are measurable, are not hidden from men (V.3 and X.35). But the judgment of God with respect to souls is an unsearchable abyss: "To whom let not a man say 'What is this?' or 'Why is that?' Let him not say so, he must not say so: for he is a man" (VII.6). God's action is completely pervasive and ultimately mysterious: "For you . . . are most secret and most present" (VI.3).[18]

What can be seen in these stories of Augustine's move from Carthage to Rome and of his turn from astrology, indeed what underlies the story of Augustine's whole life, is the effectiveness of God's action in bringing good out of evil. Not only is God not the cause of evil, he even brings good out of evil, out of the evil that men do. This does not mean that evil has no existence. It is not a substance but neither is it an illusion. Augustine can say, on the one hand, "To you there is nothing at all evil" (VII.13) and on the other hand, that the idol in Augustine's heart was "abominable to you" (VII.14). The Incarnation and Redemption, God's delivering up his only son, make no sense if evil has no existence of any kind.

God's bringing good out of evil is Augustine's "way out" of the question of the origin of evil. Sin is entirely due to the will (VII.3), at the level of human action. On the level of God's action, good is being brought out of evil. The greatest example of this is Christ: "O happy fault that gave to mankind. . . ." This is the manifestation of God's compassion, a compassion of which the philosophers cannot conceive.

It is also the Incarnation that saves us from the terror that might result from the thought of a God whose power is so great, whose will is so irresistible, and whose action is so pervasive as to bring good even out of evil. That terror might arise from the fact that God "uses" men to accomplish his designs. And he uses them in spite of their own intentions. Firminus intends to consult with Augustine about his future. What he brings about is Augustine's decisive turn away from astrology. God "procured" Firminus for Augustine. And later he "procures" the unnamed man who introduces Augustine to the books of the Platonists.

In the earlier story of Augustine's move from Carthage to Rome, it is explicitly stated that God uses men and their evil actions: "You made secret use of their perverseness and my own" (V.8). To know oneself to be in the power of such a God gives rise to the truly terrifying thought that we are simply instruments being used in some divine scheme of which we know nothing. And if we are merely instruments, means to an end not our own, then we are completely unprotected from a God who can do anything. What saves us from this terror is the firm belief in the Incarnation and Redemption: "*In due time he died for the ungodly, and thou sparedst not Thine only son but deliveredst Him for us all*"(VII.9). Christ is the "instrument" of salvation.

Augustine knows that the end toward which God is working is salvation. The initial terror at the thought of being a mere instrument is replaced by confidence, but this confidence is in God and not in oneself: "When the confessions of these past sins are read and heard, they rouse up the heart lest it sink into the sleep of despair" (X.3). God's "use" of men is not a use based on need. Creation is entirely free and so also is salvation. Christ was "willing" to let death be common to him and us. Because there is absolutely no need, God's love for man is totally "disinterested." And because God needs nothing from man, God alone is truly Lord: "And you are my Lord *because* you do not need my goods" (VII.11). [Emphasis added.]

But what, then, can man's position be with respect to God? Can man's love for God possibly be disinterested? It seems at first that man's love for God cannot possibly be disinterested. Augustine trembles with both love and terror (VII.10). Submission on account of fear would hardly be disinterested love. Even the practice of addressing God as Lord suggests that love cannot be disinterested, for disinterested love seems to presuppose freedom and thus a kind of equality. Finally, since man's whole happiness depends on God, the love of God appears to be totally interested and unavoidably so. Man does need God but God needs nothing from man. So at the very center of Book Seven, immediately after his turn "within" and his trembling with love and terror, Augustine points to this asymmetry: "It is good then for me to cling to God: for if I remain not in him, I shall not be able to remain in myself: whereas he remaining in himself, renews all things. And you are my Lord, because you do not need my goods" (VII.11).

The reason why Augustine can cling to God is that God is unchangeable. He can be held onto, trusted, because he is eternally the same and "that truly is which remains unchangeably" (VII.11). Thus, the question of the being of God is no more a "merely" theoretical matter than the question of the origin of evil. Augustine is not the disinterested spectator of the divine. But this very fact leads us back to wondering whether he can, then, be disinterested in his love for God.

We can begin to answer this question by approaching Book Seven in terms of its context, as coming between the discussion at the end of Book Six and the "conversion" of Book Eight. Augustine's clinging to God then appears as not only the recognition of what is good for him but also as the beginning of disinterested love.

The latter part of Book Six is dominated by his account of events having to do with his friends and his mistress. In Chapter Fourteen, he tells of the plan that he and his friends had made, a plan to withdraw from the ordinary occupations of life, to put all their goods in common, and to live a common life of tranquillity. But the plan falls to pieces and is eventually put aside, mostly because of complications due to their wives. This is the plan that God derides. In the next chapter we are told of his suffering when his mistress is taken away from him: "My heart clinging to her was broken and wounded." Augustine is a "slave to lust" and not a "lover of marriage." He finds another mistress but the pain of losing his former mistress becomes more and more desperate. So, in keeping with his account of the state of his soul at that time, he concludes Book Six with a discussion of what he then thought about happiness: "And there was nothing to call me back from that deeper gulf of carnal pleasures, except the fear of death and of your judgment to come. . . . I used to discuss the nature of good and evil with my friends, Alypius and Nebridius, and certainly in my judgment Epicurus would have won the palm if I had not believed (as he refused to believe) that there was a life for the soul after death and treatment in accordance with its deserts. And I would put the question: 'Suppose we were immortal and could live in perpetual bodily pleasure without any fear of loss, why should we not be happy, or what more could we want?'" (VI.16).

In Book Eight, we are told of what is called the "conversion" of St. Augustine, the well-known scene in the garden when he opens the Scriptures to the words of St. Paul: "*Not in rioting and drunkenness, not in chambering and wantonness, not in strife and envying; but put ye on the Lord Jesus Christ; and make not provision for the flesh in concupiscence*" (VII.12). What happens in the struggle in the garden is the breaking of his bonds, the bonds that tie him to a woman. At the very beginning of Book Eight, he tells us that he no longer seeks honor and money. He has already turned away from these hopes: "But very strongly yet was I enthralled with the love of a woman" (VIII.1). It is not that marriage is evil or in any way forbidden. But the Apostle exhorts him to a better course. The conversion of Book Eight is a struggle within himself from which he emerges "chaste."[19]

What has happened between his clinging to his mistress and the breaking of his bonds is the "clinging to God" of Book Seven. The chaste love of Book Eight is free, disinterested. It is not demanded; it is not extracted by fear of punishment, the fear of judgment expressed at the end of Book Six where he speaks of happiness as carnal pleasure. The foreshadowing of this chaste love is precisely what he did not see in his discussions with Nebridius and Alypius. While he is miserable and desperate on account of being torn away from his mistress, he discusses the nature of good and evil with his friends and concludes that happiness is bodily pleasure: "And I never realized that it was just this that made me so miserable, that in my drowned and sightless state I was unable to form an idea of the light of honor and of a beauty that is embraced *for its own sake* which is invisible to the eye of flesh and can only be seen by the inner soul. I was wretched enough not to consider why and from what source it was that I found it a pleasure to discuss these ideas (shabby though they were) in the company of friends and that I could not be happy, even in the way I then understood happiness, without friends, however great the amount of carnal pleasure I had in addition. For certainly I loved my friends *for their own sake*, and I knew that they too loved me for my own sake" (VI.16). [Emphasis added.]

The "beauty that is embraced for its own sake" points to the fact that the response to what is beautiful is caused by the worth of the beautiful thing. The response to the beautiful is disinterested. Yet he can speak of embracing this beauty, of being united with it. So, too, friendship is loving one's friends for their own sake, not as instruments. Friendship is disinterested but clearly this disinterestedness does not imply any lack of feeling or enjoyment that comes from the union of friends. We might say that friendship is disinterested union. Augustine describes his life with his friends while he was at Carthage. They talked, laughed, did kindnesses for each other, read books together, joked and were serious, waited impatiently for the absent and welcomed them home with joy: "These and other similar expressions of feeling, which proceed from the hearts of those who love and are loved in return, and are revealed in the face, the voice, the eyes, and in a thousand charming ways, were like a kindling fire to melt our souls together and out of many to make us one" (IV.8).

The union of friendship is a union of souls but a union of souls that is revealed and accomplished by "the face, the voice, the eyes." The love that is friendship can only be expressed by means of speech and action. Augustine longed for the company of his absent friends. The union of friendship is not bodily and is not destroyed by the absence of the other, but it cannot come into being except through the presence, to the senses, of the friends.

Augustine describes his life with his friends at Carthage to show how he lived after the death of the friend who had been his "other self." He went to Carthage so as to flee from Tagaste where everything reminded him of this friend. Augustine became a "place of misery" to himself. His great misery is due to his not knowing how to love men as they should be loved (IV.6.7). He had loved his friend, not in God, but as if his friend would never die: "For the reason why that great sorrow of mine had pierced into me so easily and so deeply was simply this: I had poured out my soul like water onto sand by loving a man who was bound to die just as if he were an immortal" (IV.8). The absence of his friend makes him flee to another place. But God is everywhere present and "He does not pass away because there is nothing to take his place" (IV.11).

Friendship as the love of the other for his own sake points to the possibility of the disinterested love of God, of the union of God and the soul. But this union is not revealed or accomplished by the body and is not dependent on the body. The presence of God to the soul is not the presence of two bodies to each other or even precisely of the souls of friends to each other. We see this at the very point where Augustine's "turn" begins, the point which he did not even recognize as a beginning. He is tormented in his search for the origin of evil. God hears his groans and takes his silent contritions as cries for mercy: "You knew what I was suffering, and no man knew it. For how little there was of it which I could put into words even for the hearing of my most intimate friends! How could they hear the tumult of my soul when I had neither time nor language sufficient to express it? Yet all of it reached your hearing, all the roarings and groanings of my heart" (VII.7).

The presence of the soul to God is total: there is nothing hidden, even if the soul does not wish to reveal it or indeed cannot reveal it. But God is "most secret and most present." This is not the self-revelation to each other of equals. The union of the soul with God is initiated by God and accomplished by God's irresistible action. Yet the soul is free, its love disinterested. This is, in part, what causes Augustine's wonder when he gives expression to the change that has taken place in him: "I wondered that now I loved you. . . ." The soul finds itself to be at the same time totally dependent and yet free. Man is not the mere instrument of God;

the relationship of God and man is not that of master and slave.

The terror inspired by the notion that man may be the mere instrument of an all-powerful God is the fear of death. Man, created out of nothing, both is and is not: he has nothing good of his own. Pride begins to show itself as an attempt to escape from this human manner of being. And philosophy is such an attempt to escape the limits of the human, to seize what it takes to be the divine existence.

Pride and Humility

It is because God is Lord, but not the master of slaves, that the most proper form of prayer is praise. The worship of God is essentially the prayer of praise, and worship is disinterested. It is "for God's sake" even though God does not need it in any way. At the same time, it is the submission of oneself wholly to God. Praise, as the most proper way of addressing God, reflects man's true "place" with respect to God. Augustine begins *The Confessions* by speaking of man's desire to praise God: "*Great art thou, O Lord, and greatly to be praised; great is thy power and thy wisdom is infinite.* And man wants to praise you, man who is only a small portion of what you have created and who goes about carrying with him his own mortality, the evidence of his own sin and evidence that *Thou resistest the proud.* Yet still man, this small portion of creation wants to praise you" (I.1). And in Book Seven, the change that takes place in his judgment about the goodness of all things has to do with his coming to see that all things praise God (VII.13).

Man's "place," as described in the opening sentences of *The Confessions*, is as a small portion of creation, that small portion which carries about its mortality as evidence that God resists the proud. The praise of God is the prayer of humility because it recognizes the complete dependence of man on God; it manifests man's place as a created being. All created being both is and is not, and this is shown in its changeability. Immediately after the "entering within" that leads him to trembling with both love and terror, Augustine presents his new understanding of created being: "And I considered the other things beneath you and I saw that they neither are totally nor are not totally. They certainly are because they are from you; yet they are not because they are not what you are. For that truly is which remains unchangeably" (VII.11). It is here that Augustine recognizes God as his Lord because he does not need anything from Augustine. Created being, simply by virtue of its being created, *cannot* be God or equal to God. God does not create out of his own substance: he creates out of nothing. No created thing can be equal to God because no created thing can be "made" of God's substance, which is uncreated (XII.7).

The sin of Adam and Eve is in wanting to be like gods, to take for themselves the divine nature. That is, they try to "steal" the nature that does not belong to them.[20] This is the sin of pride and their disobedience is due to pride. Augustine attributes this sin to man's having been created out of nothing: "Only a nature created out of nothing could have been distorted by a fault. Consequently, although the will derives its existence, as a nature, from its creation by God, its falling away from its true being is due to its creation out of nothing." Adam and Eve attempt to make themselves the ground of their own being: "By aiming at more, a man is diminished, when he elects to be self-sufficient and defects from the one who is really sufficient for him" (*City of God* XIV.13).

Man, who is created out of nothing, and who therefore both is and is not, wants simply to be. So it is his mortality that is the evidence that God resists the proud. The sin of Adam and Eve is repeated: "But I was aiming to reach you and at the same time was being forced back from you, so that I might taste death; for *thou resistest the proud*. And how could anything be more proud than to assert, as I did in my incredible folly, that I was by nature what you are?" (IV.15)[21]

But we must ask what is really wrong with the desire to be like God. Is this not the desire for something good? And certainly it would be ridiculous to claim that God's nature can really be stolen, taken away from him, so that he could cease to be God because man had become like him. Is not humility a servile groveling before God and a cowardly denial of human worth?

It is essential that we isolate the specifically Christian sense of pride and humility, that we distinguish pride and humility from their pagan look-alikes. In the first place, the sin of pride must be distinguished from the pride that is inseparable from the virtue of magnanimity. This kind of pride is not at all evil from the Christian standpoint. It is perfectly compatible with Christian humility: the humble man is surely not prevented from being great-souled.[22] Neither does the sin of pride have anything to do with striving for excellence. Christian humility is not an exhortation to mediocrity: it is perfectly compatible with being and knowing oneself to be better than others in any given endeavor. And pride is not equivalent to pagan vanity. It is primarily a matter of man's relationship to God although it also includes aspects of man's relationship to other men. But, as we will see, pride is not identical to hubris.

Humility must be distinguished from the self-depreciation and false

modesty which are the opposites of boastfulness. It is perfectly possible to
depreciate oneself and be proud at the same time, and even in the act of
self-depreciation. Humility is not a feeling of inferiority or worthlessness;
such feelings are compatible with pride and are not evidence for its
absence. Nor is humility the same as humiliation. Humiliation does not
necessarily or ordinarily bring about humility. The more usual response
to being humiliated is anger and the desire for revenge.

When we attempt to get at the Christian sense of pride and humility,
the difficulty we face is in not having the prior terms for a definition.
They are essentially different from their pagan look-alikes and cannot be
defined in those terms. In Augustine, they seem to have a special status
among the vices and virtues, a preeminence which suggests that they are
the foundation of the other vices and virtues. If this is so, then Christian
morality cannot be understood, according to Augustine, as a simple taking over of the pagan catalog of virtues and then making the addition of
humility.

Pride and humility seem to have, for Augustine, a kind of ontological
status. That is, they have to do with the very manner of being of man and
not at first with habits of action. All created things are from nothing; they
both are and are not. Pride is a swelling, a being puffed up, and thus an
emptiness (VII.7.8.9.16). It is a turning of the will toward lower things
and thus toward nothingness. In this way it is equivalent to iniquity as
such: "And I inquired what iniquity should be: but I found it not to be a
substance, but a perversity of the will, twisted away from you, God, the
supreme substance, towards lower things; casting away its most inner
parts and puffed up outwardly" (VII.16).

We can see the special character of pride in Augustine's discussion of
the temptation called "the ambition of the world." The ambition of the
world has to do with man's relationship to other men and is not the
whole of pride. But it is in terms of this temptation that Augustine
provides us with the most concentrated discussion of pride in *The Confessions*. This temptation is the third kind of temptation, the third of three
headings under which he considers the whole question of "incontinence"
as dispersion. The lust of the flesh, the lust of the eyes, and the ambition
of the world are all forms of incontinence: "Certainly it is by continence
that we are brought together and brought back to the One, after having
dissipated ourselves among the Many" (X.29). But the ambition of the
world presents a special difficulty for him in his confession and it is this
special difficulty that lets us glimpse the ontological status of pride and
humility.

Augustine defines "the ambition of the world" as the desire to be feared and loved by other men, not because of God but instead of God. It is the desire to replace God or be God in the lives of other men. This in particular is the reason why God is not purely loved or feared and why God "*resist[s] the proud and give[s] grace to the humble*" (X.36). But Augustine's special difficulty with this temptation is that, unlike the others, he cannot know himself with respect to it. That is, with the pleasures of the body and the idle curiosity which is "the lust of the eyes" he can see how far he has advanced in the ability to control himself. He can test himself to determine how much these things have a hold on him by observing how much he is troubled by being without them. But when he asks God for continence with respect to "the ambition of the world," he says: "You know how on this matter my heart groans to you and my eyes stream tears. For I cannot easily discover how far I have become cleaner from this disease, and I much fear my hidden sins which are visible to your eyes, though not to mine" (X.37).

Augustine cannot test himself because the pleasure at issue is the pleasure of hearing oneself praised; to deliberately set out to be blamed, to do things that are blameworthy in order to see how much one minds not being praised, would be mad. Indeed, God commands us to love our neighbor and the actions that manifest the love of neighbor are praise-worthy actions. What Augustine wants is to take pleasure in the praise of others not for his own sake but for God's sake. But he cannot be certain that this is in fact the true reason for the pleasure he feels when he hears himself praised. Augustine fears his "hidden sins," sins which he himself has committed but which he does not know about.

While it is certainly possible to be lazy, or to take too much pleasure in eating and drinking without realizing that one is immoderate, there is the possibility for self-observation and there are means for bringing one-self under control. But pride has "levels" at which it can act and these levels are inaccessible to self-observation. Augustine calls the love of praise "a most dangerous temptation" and reveals the secret depths that make it especially dangerous: "It still tempts me even when I condemn it in myself; indeed it tempts me even in the very act of condemning it; often in our contempt of vainglory we are merely being all the more vainglori-ous" (X.38). Because the ambition of the world has to do with being praised by others for the good things we do, it is not possible to simply withdraw oneself from the temptation. Even the hermit can glory in what he thinks are the opinions of other men about him. There is no way to avoid the temptation and there can be no certainty about oneself with respect to it.[23]

Finally, there is a kind of pride which is not concerned with pleasing others but which consists in being pleased with oneself. This means taking pleasure in good things which come from God as if they came from oneself. Or, if they are acknowledged as coming from God, it means assuming that one deserves to have these good things; it is the assumption that God gives these good things because one is worthy of them of oneself. Here we see the failure to acknowledge that one has nothing, *is* nothing, of oneself, that one's very being is from God. Creation is out of nothing.

The possibility of being proud without knowing that one is proud is revealed in Augustine's doubts about himself and ultimately in the question he must address to God: "Or is not the fact simply this, that I deceive myself and in your presence fail to be truthful in heart and tongue?" (X.37). The most rigorous and ruthless self-examination can fail to uncover these secret recesses where the soul tries to keep something of itself hidden for itself.

Pride can have some manifestations, observable at least to oneself: the desire for revenge against those who have offended us is a clear example (X.36). And envy, which has its own character, goes along with pride (X.39). But pride is not a *feeling*. It cannot be brought under the control of reason in the way that anger and fear can be, except in those cases where it manifests itself as, for example, the desire for revenge. If pride is not a feeling, then it seems that it must be an opinion and specifically, a false opinion. But what would this false opinion be about? Certainly, a proud man might have the opinion that he is better morally or intellectually than others when in fact he is not. False opinion about one's superior worth is not excluded but neither does it account fully for the sin of pride. It is possible to have too low an opinion of oneself in relation to others, but this does not constitute humility.

The sin of pride cannot consist in true opinion about one's worth. If we take Augustine himself as our example, we see that he has no hesitation about affirming his own superior intellectual abilities (see for example, IV.16) without in any way accusing himself of pride on that account. True opinion about one's worth is perfectly compatible with humility. But true opinion is not identical with humility either. One might have a false opinion of one's worth and yet be humble.

If pride and humility are neither feelings nor opinions, can we go further and say that they must be ignorance and knowledge respectively? But this is where we reach the limit of our inquiry. For only God has this knowledge of us: "For *Thou, Lord, dost judge me*; because although *no man knoweth the things of a man, but the spirit of a man which is in him,* yet there is still something of man which even the spirit of man that is in him does not know. But you, Lord, know all of him, you who made him. . . . So I will confess what I know of myself, and I will also confess what I do not know of myself; because what I know of myself I know by means of your light shining upon me, and what I do not know remains unknown to me until *my darkness be made as the noonday* in your countenance" (X.5).

What we see in Augustine's treatment of pride and humility is that it is perfectly possible to say and to mean all of the things that express a true, and truly humble opinion of oneself and yet to be lying. The man who wants to be humble knows this. In the end, he must be uncertain. But we cannot turn this into a definition of humility. For there is indeed an absolutely true perspective on the soul. This is the perspective of the most just judge: ". . . out of the abyss of your just judgment . . . in accordance with the secret deservings of souls" (VII.6).

Humility is not in our power, at least not in the way that other virtues may be. There is no pagan virtue of humility because there is no notion of creation out of nothing. And because there is no notion of creation out of nothing, there is no sense of an absolutely true perspective on the soul. The Christian virtue of humility is the properly human manner of being in the presence of the creator who has brought us out of nothingness, the manner of being of what both is and is not in the presence of what is simply. Pride, then, is a being puffed up, an emptiness that gives the false appearance of fullness. It is a kind of lie to one's self, a self-deception that belongs to the human in the most intimate possible way.

The enormity of the sin of pride—we might even say its awesome-ness—causes Augustine to tremble (X.39) as he considers this "danger." For what puts pride in its true perspective is the realization that God is not proud. The God whom the proud man wants to be and to replace in the lives of others is not proud.

When Augustine begins to examine himself with respect to the ambi-tion of the world, he addresses God as "Lord, you who alone are Lord without pride, because you are alone the true Lord, who has no other Lord" (X.36). God's rule is radically different from the rule that men exercise over each other for God alone is Lord without pride. Augustine says that this is because God alone is true Lord, that is, he has no other Lord. Because God has no one superior to him, he is not proud. Pride occurs, not from the recognition of one's power over others, but only from the recognition of something superior. Pride asserts itself only in the presence of what is higher. This, of course, does not mean that the subjects of the proud ruler do not suffer for his pride. But they suffer because he needs something from them, the recognition of his superiority which he will extract by force if necessary. This is the other side of the matter and, again, we see that God is not proud: "And you are my Lord, *because* you do not need my goods" (VII.11). [Emphasis added.]

It is not God's pride that makes human pride wrong. That is, it is not a case, as it is with men, of two prides coming up against each other. God does not punish pride so as to preserve his own superiority or to extract recognition by force. God does not create in order to be superior to what he creates; he gets nothing out of what is inferior to him and he needs nothing. He has no superior and he needs nothing from what is inferior.

The proud man wants to be God but he accomplishes precisely the opposite: he becomes closer to nothingness. He is ruled by what is inferior to him (VII.7). For God shows himself to be compassionate: "You have humbled the proud as one that is wounded . . . (VII.7). . . . You, Lord, abide forever, and you are not angry with us forever, because you have pity on dust and ashes" (VII.8). The proud man is angry and seeks revenge for insult and rebellion. God's response to the sin of Adam and Eve is to punish them and then to show compassion. The Incarnation and Redemption are the wonderful manifestations of God's compassion. Christ *"thought it no robbery to be equal with God because in nature he was the same with him. But . . . He emptied Himself, taking the form of a servant, being made in the likeness of men, and found in fashion as a man, humbled Himself, and became obedient unto death, even the death of the cross"* (VII.9).

God's compassion is precisely what is missing from the books of the Platonists. And God shows his compassion for Augustine by bringing him into contact with the proud man who gives him these books. Augustine learns how God resists the proud. The God whom the philosophers seek to be turns out to be a God who does not despise the human. The Platonists know that *"In the beginning was the Word"* but not that *"the Word was made flesh"* (VII.9).

Christ, as both fully divine and fully human, is the mediator who reconciles us with God. Our mortality is the evidence that God resists the proud (I.1), and our mortality is precisely what Christ is willing to take upon himself: "We need a mediator linked with us in our lowliness by reason of the mortal nature of his body" (*City of God* IX.17). Christ's mediation accomplishes the overcoming of death: "Those for whose liberation he was made a mediator, should not themselves remain forever in death, even the death of the flesh" (*City of God* IX.15).

The overcoming of death is precisely what first attracted Augustine to the study of philosophy. When he was a very young man, he came upon Cicero's exhortation to philosophy in *Hortensius*: "My spirit was filled with an extraordinary and burning desire for the *immortality* of wisdom." The only thing that holds him back from the life of philosophy is that the name of Christ is absent (III.4). [Emphasis added.] But when he turns to the Scriptures, they seem unworthy of comparison with the grand style of Cicero: his pride keeps him from seeing the depth of wisdom that is in these Scriptures (III.5). The "immortality of wisdom" is due to the divine character of philosophy: it represents an overcoming of the human as such. But "*the Word was made flesh*"; Christ became "*obedient unto death*" so that "those for whose liberation he was made a mediator, should not themselves remain forever in death, *even the death of the flesh.*" The Christian belief in the immortality of the soul is not based on the overcoming of the human as such. The resurrection of the body means human immortality, not the immortality of the "purified" disembodied mind.

Pride, then, turns out to involve a kind of despising of the human in favor of the divine. The radical change that takes place in Augustine, the change recounted in Book Seven, is due in great part to his finally accepting his "place." He trembles at the unlikeness between himself and God. Thus, he defines himself in terms of the distinction between himself and the Platonists who are proud and in whose books there are no tears of confession and no look of pity. For Augustine trembles with both love and terror: the God from whom he is so distant is at the same time the God to whom he can cling.

It is only from his proper "place" that man can "see." Augustine constantly connects pride with blindness and with being "outside." This is especially clear in Chapter Seven where he tells us that God took his silent inquiry as a cry for mercy. What is wrong with Augustine is that the entire direction of his inquiry is mistaken. He is turned toward things that are in places, to things that are inferior to him and which should have been subjected to him. Instead, he is ruled by these inferior things because he is proud. His pride is a swelling that "blinds his eyes." What Augustine did not then know was "the due proportion and the middle region of my salvation, that I might remain in your image, and serving you, have dominion over my body" (VII.7). His search for the origin of evil is not a purely intellectual matter. It is inseparable from the moral state of his own soul. His failure is not a purely intellectual failure but is due to his pride and his not ruling his body. Pride is the great danger; the "middle region" is the place of safety and this middle region is between God and body: " . . . serving you have dominion over my body." Seeing is inseparable from ruling the body. And ruling the body is accomplished by serving God. This is being in the image of God.

The middle place which is proper to man is arrived at by turning "within," away from the things that are in places. Augustine is admonished to return to himself by the books of the proud Platonists but his own turn within is only possible because God is now his helper and his leader.[24] His own turn within is also his humbling (VII.10). The books of the Platonists, in which there are no tears of confession, admonish him to seek for incorporeal truth (VII.20), but the Truth that Augustine finds when he enters "within" causes him to tremble with love and terror. This is why God provided that he should first come upon the books of the Platonists before he took up St. Paul, that he "might discern and distinguish what a difference there is between presumption and confession" (VII.20).

Truth and Self-Deception

It is only when he turns "within" himself that Augustine finds truth. He is admonished to turn within by the Platonists, yet his turning within is also a turning to his proper "place"; he not only turns away from things in places, he also ceases to come up against God as in battle. This twofold change in him is accounted for by what he discovers when he enters within. He discovers "above" the eyes of his soul, "above" his mind, "the unchangeable light." This light is superior to him because it made him. He owes his entire being to this light and it is in the presence of this light that he trembles with love and terror. "He who knows truth knows that light" (VII.10).

This discovery of the unchangeable light above his mind is the realization of the existence of truth: "And I said, Is truth therefore nothing at all, seeing it is neither diffused through infinite spaces nor through finite?" Augustine is now able to think of the incorporeal, of the nonspatial. The books of the Platonists have put him onto the search for incorporeal truth. This change in him must be seen against the background of Chapter One. He had not been able to think of any kind of substance except what he was accustomed to seeing with his eyes. He thinks of God as a kind of

light that is diffused through infinite spaces because he thinks that anything not in space is truly nothing. He is himself "gross-hearted" and
unable to discern his own self (VII.1).

Now, when he enters "within" himself, he finds a completely different kind of light and discovers that truth exists. Clearly, then, Augustine's
turn within is *not* spatial and is not a turn to what is in space. At the same
time that the spatial word is used its spatial sense is being denied. A turn
within the body could only be a turn to something bodily: only body is
"in" body. Nor is Augustine's turn "within" a turn to what is private, to
what is unshareable and not common. What he refers to as "within" is
hidden from other men but not from God. His interior can be revealed to
other men and in the presence of other men, but even this revelation
cannot be complete: Augustine cannot know himself completely. But "to
your eyes the very depths of man's conscience are exposed. . . . Whatever
I am, then, Lord, is open and evident to you" (X.2).

The locus of truth, then, is God. Augustine's turn "within" brings
him into the presence of truth, of the "unchangeable light." It is not truth
which is private but rather the lie. The lie is entirely one's own possession:
"And therefore, Lord, your judgments are terrible, because your truth is
not my property nor the property of this man or that man; it belongs to
all of us whom you publicly call into communion with it, warning us in
most terrible terms that we must not hold it as private to ourselves lest we
be deprived of it altogether. For whoever claims as his personal possession what you have given for the enjoyment of all, and wants to have as
his own what belongs to everyone, is driven out from what is in common
to what really is his own, that is, from a truth to a lie. For he *that speaketh
a lie, speaketh it of his own*" (XII.25)

Truth is to be shared, to be held in common. The desire to hold truth
as one's private possession is the desire to distinguish oneself, to appear
to be wiser than other men. This is a lack of the charity that has its
foundation in humility (VII.20). The truth that Augustine has in mind
when he speaks of the obligation to share is the truth of faith. There is no
obligation to publicly reveal oneself and, in particular, one's sins. Sin, like
a lie, is entirely one's own (VII.3). But Augustine, in his *Confessions*,
carries out the obligation to share the truth to the extent that he reveals
his own sins, sins which could be kept entirely hidden from other men.

Action is visible to others, although some actions are covered and
unseen. These actions have to be revealed in speech by the one who
confesses. Thoughts can also be sinful and these can be kept entirely
hidden. They can only be made known to others through speech. It is in

the realm of the revelation through speech of hidden actions and thoughts and intentions that the lie is possible. The hearer must judge of the truth or falsehood of what is told as the judge must make some determination about the veracity of the witness in a law court. In addressing himself to the question of why he makes his confession publicly, Augustine recognizes the position that his hearers are in: "And when they hear my own account of my own self, how do they know that I am telling the truth, seeing that *no man knows what is in man but the spirit of man which is in him?*" Just as charity is in some sense at the basis of the obligation to tell the truth, to share it, so also "*charity believeth all things* (that is, among those whom it binds together and makes one), and so, Lord, I make my confession to you in such a way that men may hear it, though I cannot demonstrate to them that I am telling the truth; yet those whose ears are opened to me by charity believe what I say" (X.3).

Augustine's entering "within" brings him into the presence of truth, not into contact with what is entirely hidden. But truth can only be made known to other men through speech. In discussing the reasons for confessing publicly what he is now as he writes his *Confessions*, he refers to those who want to know this: "But their ear is not laid against my heart, where I am whatever I am. And so they want, as I make my confession, to hear what I am inside myself, beyond the possible reach of their eyes and ears and minds" (X.3). And while *The Confessions* itself shows us that this revelation through speech can be accomplished, it also points to the radical incompleteness and limitations of this project. For even the one confessing does not know what is visible only to God. This contrast between the truth that God has and the truth that men have lies at the very beginning of Augustine's turn. He tells us that he sought for the origin of evil and he sought with great anxiety: "What agonies I suffered, what groans, my God, came from my heart in its labor! Yet your ears were open, though I knew it not. And when in silence I so vehemently sought after it, the silent contritions of my soul were great cries for your mercy. You knew what I was suffering, and no man knew it. For how little there was of it which I could put into words even for the hearing of my most intimate friends! How could they hear the tumult of my soul when I had neither time nor language sufficient to express it? Yet all of it reached your hearing, all the roarings and groanings of my heart, and my desire was before you" (VII.7).

The sharing of truth with other men can only be accomplished by words. And this sharing is incomplete. But God does not need our words. And even our own words to ourselves about ourselves do not completely reveal us to our own selves. Augustine does not know that his silent contritions are cries for mercy. At the most intimate point of oneself lies what is open and evident to God. Truth is what God sees. Augustine's turn "within" is the turn to incorporeal truth, to the unchangeable light that is above the mind (VII.10).

Augustine presents a second version of the turn "within" in Chapter Seventeen. Here, it is described as an ascent to "that which is." He passes from bodies to the soul and, within the soul, from the senses to the reason that judges, to the understanding itself. This is essentially a movement from the changeable to the unchangeable. In its final stage, the soul withdraws its thoughts from "custom" and from the confused crowd of phantasms which have been presented to the variable reason for judgment: "Thus in the flash of a trembling glance it came as far as that which is." But this is not a condition in which a man can remain. Augustine falls back from this sight, back to the customary. In Book Ten, where he again presents an account of this ascent, he gives us a similar description of the inevitable falling back: "But my sad weight makes me fall back again; I am swallowed up by normality; I am held fast and heavily do I weep, but heavily I am held. So much are we weighed down by the burden of custom!" (X.40).

The turn "within," especially as it is detailed in Book Seven, Chapter Seventeen, is remarkably similar to what I called "the approach of sight" in the *Phaedo*, even in its emphasis on moving from the changeable to the unchangeable. But while Socrates gives the impression that the ascent is accomplished once and for all, that the soul of the philosopher must not be like Penelope, Augustine is quite explicit about the inevitability of falling back.[25] He keeps a loving memory of his ascent but his falling back makes him weep.

The unchangeable light which he finds when he enters within, the being of whom he catches a glimpse, is secure and safe because unchangeable. This is the God to whom he can cling. The visual metaphors are clearly dominant in these accounts. And other men are clearly absent. The approach of sight to truth is made alone, at least as far as other men are concerned. The separation of soul and body in the *Phaedo* is at the same time a separation from other men. Augustine, though, has God as his leader and helper (VII.10).

The presence of other men in *The Confessions* and especially in Book Seven is largely in terms of speech. In Book Seven we find several important instances of this, among them the two cases where God "uses" other men to lead Augustine to the truth. In these accounts, it is hearing that dominates, and in the first case the speech produces certitude. "As to those deceived deceivers, those dumb talkers (dumb because they never uttered your Word), I had a perfectly good argument to oppose them. . . . It was put forward by Nebridius, and all of us who heard it were much taken aback by it" (VII.2). Nebridius provides the argument which shows the impossibility of the Manichean position: Nebridius's argument gives the Manichees no way out. Augustine is careful to mention that Nebridius came up with this argument "long ago" while they were in Carthage. The argument still stands, unchangeable.

What Nebridius's argument shows is that God cannot be affected by evil, that God is unchangeable in this respect. On the basis of this argument, Augustine is "secure" in his search for the origin of evil: he is "certain" that what the Manichees say is not true (VII.3). The anxiety that he expresses later, in Chapters Five and Seven, has to do with his search for the origin of evil within the context of his thinking of God as creator. What he must learn is that God creates and acts without changing (VII.15).

The second instance in which we see him led to the truth by another man through speech is the story of Firminus about the astrologers. Augustine's friends, Nebridius and Vindicianus, had both been trying to persuade him that there was no art whereby men could foresee the future, that when the astrologers did say something true it was by chance. Augustine is almost convinced but the story told by Firminus convinces him completely: "After hearing this story and (since Firminus was a perfectly reliable witness) believing it, all my previous resistance collapsed" (VII.6). Now he tries to persuade Firminus and to find other instances or examples with which to refute the claims of the astrologers.

The third case is that of the unnamed proud man whom God uses to bring Augustine into contact with the books of the Platonists (VII.9). On account of reading these books Augustine turns "within" to truth (VII.10). The books of the Platonists put him onto the search for incorporeal truth (VII.20). The speech of other men, including the written, plays an important role in Augustine's turn.

So too does the content of faith that is given in hearing. Augustine begins from a foundation different from that of the Platonists. As much as he was inflamed by Cicero's *Hortensius*, he is held back by the absence of the name of Christ: "For this name, Lord, this name of my Saviour, your son, had been with my mother's milk drunk in devoutly by my tender heart, where it remained deeply treasured" (III.4). It is by faith that he believes that God exists, that his substance in unchangeable, that he judges men, and that Christ and the Scriptures show the way of salvation:

"With these beliefs firmly and irrevocably rooted in my mind, I sought with fierce agitation whence evil might come" (VII.7). He tries to understand what he has "heard," that free will is the cause of the evil that we do (VII.3). From the time he began to "hear" anything of wisdom he has avoided the thought that God is in the figure of a human body and he rejoices to find this in the faith of the Catholic Church (VII.1). Finally, the Bible itself, the word of God, shows itself as containing whatever truth he had read in the books of the Platonists (VII.21).

The question of the relationship between truth and words in Augustine is perhaps best approached in terms of the truth of the word of God in the Scriptures. In Book Eleven of *The Confessions*, Augustine begins his consideration of the first verses of Genesis. Here and in the remaining books of *The Confessions* he takes up the problem of the interpretation of Scripture, specifically, the possibility of variety of interpretation of the same words. This variety springs from the depth of meaning of the word of God: "How amazing is the profundity of your utterances! See, they lie before us with a surface that can charm little children. But their profundity is amazing, my God, their profundity is amazing. One cannot look into them without awe and trembling—awe of greatness, trembling of love" (XII.14). And after discussing a variety of possible meanings of "In the beginning God made heaven and earth," he writes: "Now after I have heard all this and thought it over, I have no wish to *strive about words*. That is *profitable to nothing, but the subversion of the hearers*. . . . Now, as with burning heart I confess these things to you, my God, light of my eyes in secret, what harm does it do me if different meanings, which are nevertheless all true, can be gathered from these words?" (XII.18).

It is beyond my immediate concern to examine the whole matter of the possible identity or difference between God's meaning and Moses's meaning in the words of the Bible. The point I wish to make here is that the words of the Bible are true simply and that only true statements can be valid interpretations: the meaning of the Scriptures can only be expressed in true statements.

Until he finally turns to St. Paul, after having read the proud Platonists, Augustine had despised the Scriptures on account of their simple surface. He expected from the word of God what he had found in the best human books. As a young man, he had admired the style of Cicero but what moves him is the matter, not the style of the *Hortensius*. Yet when he turns to the Scriptures on account of the absence of the name of Christ from the *Hortensius*, his pride finds them unworthy of comparison with Cicero's grand style (III.4).

Later, Augustine wins the post as professor of rhetoric at Milan and thus God brings him from Rome to Milan where he meets Bishop Ambrose. Ambrose is renowned for his eloquence and Augustine listens to his preaching only to hear his style and to test his reputation. He was not at all interested in what was said and even held it in contempt. In fact, Augustine finds the style of Faustus more warm and winning than that of Ambrose. But gradually Augustine begins to see the truth of what Ambrose says: "For although my concern was not to learn what he said but only to hear how he said it (this empty interest being all that remained to me, now that I had despaired of man's being able to find his way to you), nevertheless together with the language, which I admired, the subject matter (*res*) also, to which I was indifferent, began to enter into my mind. Indeed I could not separate the one from the other. And as I opened my heart in order to recognize how eloquently he was speaking it occurred to me at the same time . . . how truly he was speaking" (V.14). In particular, Ambrose interprets the Scriptures in such a way, namely in their "spiritual" and not literal sense, that Augustine sees how the Law and the Prophets can stand up to hostile and mocking criticism.

After reading the books of the Platonists and becoming puffed up with knowledge, Augustine finally recognizes the "chaste eloquence" of St. Paul and sees that Paul does not, as he had thought, contradict the Law and the Prophets (VII.21). In the Scriptures and in St. Paul especially, Augustine finds whatever truth he had found in the books of the Platonists. In the books of the Platonists he had found much of the Prologue of the Gospel according to St. John. What Augustine is pointing to is a relationship between words and "things" that allows for what might be called "translation" on different levels. The books of the Platonists have been "translated out of Greek into Latin." When he reads them he finds "In the beginning was the Word. . . ." This is in the Platonic books "not of course in the same words but to precisely the same effect and with a number of different sorts of reasons" (VII.9). The first kind of translation is from Greek to Latin, the second is from the philosophical writings to Scripture. The words are not the same but the meaning is identical. And from the question of meaning we must move to the question of the truth of what is said.

In a different context, we learn that the judgment of the truth of what is said is not itself a matter of words. When Augustine begins his discussion of Genesis, he describes what it would be like if he could question Moses and ask him to explain "In the beginning you made heaven and earth." If Moses spoke in Hebrew, Augustine would merely hear sounds, but if he spoke in Latin, Augustine would know what he was saying. "But how should I know whether what he said was true? And if I did know it, would it be from him that I knew it? No it would not; it would be from inside me, from that inner house of my thought, that Truth, which is neither Hebrew nor Greek nor Latin nor Barbarian, and which speaks without the aid of mouth or tongue, without any sound of syllables, would say: 'He is speaking the truth,' and at once I would be sure" (XI.3).

Words, human words, may be either true or false depending upon whether or not the assertion or denial expresses what is indeed the case. But truth is not reducible to words. When Augustine searches in *silence* for the origin of evil, God takes his *silent* contritions as cries for mercy: "You knew what I was suffering, and no man knew it. For how little there was of it which I could put into words even for the hearing of my most intimate friends! How could they hear the tumult of my soul when I had neither time nor language sufficient to express it?" (VII.7).

The limitations of speech also show themselves in the way it is necessary to speak about God. On the one hand, God is unchangeable; on the other hand, he creates and rules the universe even to the fluttering of the leaves. On the one hand, God remains the same; on the other hand, he goes from anger to pity: "You, Lord, abide forever, and you are not angry with us forever, because you have pity on dust and ashes" (VII.8). On the one hand, "there is nothing at all evil to you" (VII.13); on the other hand, the idol in Augustine's heart is "abominable to you" (VII.14) and on account of the wicked "Thou sparedst not Thine only Son but deliveredst Him for us all" (VII.9). Even in speaking about the soul, we must use words while at the same time denying their meaning. Augustine's turning "within" is not a turn to a place, to a "thing" in a place; it is a turn away from "things that are contained in places" (VII.7). And the very opening words of Genesis, "In the beginning," have to be understood in such a way as to preserve the eternity and unchangeability of God (see for example, XI.10.11.12.) The Bible is composed of merely human words. One important difference between the Bible, which has God as its ultimate author, and other human speech is that the interpretation of the Bible must consist of only true statements.

But there is another Word of God which is "in silence" (XI.6), the eternal Word "which is spoken eternally and by which all things are spoken eternally" (XI.7). Human speech is about "things" and soon reveals its radical limitations in speech about God and the soul especially.[26] But God's Word is creative. It makes things to be what they are. Hence, Augustine's new understanding of God's presence, of the relationship of

God and creation, is in terms of truth and not in terms of space: "And I looked at other things and I saw that they owe their being to you and are all bounded in you, not in a spatial sense, but because your being contains everything in the hand of your truth,[27] and all things are true insofar as they are." Falsehood belongs not to things but only to man: "And the only meaning of falsehood is when something is thought to exist when it does not" (VII.15). St. John says of the Word that it was "in the beginning with God." "All things were made by him and without him nothing was made." This is also, "in other words," in the books of the Platonists (VII.9). And when Augustine enters within he finds the unchangeable light above his mind, and this light made him. The source of the truth of created being is in its having been created by God. But this does *not* imply a notion of being as such and of truth based on production.[28] For at the same time that we speak of God as making, we have in mind the radical distinction between God and the craftsman. Indeed, this is the change that occurs in Book Seven, from Chapter Five where he thinks of creation as production, to Chapter Fifteen where he is able to distinguish the two: "And that you, who only are eternal, did not begin to work after [the passage of] innumerable spaces of time, for all spaces of times, both those which are passed already and those which are to pass hereafter, may neither come nor go, but by you, who are still working and still remaining" (VII.15).

The notion that the source of the truth of created being is in its having been created by God becomes, in Descartes, the very foundation for the practice of the sciences. As we will see, Descartes takes God's action in creation as production, and this making becomes the model for knowing the things of nature. But for Augustine it is precisely the identification of creation and production which must be overcome.

God's activity in creating is not that of the craftsman. In particular, God does not create because creation is in any way necessary or useful for him. The whole of the activity of production is meaningful only in terms of the usefulness of the product. Even if one excludes the productions of the fine arts from the domain of the useful, these productions do exist for the sake of satisfying some human desire. But God fulfills no desire in creating. It is written in Genesis that God made all things good. And Augustine comes to realize this in his "bettered judgment." He does not now "desire better" because he sees that all things praise God (VII.13). But God needs *none* of it, lower *or* higher. And he needs nothing from man: "And you are my Lord because you do not need my goods" (VII.11).

Not only must creation be distinguished from production, human production must be viewed with suspicion. That is, it cannot be regarded as simply good: "And to the temptations of the eyes, men themselves in their various arts and manufactures have made innumerable additions: clothes, shoes, vases, products of craftmanship; pictures too and all sorts of statues—far beyond what is necessary for use, moderate, or with any religious meaning. *So men go outside themselves to follow things of their own making*, and inside themselves they are forsaking Him who made them and are destroying what they themselves were made to be" (X.34). [Emphasis added.]

With respect to music, the difficulty Augustine experiences is not unlike the dangers associated with eloquence. And Augustine raises this issue with respect to the praise of God in song. The melodies of sacred music demand a place of dignity in the heart "so that they may be received into me together with the words that give them life" but sometimes he is more moved by the singing than by what is sung (X.33).

There is a further sense in which human making must be viewed with suspicion. God creates what is, and all things are true insofar as they are. But man creates what is not.[29] Throughout the first part of Book Seven, especially in Chapters One and Five, Augustine presents himself as producing phantasms. In Chapter Five, he "sets up" the whole of creation before the eyes of his spirit and then imagines God as surrounding it. In Chapter Fourteen, he refers back to this. His soul had "made for itself a God to fill the infinite distances of all space, and it had thought this God to be you and had placed it in its own heart, thus again becoming the temple of its own idol." What causes Augustine to wonder is that "now I loved you and not a phantasm instead of you" (VII.17).

But, again, this is no purely intellectual change. In coming to love God and not a phantasm instead of God, he comes to love what he cannot manipulate. He has no power over God or over creation. He no longer "sets up" the whole creation and God around it in his mind or the idol of infinite spaces in his heart. The movement "within" to truth is at the same time a humbling: "I trembled with love and terror" (VII.10).

When he has been humbled, Augustine can recognize the "chaste eloquence" of St. Paul, and he learns to "*rejoice with trembling*" (VII.21). Most of his life until then had been devoted to the study and the enjoyment of eloquence. One of the most significant things that happens as a result of his conversion is his abandonment of the teaching of rhetoric. This parallels his turn away from the attempt to manipulate God: eloquence is an instrument of power over other men. In explaining his decision to quit "the talking-shop," Augustine says that his students were mostly interested in absurd deceptions and legal battles. They were learning from him how to use words in order to deceive and persuade others to do their will. Augustine refers to his work as "my professorship of lies" (IX.2).

This is not to imply that Augustine's preaching and his writing after his conversion are not eloquent. *The Confessions* itself is beautifully written and, in many ways, is a rhetorical work. The distinction to be made is that between words which are true and thus inseparable from the "things," and words that are false and thus inseparable from what is not. If we look back over his experiences with Cicero, Faustus, Ambrose, and the Scriptures, we see this distinction at work. Faustus is more eloquent than Ambrose but, listening to Ambrose simply for the sake of his eloquence, Augustine gradually becomes unable to separate the words and the "thing." Earlier, he had been struck by the "matter" (*quod loquebatur*) of *Hortensius*: he had been interested in Cicero's style but finds that what Cicero says about philosophy persuades him, indeed inflames him. At the same time, he disdains the Scriptures because they cannot match Cicero's style and this disdain is due to his pride. Now, after his turn in Book Seven, he recognizes the "chaste eloquence" of St. Paul: "And there appeared to me but one face of chaste eloquence" (VII.21). And after the conversion to chastity in Book Eight, he gives up his professorship of lies and he now "chatters" (*garrire*) easily to God (IX.1).[30]

Augustine now talks *to* God. This is the mode of discourse which allows him to be in the presence of truth. His talking to God is in no way an attempt to persuade God, to exercise power over him. His trying to know God is no longer for the purpose of manipulating God by possessing him in thought. After reading the books of the Platonists he had been puffed up with knowledge and wanted to appear wise in the eyes of other men: he "chattered" as if he were clever, and he could not weep because he did not yet see the difference between presumption and confession (VII.20).

Confession is the state in which the soul is most deliberately and knowingly in the presence of God and thus in the presence of truth. In confession, the soul comes closest to the truth about itself for it knows itself to be open and evident to another: "Indeed, Lord, to your eyes the very depths of man's conscience are exposed, and there is nothing in me that I could keep secret from you, even if I did not want to confess it" (X.2).

Augustine can say, then, that in confessing "I will not deceive myself" (I.5) and that "I am in your presence and I do not lie. As I speak, so is my heart" (XI.25). But this very truthfulness demands the confession of ignorance and even of the possibility of self-deception. In discussing the diversity of true opinions about the meaning of the Scriptures, Augustine makes explicit the spirit in which he writes his *Confessions*: "So if anyone asks me which of these meanings was in the mind of your servant Moses, I should not be speaking in the language of my *Confessions* if I did not confess to you: 'I do not know'" (XII.30).

This not knowing extends to the state of his own soul even though nothing can be more present to him (X.5). As we have seen, uncertainty about the state of the soul is especially acute with respect to pride and humility. Augustine fears his "hidden sins" in this matter, and finally, after arduous self-examination, he must ask: "Or is not the fact simply this, that I deceive myself and in your presence fail to be truthful in heart and tongue?" (X.37).

Augustine's uncertainty is not only about the present state of his soul but also about the future. He does not know what he will do or what he will become. And, ultimately, he must be uncertain about his own salvation. Augustine's doubt, then, is not purely or "merely" theoretical. It is no device for arriving at certitude. The doubts about his own soul cannot be overcome or replaced by certain knowledge.

Augustine's anxiety is the fear of death. His doubt is *serious*, not merely instrumental. His doubt goes to the very ground of his being, for he recognizes that he is from nothing. Any attempt to identify Augustine's certitude of existence with Descartes's first principle has to overlook an essential difference. Augustine's assertions of certitude about his existence are of no importance for the conduct of his life. Certitude of existence does not eliminate doubt about his soul, the genuine doubt which is the fear of death. It is not the certitude of his present existence but rather his creation from nothing, his not-being, which is of the greatest importance for his life and thought.

The source of Augustine's uncertainty about himself is his recognition of his own changeability. He feels this changeability chiefly with respect to sin and this recognition is a sign of his having been humbled. He now knows the difference between presumption and confession. But confession is not only the revelation of one's own sins: it is also the revelation of God's mercy.

The last word about Augustine's fundamental uncertainty must not suggest a condition of unmitigated anguish and terror. For as uncertain as he is about his own self, about his own future, he is perfectly certain of God. And this certitude is, in the end, more fundamental than any doubt about himself: "I should more easily doubt that I did not live than that truth is not" (VII.10).

Uncertainty about himself is always accompanied by certitude about

God.[31] This is the inseparable pair that lies at the basis of *The Confessions*. We see it at precisely the point where his "turn" is accomplished: "For that truly is which remains unchangeably. It is good then for me to cling to God: for if I remain not in him, I shall not be able [to remain] in myself" (VII.11). Just as Augustine's doubt about his own self is not merely theoretical, so too the question of God's unchangeability cannot be for him a purely theoretical question. It is God's unchangeability that enables man to be certain about him and this certitude determines the whole character of Augustine's life.

But this does not mean that Augustine now lives a life of certitude. Certainty about God does not eliminate doubt about oneself, for God's knowledge and action do not negate human action.[32] And sin and the lie are entirely one's own. Augustine's life might best be characterized, not as a life lived in certitude, but as a life lived in hope. Hope preserves both members of the pair.

Uncertainty by itself can lead only to despair and terror: "We might have thought that your Word was far from any union with man, and we might have despaired, unless it had been *made flesh and dwelt among us.* Terrified by my sins and the mass and weight of my misery, I had pondered in my heart a purpose of flight to the wilderness. But you forbade me and gave me strength by saying: *Therefore Christ died for all*" (X.43). Augustine writes this after he has gone through his self-scrutiny with respect to the temptations of the lust of the flesh, the lust of the eyes, and the ambition of the world. His uncertainty about himself, especially concerning pride, makes him consider fleeing to the wilderness, separating himself from others. Such a flight would have been, for him, a search for greater certitude, an escape from doubt. Instead, he remains among men and even goes so far as undertaking the very dangerous task of writing his *Confessions*.

We see the inseparable pair emerge in Book Seven and we see it clearly at work in Book Ten where he shows us how he is as he writes his *Confessions*, as he "does the truth" in the presence of God and in writing before many witnesses (X.1). Indeed, this very dangerous enterprise can only be dared because he is secure in the hope of God's mercy and mistrustful of his own innocence: "I know that you are not in any way subject to violence, whereas I do not know in my case what temptations I can and what I cannot resist. And there is hope, because *Thou art faithful*" (X.5). God's unchangeability is no mere abstraction unrelated to the conduct of life.

Even where Augustine feels most sure of himself, where the dangers seem least, he is careful to remind us of his doubt. In fact, this is where he is most explicit. In examining himself with respect to the pleasures of the senses, he takes up the sense of smell, surely the least troublesome. The pleasures of smell concern him least for he is untroubled by either their absence or presence. "So it seems to me, though I may be deceiving myself. For here too there is a sad kind of darkness in which the abilities that are in me are hidden from me, so that when my mind questions itself about its own powers, it cannot be certain that its replies are trustworthy, because what is inside the mind is mostly hidden and remains hidden until revealed by experience, and in this life, which is described as a continuous trial, no one ought to feel sure that, just as he has been worse and become better, he may not also, after having been better, become worse. Our one hope, our one confidence, our one firm promise is your mercy" (X.32).

Insofar as sin, and pride in particular, is a turning toward nothingness, Augustine's uncertainty goes to the very ground of his being. But that ground turns out to be the unchangeable God. Insofar as Augustine's hope rests on God's promise, it is a trust placed in words, not in the certitude of sight: "But up to now it is still by faith and not by sight, for by hope we are saved; but hope that is seen is not hope" (XIII.13).

Transition: From Christian Hope to Modern Certitude

Before the decisive turning point in Augustine's life, he is drawn to the life of philosophy by the promise of immortality: he is tormented by the fear of death. But Augustine learns that the immortality that philosophy offers is grounded in a view of man which attributes divinity to what is highest in him. Pride is at the very heart of the philosopher's attempt to escape death. Hope is possible only on account of God's compassion.

This change in the notion of the divine, the change from disinterested spectator to compassionate actor, makes possible (but not inevitable) the modern project undertaken in Descartes's *Discourse*. Descartes attempts to begin from nothing, to re-begin philosophy as a purely human activity and as an imitation of the divine compassion. The hope that he offers for the conquest of death is a hope grounded not in faith but in the certitude of the *je pense, donc je suis*. Descartes rejects both the Socratic notion of philosophy as an endless task and the Augustinian dependence on a compassionate God. The certitude of his self-assertion is the beginning of the task of reversing the effects of original sin.

CHAPTER III

Descartes: Occupation and Pre-occupation

The *Discourse* as Apology

The full title of the *Discourse on Method* suggests that the purpose of the work is the presentation of "the method." This method is the one whereby the reason can be conducted well and truth sought in the sciences; and it is presented in the Second Part of the *Discourse* in the form of four rules. While it is undeniable that the method of the Second Part is of the greatest importance for understanding the *Discourse*, the context in which this method is set reveals the character of the work as a whole. The *Discourse on Method* is first and foremost an apology. The four rules of the method of the Second Part are given as part of the story of Descartes's life.

The purpose of the *Discourse*, the purpose which gives it its character, is presented early in the First Part, immediately after the initial discussion of the equality of *le bon sens* in all men. This equality is said to be natural; it is based on the view that the "form" must be completely present in each member of the species. If reason is equal in all men by nature, then it begins to seem presumptuous of some men to write books in which they express their thoughts. Such men set themselves apart, think themselves superior, and want to be looked upon as superior by others. So Descartes begins his justification for writing this work by telling us that he is different from others not on account of nature but on account of fortune.

His method, he tell us, is not the result of any natural superiority of his intellect but is due to what can only be understood as a series of accidents. Indeed, his mind is mediocre; but the method gives him the means of increasing his knowledge, little by little, to the highest degree permitted by the mediocrity of his mind and the brief duration of his life (AT 3; HR 82). Descartes is careful to say that he is not presenting this method as the way that each man should follow in conducting his reason. He is not a busybody, telling everyone what to do and how to think. But then, why present the method at all?

Descartes believes that the search for truth by means of the method is a solidly good and important "occupation," indeed the best and most important of the occupations "of men purely as men" (AT 3; HR 82). But he may be deceiving himself (although the method itself should guarantee against this): our judgments concerning ourselves and our friends' favorable judgments must be regarded with suspicion. So, in this discourse, he will make us see "the ways" he has followed. He is presenting not simply "the method" of the Second Part but his whole life for judgment: "In this Discourse I shall be very happy to show the paths that I have followed, and to set forth my life as in a picture, so that everyone may judge of it for himself; and thus in learning from the common talk what are the opinions which are held of it, a new means of obtaining self-instruction will be reached, which I shall add to those which I have been in the habit of using" (AT 3-4; HR 83). Descartes is setting forth his life for judgment. And the central issue in the making of this judgment is whether or not his "occupation" is good and important.

The *Discourse* is a picture (*tableau*) that represents Descartes's life.[1] But it is also a history (*histoire*) or a fable. After assuring us that he is not proposing that each man follow his method, he tells us how the whole work should be taken: "But in proposing this work only as a story (*histoire*), or, if you prefer, as a fable, in which, among some examples that one can imitate one will find perhaps also many others that one will be right not to follow, I hope that it will be useful to some, without being harmful to anyone, and that all will be grateful to me for my frankness" (AT 4; HR 83).

This last clause ("and that all will be grateful to me for my frankness") can be seen in all its irony if we take seriously Descartes's characterization of the *Discourse* as a picture, a story, and a fable. Indeed, the opening discussion of the equality of *le bon sens* in all men is ironic in a way that could hardly be called subtle.[2] Whether the *Discourse* as a whole is ironic is another question. But once we have caught a glimpse of irony, of dissimulation, we should not be shocked to find other instances or even to find that the whole work is written in this spirit.

Descartes, of course, does not tell us if or when he is being ironic. But he does explicitly tell us that the *Discourse* is a picture, a story, a fable, and that what is represented in this way is his life. The *Discourse*, then, must be understood in terms of what Descartes says, within the work itself, about pictures, stories, and fables.[3]

The First Part is devoted primarily to a discussion of his education and his dissatisfaction with it. His remarks on stories and fables are made within the context of what he says about the books of the ancients: "The charm of fables awakens the mind, the histories of memorable actions exalt it, and, read with discretion, they help to form the judgment" (AT 5; HR 84). Reading the ancient books and their histories and fables is like having a conversation with their authors. But conversing with those of other centuries is like traveling; it has the same advantages and dangers. On the one hand, it is good to know the customs (*moeurs*) of other peoples in order to better judge our own and so that we do not think that everything contrary to our own ways is ridiculous and contrary to reason. On the other hand, too much traveling can make one a stranger in one's own country, and being too curious about the past can keep one ignorant of what is practiced now. These comments apply to the ancient books in general. But Descartes is more specific about fables and histories: "Besides, fables make us imagine many events as possible which are not; and even the most faithful histories, if they do not change or augment the worth of things in order to make them more worthy of being read, at least almost always omit the most base and less illustrious circumstances. Hence it happens that the rest does not appear as it is. And those who rule their morals (*moeurs*) by the examples that they take from them are subject to fall into the extravagances of the knights errant of our novels and to form projects beyond their strength" (AT 6-7; HR 84-5).

When Descartes characterizes the *Discourse* as a history or fable, he does not excuse it from these limitations. It seems undeniable that we are meant to read the *Discourse* with these cautions in mind, to take it in this spirit, and to be "awakened" and "exalted" by it. For all his criticisms, he himself is a writer of both.

It is not until the Fifth Part that we are given Descartes's description of what the painter does. Descartes is about to present a kind of summary of a treatise that he has decided not to publish. In this treatise he had intended to include all that he thought he knew, before writing it, about "the nature of material things." He goes on to describe the manner in which he treated this subject. He imitated "the painters, who, not being able to represent equally well in a flat picture (*tableau*) all the different faces of a solid body, choose one of the principal ones that they put alone toward the light, and shading the others, make them appear only insofar as one can see them while looking at [the one side they have chosen]. . . ." What this means in terms of his writing is that, because he is afraid to put in his discourse all that he had thought about the subject of material things, he exposes quite fully only what he thinks about light and treats everything else indirectly in terms of light. And in order to protect himself further from dispute, he does not talk about this world but about an imaginary new world. Thus, he "shades" everything and can say more freely what he thinks (AT 4l-42; HR 107).

Histories and paintings both leave things out or do not make some things explicit. In a history, the things left out may be only the most base and least illustrious, but the effect is that what is shown cannot appear as it is. The noble and illustrious things are somehow distorted in this kind of report. Paintings may shade both trivial and important things. But shading is not the same as hiding completely. The painter chooses one face of the solid—and not necessarily the best or most important face— and puts only that face in the light and leaves the rest unspecified. He chooses one time of day with its own peculiar slant of light and shows the whole from that angle. This means, of course, that we are not at all free to fill in whatever we please in the shadowed places. We do have at least one face of the solid to go by and even the parts in shadow are not entirely hidden: there is at least the suggestion of what is there. The distortion in painting is due in part to its representing solids on a flat surface. But this distortion is overcome at least to some extent by the techniques of the painter, particularly in shading.

The danger of both history and painting is that we are tempted to take the part for the whole. But the part is only an "appearance" of the whole or a "face" of the whole. If we forget this, we are deceived: we take the appearance for the thing simply and are thus deceived by a false appearance. One of the chief tasks of the reader of the Discourse, then, is to fill in what is missing so as to reconstitute the whole. But what is to be filled in is determined by what is already there, even though what is there in daylight is by itself a distortion.

Fables present different dangers and different tasks. The difficulty with fables is that they "make us imagine many events (événements) as possible which are not possible." It is not immediately clear whether the events in question are human events only or whether they might include natural events. In any case, what he says about histories may also be meant to apply to fables: "Those who rule their morals by the examples that they take from them are subject to fall into the extravagances of the knights errant of our novels and to form projects beyond their strength." The task of the reader, with respect to this aspect of the *Discourse*, is to determine what is possible and what is impossible, either simply or in relation to different degrees of strength.

The term '*événement*' is used in Part Six (AT 65; HR 121) to mean 'result.' There he is speaking of the conduct of experiments. In the *Discourse* as a whole he is speaking not only and not even primarily about the conduct of reason in the sciences but about the conduct of life, of the whole of life.[4] To characterize the *Discourse* as a fable, then, may be to ask of the reader that he distinguish between what can and what cannot be accomplished by means of the "occupation" that Descartes is engaged in. With respect to the sciences, Descartes himself makes this distinction explicit. In the Sixth Part, where he discusses his reasons for writing the *Discourse*, one of the things that he says he wants to make clear is "what I can or cannot do in the sciences" (AT 75; HR 128).

But Descartes's "occupation" is not limited to the search for truth in the sciences. In spite of the title of the *Discourse*, it is clear that Descartes's occupation is the search for truth simply and that this search extends to every aspect of life. That is to say, the *Discourse* is chiefly concerned with human action and with moral action in particular. This is why he presents his life for judgment (AT 3-4; HR 83) and why he describes his purpose as, in part, "to give to the public some account of my actions and designs (*desseins*)" (AT 74; HR 127). The distinction between what is possible and what is not possible must be made not only with respect to what can be accomplished in the sciences but also with respect to moral action and to action as such. And we must expect that, since the *Discourse* is a fable, some events or results are made to appear possible but are really impossible.

Because the *Discourse* is a history, we must take into account its "autobiographical" details, but always remembering that the most base and least illustrious are omitted and that the most noble and illustrious do not appear as they really are. With respect to these autobiographical details, we can identify the pattern in terms of which they are connected as that of motion and rest. Specifically, the story of his life is told, in the broadest terms, as an alternation of traveling and staying put. This is echoed in the dominant metaphors of the *Discourse*: reading the books of the ancients is like traveling, and Descartes's own task is that of architect, building a new home for himself.

The autobiographical details give us Descartes in time and space. And they have the effect of structuring the *Discourse* in terms of a temporal sequence, beginning with his childhood and ending with an account of his plans for the future. This temporal sequence, in turn, gives the appearance of naturalness to Descartes's thought.[5] The impression is that one thing follows naturally from another in this particular order in much the way that childhood follows infancy. But fortune, too, plays a decisive role, or at least is said to be decisive, even in the formation of the method (AT 3; HR 82). The *Discourse* begins from the equality of the species 'man' with respect to *le bon sens*, from Descartes's sameness, and then separates him from the rest on account of fortune.

Telling the story of one's life in terms of nature and fortune seems a perfectly unobjectionable and even unavoidable way to proceed. Nature and fortune are surely the chief causes operating in any life and can be called upon to explain a great deal of what has happened to us and what we have become. But there is also a third cause at work in any human life and Descartes is very much concerned to show this: he wishes to give an account of his "actions and designs." The impression of the *Discourse* as a presentation of Descartes's *thoughts* must be moderated so as to take into account his actions and plans and, on another level, to watch the relationship between thought and action. That is, the reader must not separate the autobiographical aspects from the thoughts presented along with them, even though the autobiographical details are quite sparse and the actions seem less than "illustrious."

We are led, then, to wonder what are the "memorable actions" (AT 5; HR 84), and the most noble and illustrious things (AT 7; HR 85) that are being shown to us in the *Discourse* as history. In what way is the mind "exalted" and the judgment formed? (AT 5; HR 84) Such descriptions lead us to expect heroic deeds like those of the knights in novels. Instead we find that the great struggle of the *Discourse*, the great decision, concerns whether or not he should publish his treatise and reveal the first principles of his physics. But this is indeed a moral struggle and in the account presented in the Sixth Part, we are shown the reason at work, not in the sciences, but in the conduct of life.

If we again consider the *Discourse* as the representation of a human life and not simply as the presentation of a method for the conduct of reason, we begin to notice the *almost* total absence of things that should be there. Here we are in the risky business of filling in what is shaded, and we are not entitled to argue that *anything* missing must be important. Painters choose one side of a solid body and put that one side in the light and "shading the others, make them appear only insofar as one can see them in looking at [the side that is put in the light]" (AT 41-42; HR 107).

The things that are shaded do appear; they are not totally absent. But they appear only in relation to the side that is put in the light. They do not appear as they are "in themselves."

The side of Descartes that is put in the light in the *Discourse* is the side of reason. Were it not for the scant autobiographical details, the *Discourse* would be the representation of reason alone. But such things as the "stove" of the Second Part remind us that Descartes is not really a disembodied mind, that the *Discourse* is about a whole man. The human aspects of the picture other than reason, which is turned toward the light, are not, however, treated "in themselves." They appear only in relation to the reason; but if we do not take them into account, we will see only a distortion, a grotesque picture of a life that could hardly be called human. Indeed, without the shaded parts, the *Discourse* as the representation of a life would give us the picture of a monster.

The most significant aspects of human life that are shaded in the *Discourse* are the passions, the body, and the relationship with other men. These parts of any ordinary life are present in the *Discourse* but are only alluded to in passing and only in relation to the activity of reason. This is true even of the body, for, although the question of material things is taken up explicitly and at length, Descartes's own body is only suggested. The human body is treated in the *Discourse* as an object of thought, as a material thing to be investigated by the sciences, and only indirectly as a part of Descartes's own life.

Similarly, the place of other men in the *Discourse* is not what one would expect in the story of a human life. On the one hand, there is much concern with "all men." This is especially evident at the very beginning, where he speaks about the entire species, which, of course, includes all men at all times. And in the Sixth Part there is frequent explicit reference to the good of mankind in general. But, on the other hand, the *Discourse* shows us a man with no ordinary human ties. Even when Descartes is not traveling, he is detached from the society in which he lives: "I have been able to live [in a city] as solitary and withdrawn as in the most far-off deserts" (AT 31; HR 100). He says nothing of his family, except perhaps to indicate, indirectly, that the financial situation was such that he did not need to practice a trade. His friends are mentioned only twice, both times in connection with their judgments of his work. In the First Part, we are told that "the judgments of our friends must be suspect" (AT 3; HR 83). In the Sixth Part, three kinds of judges are distinguished: his friends, the indifferent, and those whose "malignity and envy would try to discover what affection would hide from [his] friends" (AT 68; HR 124). This is the only hint of any ties of affection in the *Discourse*.

Equally surprising in what is supposed to be the story of a human life is the absence of passion. The "interior passions" in general are mentioned in connection with the discussion of the relationship between soul and body (AT 55; HR 115); the feelings and appetites are said to imply that soul and body are joined and united in a way not sufficiently expressed in the metaphor of the pilot in his ship (AT 59; HR 118). Otherwise, the passions as such are not discussed. And Descartes himself is painted as a man without passion, except for the slightest hints of their presence. One such hint is the very mention of their absence at the beginning of the Second Part: ". . . neither cares nor passions . . . troubled me" (AT 11; HR 87).

If these shaded aspects are brought into the light, and if we fill in the least illustrious but ordinary human things, the *Discourse* begins to appear as less a plane surface and as more textured, as less concerned with the mathematical and more concerned with the moral, as less a guide for speculation simply than for reason as the source of action, as less the presentation of a method and more the representation of a human life. Finally, and ironically, if the *Discourse* must be read as a fable, in which impossible things are made to appear possible, Descartes begins to look like a conjurer. The champion of clarity, distinctness, and certitude, by characterizing the *Discourse* as a fable, throws everything into doubt, creates a condition of mistrust, and makes the reader wary of illusion. Descartes's hope that "all will be grateful for my frankness" (AT 4; HR 83) is perfectly ironic.

Laughter, Tears, Trembling, and Wonder

In keeping with the almost total absence of passion, of body, and of other men, the *Discourse* shows us no laughter, no tears, and no trembling. Again, these are striking absences in what is supposed to be the story of a *human* life. What we do find are the barest hints to suggest even Descartes's awareness of these manifestations of the human. He never presents himself as laughing, weeping, or trembling.

At the end of the Third Part, he tells us that after his stay in the stove-heated room, he returned to his travels: "And in all the nine years following, I did nothing else but roam here and there in the world, trying to be a spectator rather than an actor in all the comedies which are played there" (AT 28; HR 98-99). This is the only mention of comedy and one of the few suggestions of the possibility of laughter in the *Discourse*.[6] The suggestion is of Descartes's own laughter as he tries to be the spectator of the comedies and not the object of laughter himself. The reason for Descartes's traveling is that he might now undertake to doubt all of his opinions (except the maxims of Part Three and the truths of faith). He hopes to carry out this doubting not by remaining alone in the room where he had constructed the method but by "conversing with men" (AT 28; HR 98). Descartes does not specify in what the comedies consist but we can gather from the context that they have to do with doubt and error. By wandering around trying to be a spectator of comedies, he succeeds in uprooting from his mind "all the errors which had been able to slip in previously" (AT 28-29); HR 99). In each matter, he reflects on what might make it suspect and what might give us occasion to be mistaken.

The only other suggestions of comedy have to do with the ridiculous. Here, too, the context is that of traveling: "It is good to know something of the morals (*moeurs*) of different peoples in order to judge more soundly our own and so that we do not think that everything contrary to our ways is ridiculous and contrary to reason, as those who have seen nothing usually do" (AT 6; HR 84). And in the Second Part, he speaks of the variety of opinions and sentiments that one encounters in traveling and of the changes of opinion that occur even within one people: "And even down to the fashions of our dress, the same thing which pleased us ten years ago and which will please us perhaps again in ten years, now seems to us extravagant and ridiculous" (AT 16; HR 91).

These appearances of the ridiculous show that we are usually more persuaded by custom and example than by any certain knowledge (AT 10; HR 87). Things seem ridiculous in relation to our own customs and these customs themselves change over time: we can even appear ridiculous to ourselves. But from the standpoint of "certain knowledge" it is variable custom itself that can appear laughable, especially when it takes itself seriously. Descartes in his travels is the spectator of custom and from this standpoint all customs are equal. None is ridiculous in relation to any other, and all are laughable in relation to certain knowledge.

But Descartes's travels as the spectator of comedies are undertaken after he forms his provisional morality. And the first maxim of this code establishes him as the most conventional of men: "The first was to obey the laws and customs of my country, keeping faithfully the religion in which God has given me the grace of being instructed from my childhood, and ruling myself in all else, according to the most moderate opinions, and the furthest from excess, which would be commonly admitted in practice by the most sensible of those with whom I would be living" (AT 22-23; HR 95). This conformity to local and current custom keeps him from being an object of ridicule, while his stance as seeker of certain knowledge makes him the spectator of comedies. Descartes is the unnoticed and detached observer of other men. He is like a spy among men.

Descartes's detachment allows confusion, error, and uncertainty to appear in a comic light. There is no comparable mention of tragedy in the *Discourse*, and nothing is even described as pitiable. What comes closest is the mention of "sadness" as one among the "imperfections" not found in God and from which Descartes would willingly be free (AT 35; HR 103). And "sadness" is a very pale, weak, and distant relative of the profound and noble movements of the soul associated with tragedy. There is no mention of any tragic error in the *Discourse* as a whole or in connection with Descartes's own life. There are not even any mistakes or regrets of a more ordinary kind.

Of course Descartes does not specify a kind or degree of "sadness," and sadness can range from the trivial melancholy mood of a day to unbearable grief over the death of one most loved. Descartes chooses the weakest and least precise expression: the least emotion is expressed but the greatest latitude is permitted. Grief is not excluded. But there is no death in the *Discourse*, no mourning and no tears of grief. This is consistent with the almost total absence of any ties of affection.

Yet, the fear of death is suggested in the *Discourse*. It is there in the shadows, one of the sides of the human that is not shown in itself but only in relation to reason. There is surely no trembling in the face of death; indeed there is the apparent affirmation of the immortality of the soul. But less obviously and no less significantly, Descartes reveals a kind of "preoccupation" with death. Because it is expressed always in relation to his "occupation" of seeking the truth, the possibility of fear is never explicitly stated. In the First Part, where he sets forth his belief that his occupation is good and important, he tells us that the method he has formed is one "by which it seems to me that I have the means of augmenting my knowledge by degrees and of elevating it little by little to the highest point to which the mediocrity of my mind and *the short duration of my life* will permit it to attain" (AT 3; HR 82). [Emphasis added.] His death is considered only as a limitation on the increase of his knowledge.

This same way of talking about death occurs several times in the Sixth Part. Here Descartes presents his reasons for and against publishing his treatise on the foundations of his physics. One reason for publishing the treatise is that he can thereby communicate to the public what he has discovered and convince *"les bons esprits"* to contribute to the experiments that he still needs. The lack of experiments and the "brevity of life" are the two things that prevent the attainment of his goals in the sciences (AT 63; HR 120). At the very end of the *Discourse*, he tells us that "I have resolved to use the time which remains for me to live in nothing else than trying to acquire some knowledge of nature, such that one can draw from it rules for medicine" (AT 78; HR 127).

In at least four places in the Sixth Part we even sense a note of urgency. Publishing his writings during his lifetime would cause opposition and controversy, and he does not want "to lose time" (AT 66; HR 122). He believes that he is obliged to manage the time that remains to him, to use it well, but, if he publishes the foundations of his physics, he will lose time (AT 68; HR 123). But then he is obliged to write because he sees "every day, more and more, the delay that the plan [to instruct himself] suffers" (AT 74-75; HR 128).

In each case, death is spoken of only in relation to his occupation and in terms of the limitation of his accomplishments, the frustration of his designs. At the very end of the Fifth Part, he claims that weak minds are separated from the path of virtue when they imagine that the human soul is of the same nature as that of the beasts "and that, consequently, we have nothing to fear or to hope for after this life" (AT 59; HR 118). He never mentions any poignant fears or hopes for the life after death; there is only the casual statement: "I revered our Theology, and I intended, as much as anyone else, to win my place in heaven" (AT 8; HR 85). The claim is made that the human soul is entirely independent of the body and is therefore not subject to die with the body. But the conviction that the soul is immortal is never reflected in Descartes's account of his own life. It has no bearing on his conduct. On the contrary, death preoccupies him, and its relentless approach affects his decisions.

In characterizing Descartes's concern with the certitude of death as "preoccupation," I do not mean to suggest that he is pathologically obsessed by the fear of death. I do mean to claim that he understands the activity of philosophy in its relation to mortality. Now, it might be argued that a few references to the brevity of life do not justify the assertion that Descartes ascribes such importance to the inevitability of death. But I will try to show that Descartes is a kind of Stoic, a compassionate Stoic, and, if I am correct in this, then the claim that he is preoccupied with death would perhaps not seem too strong.

The preoccupation with death and the sense of urgency about its approach are the closest we come to any manifestation of human concerns in the *Discourse*. The awareness of the inevitability of death is a sign of a soul "in" a body, not a disembodied mind. Yet, in spite of the preoccupation with death, there is only the slightest suggestion of the recognition of fortune with respect to death. Descartes is aware that death is inevitable and always nearer, but he speaks as if he will live to old age and die a natural death. In speaking of his plans to overcome two or three crucial difficulties in his search for truth, he says: "My age is not so advanced that, according to the ordinary course of nature, I may not still have enough leisure to accomplish this result" (AT 67; HR 123). His expectation is that the duration of his life will follow the ordinary course of nature, but in saying this he is recognizing that it might not, that fortune might end everything at any moment.

This hint of the recognition of the possibility of sudden death is far removed from any trembling in the face of imminent death. And just as there is no trembling in the face of death in the *Discourse*, so too there is no trembling in the presence of God. The God who is found in Part Four is not loved or feared. And he is not addressed in prayer: Descartes speaks about him and not to him. The recognition that "all that is in us comes from [God]" (AT 38; HR 105), the acknowledgment that we are from nothing, produces no trembling of love and awe. The perfections of God do not give rise to any prayer of praise.

Descartes's wonder (or a somewhat paler version of wonder) with respect to God is expressed only once and rather indirectly. The context is the discussion of "animal spirits" and "interior passions" which move the body. He says that we should consider the body "as a machine, which having been made by the hands of God, is incomparably better ordered and has in itself movements more wonderful (*admirables*) than any of those which can be invented by men" (AT 56; HR 116). But the impression that God's work is being given unqualified admiration is marred by Descartes's pointing to the relative simplicity of man-made machines. Moving machines that man makes use only few pieces "in comparison with the great multitude of bones, muscles, nerves, arteries, veins, and all the other parts that are in the body of each animal" (AT 56; HR 116). It is difficult to escape the suspicion that there is here an implied criticism of God as craftsman: he needs something extremely complicated to accomplish what he wants to do.

Descartes's somewhat weak version of wonder is reserved for the body and in fact for all animal bodies. The rational soul, peculiar to man, is said to be created by God, but Descartes expresses no admiration for this soul and its creation (AT 59; HR 118). At least, he does not express any wonder at the creation of the rational soul. On the other hand, "it is something quite remarkable that there are no men so obtuse and stupid, not even excepting the mad (*insensés*), who are incapable of arranging together different words and composing a discourse therefrom by which they make their thoughts understood" (AT 57; HR 117). This remarkable capability is one of two things that distinguish man from the beasts. But the discussion of these distinctions occurs quite deliberately before the description of the rational soul (AT 59; HR 117). And the communication of thought by means of speech gives him occasion not to be astonished: "And I am not at all astonished at the extravagances attributed to the ancient philosophers whose writings we do not have." This absence of astonishment is due to the experience that Descartes himself has when he attempts to make his thoughts understood: "I have often explained some of my opinions to people of very good intellect and who, while I was speaking to them, seemed to understand them very distinctly; nevertheless, when they repeated them, I noticed that they changed them almost always in such a way that I was no longer able to admit them as my own" (AT 69; HR 124). What is understood by the hearer is often different from what the speaker thinks. But the only way to know this is to have the hearer repeat what he thinks the speaker meant. There is no getting outside of speech for the expression of thought. Yet speech is not identical with the thought it expresses. Descartes is not astonished at the failure of speech to communicate exactly and infallibly. That is, he is at least no longer astonished: he may have been at first, but repeated experience has dulled any surprise he might have felt.

What Descartes says did astonish him was the failure of the learned to build anything more exalted on the foundations of mathematics: "I was pleased above all by mathematics because of the certitude and the evidence of their reasons; but I did not yet notice their true use, and thinking that they served only for the mechanical arts, I was astonished that, their foundations being so firm and so solid, nothing more exalted had been built on them" (AT 7; HR 85).[7]

This situation is contrasted with the condition of the ancient moral writings in which superb and magnificent palaces are built on sand. And Christian theology is presented both as having no indispensable moral relevance and as resting on a more-than-human foundation (AT 8; HR 85). Given the dominance of the architectural metaphor for Descartes's project in the *Discourse*, it does not seem outrageous to suspect that his most important task is not the building of the sciences on the foundation of mathematics but rather the mathematical grounding of the "conduct of life."[8]

What pleases Descartes in the mathematical sciences is the certitude and evidence of their reasons. Here we are in the realm of demonstration and necessity. But the objects of mathematics may or may not exist in the world: "I noticed also that there was nothing at all in them which assured me of the existence of their object . . . ; but for all that I saw nothing which assured me that there was any triangle in the world" (AT 36; HR 103-4). When he does turn to "the world" in the Fifth Part, he finds a different pleasure and another cause for wonder. Of the formation of glass from ashes by the violent action of fire he writes: "For this transformation of ashes to glass, seeming to me to be as wonderful (*admirable*) as any other which happens in nature, I took particular pleasure in describing it" (AT 44-45; HR 109).

The pleasure of describing the transformation of ashes to glass is the pleasure of giving a report, an eye-witness report, of an amazing event. What is wonderful in this case, and what is pleasant to describe, is not certitude and firmness but change, and a change which is remarkable for its completeness. But there is also something remarkable about Descartes's locating this transformation in nature: the transformation of ashes to glass seems to him to be "as wonderful as any *other* which happens in nature."

The context of this reference to the formation of glass is the discussion of fire and especially of fire as a source of light. Descartes is summarizing the treatise which he decided not to publish and he is, like the painters, showing everything from one aspect, that of light itself. But the world about which he is speaking, even though imaginary, is imagined to have been created by God. And immediately after his reference to the transformation of ashes into glass, he reminds us of creation and of God's conserving action: "But it is certain, and this is an opinion commonly received among theologians, that the action by which [God] now conserves [the world] is exactly the same as that by which he created it" (AT 45; HR 109).

In speaking of the transformation of ashes into glass as something that happens in nature, Descartes is blurring the distinction between nature and art and the distinction between God and the craftsman. Although it is impossible to speak about the creation of nature without using the metaphor of the crafts, the essential task of the theologian is to distinguish God from the craftsman. But the point I wish to emphasize here is that Descartes's blurring of these distinctions has the effect of making the reader puzzled about the true cause of wonder. Is Descartes's wonder evoked by the works of God or by the works of man?

The *Meteorology*, which is attached to the *Discourse on Method*, begins with the observation that "we naturally have more wonder (*admiration*) for the things which are above us than for those which are at the same level or below us" (AT 232). Specifically, he mentions the clouds, which are, quite literally, above us. But then he goes on to say that the poets and painters make the throne of God out of clouds and represent God as causing winds, rain, and lightning. God is "above" us, but not literally, spatially. Descartes hopes that, if he can explain what is above us, what is most wonderful, then what is below us will no longer seem wonderful: "Which makes me hope that if I explain here the nature [of clouds], in such a way that there is no longer any reason to wonder at anything that is seen in them or that falls from them, it will be easily believed that it is possible to find the causes of everything that is most wonderful upon the earth" (AT 232).

Wonder is natural. And it is natural to wonder at natural things, especially at what is above us. Descartes's task in the *Meteorology* is the elimination of this natural wonder at natural things through the explanation of their nature. The explanation of their nature means finding their causes. Knowledge eliminates wonder, and knowledge is the finding of causes.

The goal of the elimination of wonder at natural things is also made explicit in the discussion of the rainbow. Descartes indicates that his method will be made manifest in the discovery of the rainbow's causes: "The rainbow is a wonder of nature so remarkable, and its cause has been in all ages sought out so carefully by fine thinkers, yet so little known, that I could not choose a subject more appropriate to show how, by the method I use, one can arrive at knowledge that those whose writings we have on the subject did not have" (AT 325). And Descartes concludes the discussion of the rainbow by explaining away "the appearance of signs in the sky which cause great wonder in those who do not know the reasons for them" (AT 343).

There is an essential connection between Descartes's concern with the elimination of wonder and his deliberate failure to distinguish God's activity in creating from the activity of the craftsman. This connection will be established within the context of my discussion of what the *Discourse* reveals about Descartes's notion of truth. There it will be seen that the search for true causes is at best subordinated to the task of the production of effects.

As we saw in the *Discourse on Method*, the elimination of wonder is not complete and there is even some indication of wonder at natural things. But these cases are ambiguous: the complexity of animal bodies and their movements and the transformation of ashes into glass. In the first case, the animal body is to be considered "as a machine" (AT 56; HR 116) made by the hands of God. And the transformation of ashes into glass by means of the action of fire is a work of art. Like all such works, it is dependent on nature for its material, but to call it a natural transformation is to collapse the distinction between nature and art. The collapse of this distinction is the effect of both of these cases of wonder.

Has Descartes turned from wonder at corporeal nature to wonder at the human soul? The *Discourse* moves from "the sciences," including poetry, rhetoric, and morals, in the First Part, to physics in the Fifth Part, to total dedication to medicine in the Sixth Part. The ability to communicate thought by means of speech is said to be remarkable (AT 57; HR 116) and so also is human action according to reason (AT 58; HR 117). But the mind depends so much on the disposition of the organs of the body that "if it is possible to find some means which would commonly make men more wise and more able than they have been until now, I believe that it is in medicine that one must seek it" (AT 62; HR 120). The *Discourse* seems to focus more and more narrowly on the body.

But what really astonishes Descartes is the failure to build on the firm foundations of mathematics. And, as we saw, the context for the discussion of mathematics as a firm foundation suggests that what is to be built on it is a palace of virtue to replace the one built by the "ancient pagans." The ancient pagans "raise the virtues very high and make them appear worthy of being valued *above all the things that are in the world*; but they do not sufficiently teach us to know them and often what they call by such a beautiful name is only insensitivity, or pride, or despair, or parricide" (AT 7-8; HR 85). [Emphasis added.]

It is also clear from the discussion of theology that, according to Descartes, Christian moral teaching has not succeeded where the ancient pagans failed. Nowhere in the *Discourse* does he look to Christianity for guidance in the "conduct of life." Even the provisional moral code of Part Three, which mentions the truths of faith in the first maxim, looks to the Stoics for its foundations. Theology does not teach anyone how to go to heaven, nor does it claim to: it is very certain that "the way is not less open to the most ignorant than to the most learned." And the examination of revealed truths, if it is to succeed, would require some extraordinary assistance from heaven. To examine revealed truths successfully, one would have to be "more than a man" (AT 8; HR 85). Descartes's occupation belongs to "men purely as men" (*hommes purement hommes*) (AT 3; HR 82).[9]

Actor or Spectator

Descartes characterizes his "occupation" as "the search for truth" and as the "augmenting of knowledge" (AT 3; HR 82). Expressed in these terms, his occupation seems to be speculation, a life devoted to the theoretical, a contemplative life. But we see at once that the truths or the knowledge that Descartes seeks are ultimately useful. This is especially clear in Parts One and Six. The criticism of the sciences in the First Part is chiefly a criticism of their lack of practical value, of their lack of relevance to the conduct of life. And as the focus of the *Discourse* narrows from the search for the truth simply to the truths of physics and finally to medicine, the practical end of Descartes's occupation comes more and more clearly into view. At the beginning of Part Six he makes this quite explicit. When he acquires some general notions bearing on physics, he realizes that these notions are such that "it is possible to arrive at some knowledge that is very useful for life and that instead of that speculative philosophy that is taught in the schools, one can find a practical one" (AT 61-62; HR 119). This practical philosophy will make us "masters and possessors of nature."

In addition to the theme of the practical value of the sciences, we find in the *Discourse* an overriding concern with the conduct of life as such, with the practical in its widest sense, in spite of the impression created by its title and in spite of its apparent emphasis on physics. In discussing his resolution to seek the truth in "the great book of the world," Descartes writes: "And I always had an extreme desire to learn to distinguish the true from the false, in order to see clearly in my actions and to walk with assurance in this life" (AT 10; HR 87). "The great book of the world" is not the world as it is the object of physics, not corporeal nature, but rather "the morals (*moeurs*) of other men" (AT 10; HR 87). In comparing this task to the building of a new home, he indicates that the doubting of all his opinions is for the sake of the conduct of his own life: "And I firmly believed that, by this means, I would succeed in conducting my life much better than if I built only on old foundations" (AT 14; HR 89). With respect to morals and customs, he finds such diversity of opinion that he is constrained to undertake the conduct of himself by himself (AT 16; HR 91).

Descartes's speculation is a preparation for action. His resolution to seek the truth in the great book of the world is carried out by traveling and seeing the customs, manners, or morals (*moeurs*) of other men. He tries "to be a spectator rather than an actor in all the comedies that are

played there" (AT 28: HR 99). In traveling from place to place simply in
order to see, Descartes preserves the stance of the disinterested spectator.
What is happening in these comedies does not really affect him. He is
simply an observer. And in this way he uproots from his mind all the
errors which had slipped in until then. The search for truth about morals
is carried out by means of disinterested observation.

But we must qualify the meaning of "disinterested." Descartes's task
is to build something for himself and to build on a solid foundation: he is
looking for certitude in the conduct of his life. In this sense, he is wholly
interested.[10] After saying that he tried to be a spectator of, rather than an
actor in, the comedies which are played out among men, he adds: "Not
that I imitated . . . the skeptics, who doubt only in order to doubt, and
pretend to be always irresolute: for, on the contrary, my whole design
tended only to assure myself and to reject shifting earth and sand in order
to find rock or clay" (AT 29; HR 99).

In presenting his own life for the judgment of others, a similar
distinction is made: our judgments about ourselves and the judgments of
our friends about us must be viewed with suspicion. We are not disinterested spectators of ourselves and so we may be deceiving ourselves. Descartes believes that his occupation is good and important but "it is nevertheless possible that I am mistaken and it is perhaps only a little copper
and glass that I take for gold and diamonds" (AT 3; HR 82-83). It is
noteworthy that the possibility of self-deception even about the very
worth of his life still exists as he writes the *Discourse*, that is, after the
method has been constructed and practiced. Descartes wishes to add
common opinion to the means that he already has for instructing himself.
He suggests that common opinion about him will be disinterested and
therefore true. But here, too, the meaning of "disinterested" must be
qualified. For in spite of his repeated claims that he wants only to conduct
his own life and not to teach a method for others, it becomes clear that the
Discourse has some relevance for the public.[11] In the Sixth Part, where he
presents his reasons for and against publishing, he refers to the public's
"interest" in his decisions: "And these reasons on one side and the other
are such that, not only do I have here some interest in saying them, but
perhaps also the public has some [interest] in knowing them" (AT 60-61;
HR 119).

There are, then, two sides of the *Discourse*. Descartes observes other
men and we observe Descartes. He represents his life as in a picture. But
this means that in observing Descartes we must follow his lead, the
example he sets for us in the observation of others: "For it seemed to me

that I would be able to uncover much more truth in the reasonings that each man makes concerning the affairs which are important to him, and of which the result must punish him soon after if he judged badly, than in those made by a man of letters in his study, concerning speculations which produce no effect" (AT 9-10; HR 86). This approach to the observation of others is taken before Descartes constructs the method, before he sits alone in the stove-heated room. Descartes's reasonings in Parts Two and Three, then, may well be reasonings of the first kind and not "speculations which produce no effect." In observing Descartes, the reader must be attentive to the reasonings which lead to his actions. Unless this passage is ironic, those reasonings will reveal "much more truth."

The approach to the observation of others described at the end of the First Part is modified in Part Three, in the discussion of the first provisional moral maxim. Descartes determines to obey the laws and customs of his country, to keep the religion in which he was instructed since childhood, and to follow the most moderate opinions in governing himself in all the things not covered by laws, custom, and religion. And although the Persians and Chinese also produce intelligent men, it seems to him that he should rule himself according to those with whom he would have to live. But "in order to know what were truly their opinions, I should rather take notice of what they practiced than of what they said; not only because in the corruption of our morals there are few people who are willing to say all that they believe, but also because many do not know it themselves, for, the action of the thought by which one believes a thing being different from that by which one knows that one believes it, there is often one without the other" (AT 23; HR 95).

Action reveals opinion more accurately than words do. Action reveals what the man truly believes, whereas words can deceive, either deliberately or not. This means that opinion leads to action, has its effect in action, but that it is entirely possible to hold an opinion without knowing that one holds it and even to hold an opinion that one would say is false. Holding an opinion means two things: saying the opinion and acting in terms of the opinion. So it is possible to hold two contradictory opinions, one revealed in speech and the other revealed in action, without being aware of the contradiction.

Descartes, in his nine years of wandering, examines both actions and "propositions" (AT 29; HR 99). He collects "experiments," or "experiences," (*expériences*), and tests himself (AT 9; HR 86), all the while maintaining the stance of the disinterested spectator. And this stance is one of doubt and mistrust. It is in this way that the crucial distinction between action and thought arises as the distinction between certitude and doubt. Descartes expresses his goal, the goal we see him pursuing in the life displayed in the *Discourse*, at the end of Part One: "And I always had an extreme desire to learn to distinguish the true from the false *in order to* see clearly in my actions and to walk with assurance in this life" (AT 10; HR 87). [Emphasis added.] The goal is certitude in action; the ability to distinguish the true from the false is not for its own sake but for the purpose of being able to base his actions on truth.

It is not immediately obvious what kinds of truth can serve as the basis for action. Truths about man's end would seem to be indispensable since action is incomprehensible without an end to which it is directed. This end is ultimately the human good, what is ultimately good for man as man. The *Discourse* moves from "metaphysical" truths in Part Four, to physics in Part Five, and finally to the promise of seeking truths which will be useful for medicine in Part Six. And it is there that health is said to be "the first good and the foundation of all the other goods of this life" (AT 62; HR 120). Of course, this does not mean that health is necessarily the highest good, the greatest good for man; and it even implies that health is not the only good. We also find in Part Six several assertions about virtue. Those who are really virtuous are those who "desire in general the good of men" (AT 65; HR 122). And it is "the law which obliges us to procure as much as is in us the general good of all men" that obliges Descartes to make known the general truths of physics that he has discovered (AT 61; HR 119).

The moral imperatives of Part Six must be seen in contrast with the provisional moral code of Part Three. This code is provisional: his assent to it is tentative. It gives him a place to stay while his own house is being built (AT 22; HR 95), but this means that it is intended only as a temporary guide for his actions. And, indeed, it is for the most part, if not entirely, abandoned in Part Six. This suggests that the truths discovered in Parts Four and Five do serve as the basis for a new non-provisional code, as the firm foundation for a new moral edifice.

The most striking apparent reversal of the provisional moral code concerns the third maxim. This is the maxim which requires him to try to conquer himself rather than fortune and to change his desires rather than the order of the world. These attempts are based on the belief that nothing is entirely in our power except our thoughts. The effect of this belief is that "we would not desire to be healthy when we are sick or to be free when in prison anymore than we now desire to have bodies as little corruptible as diamonds or to have wings to fly like birds" (AT 26; HR

97). The truths recounted in Parts Four and Five make it possible for him, in Part Six, to expect that we can make ourselves "masters and possessors of nature." And in sharp contrast to the third provisional maxim, we can desire the invention of an infinity of devices which would make it possible to enjoy the fruits of the earth without pain. And most importantly, we can hope for the conservation of health, the cure of an infinity of diseases, and even the prevention of the enfeeblement of old age (AT 62; HR 120). The hopes and promises of Part Six are not only a reversal of the Stoic maxim of Part Three but also a repudiation of God's punishments of man after the Fall. Christian moral teaching is not explicitly mentioned but it is clearly Descartes's target.

The second reversal is less obvious but perhaps more fundamental, for it undercuts the purpose of the provisional code as such and violates the second maxim. It is here that we see the distinction between actor and spectator emerge as the distinction between certitude and doubt. Descartes introduces the provisional moral code by speaking about the need for temporary lodgings and then goes on to say: "Thus, so that I would not remain irresolute in my actions while reason obliged me to be irresolute in my judgments, and so that I would not fail to live thereafter as happily as I could, I formed a provisional moral code (*morale par provision*)" (AT 22; HR 95). The need for decisiveness and firmness in action is the reason for the second maxim: "My second maxim was to be the most firm and resolute in my actions that I could be and not to follow less faithfully the most doubtful opinions, once I had determined on them, than if they had been very sure" (AT 24; HR 96).

The need for resoluteness in action is repeated at the beginning of the Fourth Part where the foundations of Descartes's new home are laid. These foundations are "metaphysical" and are arrived at only at the end of the most complete doubt. This doubt is first contrasted with certitude of action: "I had for a long time noticed that, as far as morals are concerned, it is sometimes necessary to follow opinions that one knows to be quite uncertain just as if they were indubitable, as has been said above; but because then I desired to be occupied with only the search for the truth, I thought that it was necessary that I do exactly the contrary, and that I should reject as absolutely false all of that in which I could imagine the least doubt" (AT 31; HR 100-101). The requirements of action are opposite from the requirements of truth: the true is the indubitable. Action can only pretend to have its beginnings in indubitable truths.

The reversal that is presented in the Sixth Part comes to light if we are noticing Descartes's own actions or, more specifically, his decisions.

Part Six shows us a vacillating Descartes, a man who is irresolute and indecisive. He goes back and forth between publishing and not publishing, between writing and conducting experiments, between tranquillity and controversy. The decision to write and publish the *Discourse* itself is carried out. But the resolution to spend the rest of his life in acquiring knowledge useful for medicine, the resolution which seems to be the culmination of his "apology," seems to have been simply dropped.[12] There is a difference between the opinion Descartes *says* he holds about action and the opinion about action that is revealed in his actions themselves. He says that action demands resolution but he is irresolute, at least in Part Six.

The provisional maxim which seems to endure and to resist the changes brought about by the metaphysics and physics of Parts Four and Five is the first maxim: to obey the laws of his country and to keep faithfully the religion in which he was instructed from his childhood. This maxim appears to be preserved in what he says at the very beginning of Part Six. He has just summarized, in Part Five, the treatise containing the principles of his physics. Now he is about to report on the way in which he arrived at the decision not to publish that treatise but to publish the *Discourse* instead. He had been ready to prepare the treatise for printing when he learned that Galileo's opinions had been criticized: "I learned that people, to whom I defer and whose authority has scarcely less power over my actions than my own reason over my thoughts, had disapproved of an opinion of physics, published shortly before by another, of which opinion I would not wish to say that I was, but that I had not noticed in it, before their censure, anything that I could imagine to be prejudicial either to religion or to the State, nor, consequently, which would have prevented me from writing it if reason had persuaded me of it; and that made me fear that there might nevertheless be found some one among mine, in which I might have been mistaken" (AT 60; HR 118).

In this passage, Descartes appears to give the authority over his actions to religion and the state, not to his own reason. The action in this case is the publication of his treatise. To give the authority over his actions to religion and the state appears to contradict the very purpose of the *Discourse*, the purpose of finding out how to conduct his own life on the basis of truth. Certainly by the time we reach the Sixth Part, we expect to find the first provisional maxim reversed.

Descartes's deference to the authority of religion and the state, however, may be less than sincere. He says that the mere expectation of censure "was sufficient to oblige me to change the resolution that I had to publish [these writings]" (AT 60; HR 119). But he has in fact already given a summary of the treatise in Part Five. In order to "shade a little all these things and to be able to say more freely" what he thinks, he speaks about an imaginary world. This allows him to avoid either following or refuting the opinions of the learned and thus to escape all dispute (AT 42; HR 107). And after telling us that his own reason does not have ultimate authority over his actions, he spends the rest of Part Six presenting "the reasons" which alternately made him decide to publish or not publish his treatise. The possibility of prejudice to religion and the state is never mentioned again. Indeed, Descartes seems convinced that his writings are harmful to no one (see for example, AT 78; HR 130).

I am not trying to suggest that Descartes is willing to disobey the laws of his country and to flout the teachings of religion. My point is that obedience and conformity are subordinated to other ends. The two strongest motives for action, for the action of publishing or not publishing, are Descartes's own "repose" and the general good of mankind. The question of the relationship between these two is the way in which the moral aspect of the *Discourse* is given its most definitive shape.

Another way of putting the question of the relationship between the repose of the seeker of truth and the general good of mankind is in the form of the very old question of whether philosophers should rule. In fact, this is another way of approaching the issue of authority over action, that is, should reason rule? Descartes has taken great pains in the *Discourse* to show that he has no intention of ruling anyone but himself. From the beginning of Part One to the end of Part Six, he very explicitly rejects the role of reformer and even of busybody. One of the reasons for the initial claim that *le bon sens* is equal in all men is to insist that he does not claim any intellectual superiority for himself. And immediately after telling us that he will represent his life for judgment he is careful to say that he is not attempting to teach the method that each should follow but only to show how he had conducted his own reason: "Those who meddle by giving precepts must esteem themselves more able than those to whom they give them" (AT 4; HR 83). And at the very end of Part Six, he chooses the life of leisure over the life of honor: ". . . and I will always hold myself more obliged to those by whose favor I will enjoy my leisure without interference than I would to those who would offer me the most honorable employment in the world" (AT 78; HR 130). Descartes's "occupation" requires leisure: it is not the occupation of philosopher-king.

But the beginning of the *Discourse* is clearly ironic. It quickly becomes evident that Descartes does think himself to be superior to his contemporaries and his predecessors, and to be the benefactor of future generations. His rejection of all that he has been taught implies that his own reason is superior to his teachers' and to the writers he studied. He must conduct himself by himself (AT 16; HR 91). The question is whether superior intelligence should rule, is entitled to rule, and whether it is obliged to rule whether it wants to or not. Descartes seems to reject all claims to rule over others. Indeed, this is one of the strongest impressions he seeks to create in the *Discourse*.

There are, however, other kinds of rule. The rule of soul over body is not explicitly discussed in the *Discourse* as a *moral* issue. But the discussions of the union of soul and body, and of the separability of soul and body certainly have moral implications. And finally, there is the rule over nature which is indeed explicitly asserted. Reason will make us "masters and possessors of nature" (AT 62; HR 119). Descartes's "practical philosophy" makes it possible to use fire, water, air, stars, the heavens, and all the other bodies that surround us. This is the rule of philosophy over body as such.

The turn from speculative to practical philosophy is the reorientation of philosophy away from the stance of the disinterested spectator. It is the turn from contemplation of nature to rule of nature. Descartes's apology, then, amounts to the claim that philosophy is, or is to be, preeminently useful for all mankind. The defense of philosophy requires that philosophy itself be changed: it is no longer the same activity.

But we cannot help wondering if Descartes seriously intends that philosophy make us masters and possessors of nature. That is, given the character of the *Discourse* as a fable, we might ask whether the mastery and possession of nature is possible or whether such mastery is really impossible. Indeed, the question is suggested by the fact that the mastery and possession of nature is the reversal of the third provisional maxim, which clearly denies the possibility of power over the things of nature.

The third maxim is "to try always to conquer myself rather than fortune, and to change my desires rather than the order of the world; and generally, to accustom myself to believe that there is nothing entirely in our power except our thoughts; so that after we have done our best, concerning the things which are exterior to us, everything which is lacking for our success is, from our point of view, absolutely impossible" (AT 25; HR 96-97). Following this maxim will make him "content," and contentment here means desiring nothing that one cannot have: "For our will, directing itself naturally to desire only the things that our understanding represents to it in some way as possible, it is certain that, if we consider all the good things which are outside us as equally separated from our power, we will have no more regrets at lacking those which seem (to be) due to our birth, when we are deprived of them through no fault of ours, than we have in not possessing the kingdoms of China or Mexico" (AT 25-26; HR 97).

If we compare this maxim, which has us regard only our thoughts as in our power, with the expectation of our being masters of nature, we must conclude either that the metaphysics and physics of Parts Four and Five have somehow brought about this reversal or that the mastery of nature is really impossible. In either case, we must look to the third maxim itself in order to see what would have to be done to bring about its reversal.

The third maxim is itself a means to a kind of mastery, the conquest of oneself and, at the same time, of fortune. The philosophers who practiced this maxim "were able to free themselves from the domination of fortune and, in spite of suffering and poverty, to rival their gods in happiness" (AT 26; HR 97). They accomplished this by "occupying themselves without ceasing in considering the limits which were prescribed to them by nature." They were thus persuaded that nothing was in their power except their thoughts and so their desires were accordingly moderated. The will carries us "naturally" to desire only the things that the understanding represents to us as in our power.

Descartes's explanation of the third maxim presents it as a way of life in accordance with nature. Meditation on the limits prescribed to man by nature shows the will what is possible and what is not, and the will, by nature, desires only what is presented to it as possible. Reason thus rules the will and its desires, and all of this is according to nature. The reversal of the third maxim, then, would seem to require a change in the understanding of what the limits prescribed to man by nature are. Again, what these new limits would have to be may be suggested by the third maxim itself.

The maxim depends on the claim that nothing is entirely in our power except our thoughts. Descartes says that he must accustom himself to believe this. Then, after claiming that the will "naturally" desires only what is represented to it as possible, that is, as in our power, he admits that the limitation of desire is difficult: "But I confess that there is need for long practice and often repeated meditation, in order to accustom oneself to regard all things from this point of view." The philosophers who rivaled their gods in happiness were able to do this because, "occupying themselves without ceasing in considering the limits which were prescribed to them by nature, they persuaded themselves so perfectly that nothing was in their power except their thoughts, that that alone was sufficient to prevent them from having any affection for other things" (AT 26; HR 97).

The conduct of life according to this maxim is not "natural," at least in the sense of happening without determination and effort. One must *accustom* oneself, practice, meditate without ceasing, and *persuade* oneself. All of this effort suggests rather an overcoming of something so persistent as to be natural to man. If the will naturally desires what the understanding presents to it as possible, then the understanding is what must be brought under control with such difficulty. By nature, the understanding does not recognize the limits prescribed to us by nature. The understanding sees no "reason" why everything should not be in our power. It must be persuaded by ceaseless meditation that nothing except thought is in our power. The will naturally follows upon the understanding's natural tendency and must be brought within its proper bounds by repeated thought. The conquest of oneself and the changing of one's desires turns out to be a kind of conquest of nature. This is not an overcoming of corporeal nature but rather of the mind and will by persuasion.

That the conduct of life according to the third maxim is a kind of conquest of nature is implied in Descartes's claim that the philosophers who did this actually rivaled their gods in happiness. There is, of course, a paradox here: the unceasing reflection on the limits prescribed to man by nature brings about the surpassing of the ordinarily human. These philosophers were richer, more powerful, freer, and happier than any other men however favored by nature and fortune (AT 26-27; HR 97). Indeed, they rivaled their gods.[13]

According to the third maxim, only our thoughts are entirely in our power and we must regard everything outside of us as equally far from our power. The crucial distinction between "outside" and "inside" is here introduced in the *Discourse* for the first time. And the distinction thus first arises, not with respect to speculation but with respect to action or power. That is, *the distinction between outside and inside arises first as the distinction between what is in our power and what is not in our power and not as the distinction between knower and known.*

Everything except our thoughts is "exterior" or "outside of us." This includes health and thus even our own bodies. We must conclude that our thoughts are to be understood as "interior." To have something entirely within our power is to be able to dispose of it as we wish. So the philosophers who lived according to this maxim did in fact dispose of "exterior" things as they wished: their desires had been so changed that they wanted nothing from and had no affection for external things (AT 26; HR 97).

In the Sixth Part, "external" things are to be brought under our power. By "knowing the force and the actions of fire, water, air, stars, the heavens, and all other bodies that surround us" we will be masters and possessors of nature. In particular we will learn how to conserve health, to escape disease and perhaps even the enfeeblement of old age (AT 62; HR 120).[14] The fear of death is to be conquered, then, not by the virtue of courage but by removing the cause of fear. We are to have power over nature, that is, over bodies, by knowing them.

Between the third provisional maxim and its apparent reversal in Part Six, the distinction between outside and inside is made again with respect to thought and body, but not explicitly with respect to what is in our power and what is not. In the Fourth Part, Descartes discusses the origin of the idea of God, and works toward the conclusion that God must exist. The idea of a being more perfect than himself must come from that more perfect being. But "as for the thoughts that I have of many other things outside of me, such as the sky, the earth, light, heat, and a thousand others," these may have come from me since they contain nothing "superior" to me (AT 34; HR 102).

Now what is "outside" of me includes God: Descartes speaks of bodily things as "other things outside of me." The thought of God seems not to be in his power. And "being in my power" now seems to mean "being caused by me," or at least "being dependent on me." Thoughts remain interior: they are "in me" (AT 34; HR 102). And I "depend" on God from whom I have all that I have.

Stoic independence seems to collapse under the weight of the idea of such a God. Yet the *Discourse* does constantly present Descartes in the light of the third maxim. There is, of course, Descartes's insistence that his whole concern in life is with his thoughts and there is the impression that he "controls" his thoughts. At the very beginning of the Second Part, the scene that is set for the construction of the method is very much in keeping with the third maxim: no conversation, no cares, no passions. He is alone with his thoughts and he decides what to think about (AT 11; HR 87).

Most significantly, the *je pense, donc je suis*, which follows so soon in the *Discourse* upon the provisional moral code, shows itself in a somewhat different light when thinking and existence are seen against the background of the third maxim. The thinking and existence of the *je pense, donc je suis* emerge out of a context of power and independence: thinking is what is entirely in my power and, as such, constitutes the "belonging entirely to me" of independent existence. The *je pense, donc je suis* is not created from nothing as it might appear to have been.

Also, the third maxim provides a context for the certitude and assurance of the *je pense, donc je suis*. There is a plausible connection between certitude and what is in one's power, between uncertainty and what cannot be controlled. This is best seen in the claim that the philosophers who persuaded themselves that nothing but their thoughts were in their power "were able to free themselves from the domination of fortune" (AT 26; HR 97). Fortune is precisely the uncertain, the unpredictable, and thus the uncontrollable.

But what can it mean to say that our thoughts are entirely in our power?[15] The very beginning of the metaphysical meditations of the Fourth Part seems rather to deny this. Descartes must doubt, must consider everything doubtful as absolutely false, because of the possibility of deception. To say that our thoughts are entirely in our power cannot mean that we can never be deceived. Or, if it does mean that we can never be deceived, it is itself false. Further, "all the same thoughts that we have while awake can also come to us when we sleep" (AT 32; HR 101). The *je pense, donc je suis* emerges as a thought that is completely in my control, that is immune to the attacks of fortune and the variableness of circumstance.

The assured existence of the thinker gives way in the Fourth Part to total dependence on the creator. Dependence on God is one of the dominant motifs of the second part of Part Four. Dependence is revealed in imperfection: "For, if I had been alone and independent of all others, so that I had had of myself all this little bit that I had of the perfect being, I could have had of myself, for the same reason, all the rest that I knew to be lacking in me, and thus to be myself infinite, eternal, immutable, all-knowing, all-powerful, and in sum to have all the perfections that I was able to notice in God. . . . I saw that doubt, inconstancy, sadness, and similar things could not be there [in God], since I myself would have been quite pleased to be free of them" (AT 34-35; HR 102-103). The existence of God is suggested by Descartes's own relative powerlessness: he cannot be what he would like to be. The imperfect cannot exist by itself but only in relation to something else on which it depends and in whose power it is. To be dependent on God is to be in God's power: "If there were some bodies in the world or even some intelligences or other natures which were not completely perfect, their being must depend on his power, so that they could not subsist without him for a single moment" (AT 35-36; HR 103).

I am not attempting here to present a complete interpretation of Descartes's discussion of either the *je pense, donc je suis* or the existence of God. Rather, I am emphasizing the shaded aspects of the "metaphysical meditations" so as to fill out the background. When seen against the darker shapes of dependence and powerlessness, the "first principle" of Descartes's philosophy (AT 32; HR 101) appears less starkly epistemo-logical, less "pure" of and less neutral to the ordinarily human.

It is precisely this certitude, the certitude of power and control, that Augustine must abandon in order to find the truth. And, for Augustine, the attempt to achieve this kind of certitude is not morally neutral. The *je pense, donc je suis* is the principle of self-sufficiency; for Augustine, only sin and the lie are entirely one's own.

Here again we can see the difficulty with identifying Augustine's certitude of existence with Descartes's first principle. Augustine's asser-tions about the certitude of existence do not constitute any attempt to establish a self-sufficient ground for his thought. (I will not discuss here his refutation of scepticism, although the same claim can be made about Augustine's so-called "*cogito*": it is not the foundation for any *self*-suffi-ciency.) In Book Seven of *The Confessions* we find two such assertions: "I was as certain that I had a will as that I had a life" (chap. 3) and "I would sooner doubt that I did not live than that truth is not" (chap. 10). The first leads him to the conclusion that his sins are his own. The second reveals, not the primacy of his own existence, but of the existence of that truth which made him.

What these two instances also show is Augustine's willingness to assert that he *lives* (*vivere*). His certitude here is not abstracted from the body. The *je pense, donc je suis* rests on Descartes's doubt about the very existence of his body. This doubt, this deliberate exclusion of his own body from the foundation of his certitude, is the exclusion of what he cannot simply control. The most undeniable, unavoidable, certain evi-dence of the inability to simply control one's body is death. Descartes's certitude about his own existence is the first principle from which he initiates the project of the mastery of nature. This mastery of nature is ultimately the conquest of death.

Descartes introduces the physics of Part Five as "the chain of other truths which I have deduced from these first truths" (AT 40; HR 106). Here in Part Five, he will provide a summary of the treatise that he decided not to publish. It is in preparing the reader for this summary that

Descartes actually makes the analogy with the painter who puts only one face of the object in the light and leaves the rest in shadow to be seen, not as it is in itself, but only in relation to what is more fully illuminated. What Descartes puts in the light is light. Then all things are taken up in the way that they are related to light: the sun and the fixed stars as the cause of light, the heavens which transmit it, the planets, comets and earth because they reflect it, all the bodies on the earth because they are colored, or transparent, or luminous, and finally man because he is the spectator of light.

We must expect, then, that the treatment of man in the Fifth Part will focus on man as spectator. Other aspects of the human will be there but less conspicuously. God is presented as actor, specifically as creator (AT 42; HR 107) and as legislator: "I have noticed certain laws that God has established in nature" (AT 41; HR 106). But it is here, in what purports to be a summary of a treatise on physics, that we sense an amibiguity in what is meant by "laws of nature." For someone versed in the Christian tradition, the notion that God has established laws in nature cannot fail to bring to mind the possibility that what is being spoken of is "the natural law" in the moral sense.

This possibility is certainly not ruled out by what Descartes goes on to say: "I have noticed certain laws that God has so established in nature and of which he has imprinted such notions in our souls that after having made sufficient reflection on them, we could not doubt that they are exactly observed in everything that is or that happens (se fait) in the world. Then, in considering the consequences of these laws, it seemed to me that I discovered many truths more useful and more important than all those that I had learned until then, or even hoped to learn" (AT 41; HR 106-107).

I would not want to claim that Descartes is not really talking about physics at all. The truths that he describes as "more useful and more important" than all he had learned or hoped to learn could be truths with direct relevance for medicine. The emphasis on medicine in Part Six makes this a plausible interpretation. But it must be noted that, immediately after his mentioning these most useful and important truths, he compares himself to the painter: "Thus, fearing not being able to put in my discourse all that I thought about it [the nature of material things], I only undertook to expose there quite fully what I conceived about light" (AT 42; HR 107). True, the considerations that prevent him from publishing the treatise could have to do simply with possible controversy over his physics.[16] This is certainly suggested by the reference to Galileo at the beginning of the Sixth Part. But this is my point: the physics and its potential for creating controversy are precisely what he is putting in the light; his physics is the face of his thought which he illuminates so as to "speak more freely" (AT 42; HR 107) about what is in the shade. Again, we are not free to decide what Descartes has put in the shade: we are bound by the clues provided in the text. And there are several indications that the less fully exposed faces of Descartes's thought are those concerned with moral action, specifically with the difficulties of natural law. These difficulties center on the problem of the effectiveness of the natural law as a law that binds human beings in moral matters. If Descartes is playing on the ambiguity of "laws that God has established in nature," the claim that these laws "are exactly observed in everything which is or is done in the world" must be ironic. He is pointing to the fact that men do not observe the moral "natural law" the way planets in their orbits observe the physical laws of nature. The constant emphasis in the *Discourse* on variations in customs also calls this difficulty to mind. And the first provisional moral maxim is one way of expressing the objection to the claim that there is such a natural law: "And even though among the Persians and the Chinese there are perhaps some just as sensible as among ourselves, it seemed to me that it was more useful to rule myself according to those with whom I would live" (AT 23; HR 95).

In the "deduction" which Descartes recounts in Part Five, he is able to move without difficulty from the heavenly bodies to the earth and its inanimate bodies. It is only when he reaches animals and especially man that he must change his procedure. Whereas he had been demonstrating effects from causes, he must now proceed from effects to causes. That is, he must take the effect, man, as the given. Deduction from nature will not work. He begins by supposing no soul, but only the body, in whose heart is heat without light. In this body he finds exactly what happens in the human body without our thinking of it. He is not able "to find any of those [functions] which, being dependent on thought, are the only ones which belong to us insofar as we are men, whereas I found them all afterwards, having supposed that God created a rational soul and that he joined it to the body in a certain manner that I described" (AT 46; HR 110).

Descartes then presents the explication of the movement of the heart in order to show how he treated "this matter." The most obvious antecedent of "this matter" is the working of the fire without light. But there is nothing to preclude the suggestion that the discussion of the movement of the heart is meant as an illustration of the manner in which the rational soul is joined to the body. At first this seems impossible because Descartes has just spoken of the fire in the heart as being present without supposing any soul. But if we recall the wider context of Part Five, we see that man is being treated insofar as he is the spectator of light and of illuminated things. The explication of the movement of the heart is an illustration not only of one of the body's motions but also of man as spectator. That is, the heart and its parts and movements are in the light, but the observer is also present. The movement of the heart and arteries is "the first and most general that one *observes* in animals" (AT 46; HR 110). [Emphasis added.]

The heart and its movements are not distinctive of man as he is different from any animal: Descartes tells the reader that he should have the heart of a large animal with lungs cut open in front of him. The movement of the heart is involuntary. In the words of the third maxim, it is not in our power and it is "exterior." But the observer who is looking at and feeling the heart is showing us the rational soul joined to a body. The joining of rational soul and body in the task of explaining the heart is perhaps best shown in Descartes's comparison of the heart with a clock: "Finally, that those who do not know the force of mathematical demonstrations and are not accustomed to distinguish the true reasons from the likely, should not dare to deny this [explanation] without examining it, I wish to alert them that this movement, that I have just explained, follows as necessarily from the disposition of the organs alone that one is able to see in the heart with the eye, and from the heat that one can feel with the fingers, and from the nature of the blood that one is able to know by experience, as does that of a clock, from the force, from the position and from the shape of its counterweights and wheels" (AT 50; HR 112).

The task of explaining the heart is the task of explaining a natural thing, taking it as a given and not as deduced from higher principles. The heart is here regarded as matter simply: its movements are not attributed to the soul but only to heat. The observer who wants to explain these movements does so by means of the senses and mathematics. This combination of senses and mathematics is a joining of rational soul and body and is unique to man, the spectator of light and of illuminated things.

Part Five also presents us with two other ways in which man is unique. Descartes distinguishes man from both natural and man-made things, that is, from animals and machines. Man is able to use words to declare his thoughts to others (AT 56, 57; HR 116-17) and he is able to act in particular circumstances: reason is a "universal instrument" (AT 57, 58; HR 116). Now, both animals and machines can say words and can do things, indeed can often do things better than we can. What Descartes focuses on is man's ability to respond specifically to what is said to him and to act in terms of particular situations. Man moves from general to particular in a way that animals and machines cannot. "By these two means, one can . . . know the difference between men and beasts" (AT 57; HR 116).

The movement from general to particular is precisely the movement of *moral* reasoning with respect to natural law.[17] Or, in somewhat different terms, it is the area in which prudence operates. And it is here, of course, that the peculiar difficulties of moral action come to light. The general principles of natural law are rather easily agreed upon and come close to being self-evident. But in the descent to particulars, that is, to action, there is less and less clarity. The distance between action, which is most particular, and first principles appears even more troublesome when we consider the claim that natural law as a moral law for man is "a participation of the eternal law in the rational creature."[18] Eternal law refers to God's rule of the universe. It is here that the ambiguity of "laws of nature" is seized upon by Descartes: the laws of corporeal nature are in the light and the moral natural law in shadow.

In remarking on the difference between man and animals with respect to action, Descartes admits that animals sometimes accomplish some things better than we do. But this, he says, does not prove that they have minds. Rather, it shows that they do not, for in some things they show no industry at all. This means that they act by nature according to the disposition of their organs "as one sees that a clock, which is composed only of wheels and springs, is able to count the hours and to measure the time more accurately than we can with all our prudence" (AT 59; HR 117). The clock counts and measures, numbers the discrete instants as they pass, and it does so with greater accuracy than we can bring to such a task. Prudence has also to do with time: it looks to the future in terms of the effect of action. It is not neutral to the passing seconds as the clock is. It does not treat them equally as the clock does. But prudence is also a kind of accuracy and measurement. Right action is done only with the greatest precision. But prudence can, of course, fail. There are always failures to anticipate accurately, factors that one failed to take into account. But even in the best cases, even for the most prudent, there is always fortune and the threat of bad fortune. This above all is beyond our control and outside our power.

Prudence can never foresee with certitude because of the ultimate particularity of action. Only God, then, would be the perfect legislator for human action. Descartes points to the deficiencies of human prudence in the Second Part, where he insists that his task is not the reformation of the state but only the better conduct of his own life. In enumerating the difficulties of any attempt to reform "the public," he cites the role of custom (*l'usage*): "Then, as to the imperfections [of political institutions]—if there are any, and the diversity among them is enough to make it certain that there are—custom has no doubt considerably softened them; and it has even avoided or insensibly corrected a number of them— something that prudence [alone] could not have supplied so well" (AT 14; HR 89).

On the basis of this comparison, we might conclude that Descartes's task in the *Discourse* is to make himself as prudent as possible, indeed so prudent as to conquer fortune in his own life. But this passage, in noting the diversity among peoples and thus inferring imperfection in their laws, points to the deficiency of natural law and of God as legislator. And it puts in an ironic light the earlier claim that "it is certain that the state of the true religion, of which God alone has made its ordinances, must be incomparably better ruled than all the others" (AT 12; HR 88). Christianity provides no set of ordinances for political life. Natural law has produced diversity and imperfection. Again, the difficulty here is in moving from general to particular, from natural law to human law.

This same difficulty of moral reasoning arises in Part Six in two ways. First, there is the display of Descartes's decision. He recounts the reasoning through which he proceeded to the determination not to publish the treatise and to publish the *Discourse*. We see reason at work in its moral dimension. He had resolved to publish his treatise, but when he learns of Galileo's trouble he changes his mind. He does not want to do anything to give even the impression of harm to religion or the state. What comes into play immediately is the possibility of conflict between obligation and inclination: "This was sufficient to oblige me to change the resolution that I had had of publishing them [his opinions on physics]. For, even though the reasons, for which I had taken the resolution before, were very strong, my inclination, which has always made me hate the trade of writing books, made me immediately find enough other reasons to excuse myself from it. And these reasons, on one side and the other, are such that not only I have here some interest in telling them, but perhaps also the public has some interest in knowing them" (AT 60-61; HR 119).

The possible conflict between obligation and inclination is, more precisely, a possible conflict between "the law that obliges us to procure as much as is in us, the general good of all men" (AT 61; HR 119) and the desire for "repose." And this can be put as the tension between "occupa-tion" and leisure. It is here, of course, that the character of the *Discourse* as apology comes closest to the surface. In the Sixth Part, philosophy itself is made to appear as morally good, as beneficent, as the opposite of useless. Indeed, it is made to appear as beneficial for all mankind and not simply for the very few who do it. Descartes seems to eliminate the possible moral conflict between duty and inclination by the claim that he is using his leisure to advance the practice of medicine. In concrete terms he decides, after much debate, not to publish the treatise but to publish the *Discourse*. This is the action that is done as a result of his moral reasoning: this is the move from general to particular.

The same movement appears again in Part Six but in what appears to be a very different immediate context. In discussing the need for experi-ments to accomplish what he wants to accomplish, Descartes provides what seems to be a second, briefer summary of his unpublished treatise. "But the order that I have held to is this: Firstly, I have tried to find in general the principles or first causes of all that is or that can be in the world, without considering anything for this effect, but God alone who created it, nor to derive them from any source except from certain seeds of truths which are naturally in our souls" (AT 63-64; HR 121). From these first principles he deduces sky, stars, the earth, water, air, fire, minerals, and other things. "Then, when I wished to descend to those things which were more particular, such diversity was presented to me that I could not believe that it is possible for the human mind to distin-guish the forms or kinds of bodies which are on the earth from an infinity of others which could be there if it had been the will of God to put them there" (AT 64; HR 121). Again as in the Fifth Part, the deduction stops at living things, and he must now proceed from effects to causes. Thus the purpose of experiments is to fill in the gap between particulars and principles: "But it is necessary also to confess that the power of nature is so ample and so vast, and that these principles are so simple and so general that I noticed almost no particular effect as to which I could not at once recognize that it might be deduced from the principles in many different ways" (AT 64-65; HR 121).

The question that an experiment is supposed to answer is how the particular is a deduction from the general. This may well be a transposi-tion of moral investigation onto the methods of scientific investigation: the moral problem that Descartes so often points to in the *Discourse* is the diversity of custom among peoples. The transposition of moral reasoning onto the investigation of nature may be the foundation for the change from speculative to practical philosophy made explicit at the beginning of the Sixth Part. It would also make the title of the *Discourse* a more adequate description of what he is doing in this work.

This is not to say that Descartes's criticisms of the sciences, especially of philosophy and theology, are not serious. Nor is it to deny the seriousness of his claim that the moral teachings of the ancients are built on sand. There is no "method" of moral reasoning that can be simply applied to physics. The diversity of customs among peoples, the confusion and error that Descartes observes, are evidence of the lack of such a method and of any firm foundation for the virtues. The transposition, then, is one of ends, not means. The sciences, and in particular the natural sciences, are turned toward the attainment of the good of all mankind.

The kind of knowledge that Descartes mentions explicitly as the model for scientific knowledge is the knowledge of the craftsman: ". . . it is possible to arrive at some knowledge which is very useful for life, and instead of that speculative philosophy that is taught in the schools, one can find a practical philosophy by which, knowing the force and actions of fire, water, air, the stars, the heavens, and all the other bodies that surround us, as distinctly as we know the various crafts of our artisans, we could employ them in the same way for all the uses to which they are proper and thus make ourselves masters and possessors of nature" (AT 61-62; HR 119).

The arts are the most universal and the first attempt by man to conquer fortune and to compensate for natural deficiencies. Their ends are unmistakably human. And each art has as its end some particular human good. Descartes turns not only physics but also philosophy, the most universal of the sciences, toward a purely human end. This end is the good of all mankind; it is a moral end to be sought after chiefly, as in the arts, by the care of the body. The reorientation of physics towards the useful requires the reorientation of the science of "all things." Thus, when Descartes finds some general notions pertaining to physics and begins to test them on various particular difficulties, he believes that he cannot keep them hidden "without sinning gravely against the law that obliges us to procure as much as is in us the general good of all mankind" (AT 61; HR 119). His discoveries in physics imply a replacing of speculative by a practical philosophy.

Descartes's reference to grave sin gives the impression of religious obligation and the reference to obligation as "law" can only suggest the natural law. It is not unthinkable that "the laws of nature" (AT 41; HR 106) are, for Descartes, first and foremost moral laws. The law that he specifies is concerned only with obligation to other men, not to God, and we must assume that this law is discovered by purely human means: theology is useless for attaining the good and requires that one be "more than a man" (AT 8: HR 85).

Pride and Humility

We are led, then, to ask what is the place of man in nature and in relation to the divine for Descartes? In particular, we must ask what is the place of the philosopher both in relation to other men and to the divine? This assumes, of course, that Descartes's "occupation" is philosophy as "the search for truth" (AT 3; HR 82).

In the first place, there is no Christian humility in the *Discourse*. The differences between Augustine's revelation of himself in prayer and Descartes's representation of his life to the public make the absence of humility in Descartes quite obvious. At most there is, in the Fourth Part, a tentative recognition of the dependence of all created things on God. But the "law that obliges us to procure as much as is in us the general good of all mankind" shows little or no confidence in a God who alone can bring about the good of all mankind. Indeed, the whole tone of the *Discourse* is one of self-reliance, or, more accurately, of the search for self-sufficiency.

On the other hand, there is a good deal of false modesty, especially evident in the ironic beginning: "As for me, I have never presumed that my mind is in any way more perfect than the ordinary" (AT 2; HR 82). It is only fortune that has led to the method by which he augments and elevates his knowledge as far as "the mediocrity" of his mind permits (AT 3; HR 82). In his judgments of himself, he tries "always to tend toward the side of mistrust rather than towards that of presumption" (AT 3; HR 82). And we cannot help being reminded of Socrates when, at the end of the Third Part, he explains how he acquired his reputation as a philosopher: "I would not know how to say on what they based this opinion; and if I contributed something to it by my discourse, this must have been in confessing more candidly what I did not know than those who have studied a little usually do, and perhaps also in making known the reasons that I had for doubting many things that others regard as certain rather than in showing off any doctrine of mine" (AT 30; HR 100).

It soon becomes evident that Descartes does not regard his mind as mediocre. Philosophy has been engaged in by "the most excellent minds" (AT 8, 30; HR 86, 100) and where these most excellent minds have failed to get beyond probability and hence diversity and dispute, Descartes appears to succeed. Knowledge of ignorance gives way to the certain knowledge of all things. Mistrust of his judgment of himself gives way to what appears to be an awesome presumption. Against the initial modest request for the readers' judgments of his life so that he might instruct himself (AT 4; HR 83), we must place the claim that "I have almost never encountered any critic of my opinions who did not seem to me either less rigorous or less equitable than myself" (AT 69; HR 124). And with respect to the carrying out of the project proposed in the Sixth Part, Descartes confesses that he alone can do it: "And I think I can say, without vanity, that, if there is someone who is capable of it, it must be myself rather than anyone else: not that there may not be in the world many minds incomparably better than mine; but because one can not conceive a thing so well and make it one's own when one learns it from another as when one discovers it oneself" (AT 69; HR 124). The "work" which Descartes has begun can only be finished well by himself (AT 72; HR 126). Descartes is in the company of those who, at the beginning of Part Two, are solitary workmen (AT 11-12; HR 87-88). And this company includes God, not as creator but as ruler. At the very end of Part Six, Descartes implies that he is worthy of being offered "the most honorable employment on the earth," and in contrast to the leisure that he prefers, this most honorable employment would seem to be ruling.

The Stoics' rivalry with their gods appears at first to be replaced, in Part Four, by total dependence on the Christian God who creates all things and by his power holds them out of nothingness. But this in turn is replaced by what is at least the most obvious if not the most important manifestation of presumption in the *Discourse*: man will make himself, on his own, master and possessor of nature. When read against the background of Genesis, Descartes's project can only be described as defiance. Adam is told that he will have his bread only by sweat and toil. The new philosophy will make it possible for man to enjoy the fruits of the earth without any pain. The so-called "effects of original sin"—sickness, death, the darkening of the intellect, and the weakening of the will—are all reversed, the first three by medicine. The last, the weakening of the will, is overcome in the imposition of the will on nature. The will is given back its power through the "universal instrument" of reason.[19]

One example of the lack of an order imposed by reason is the ancient city. These cities have grown little by little and are thus badly proportioned, their buildings badly arranged, their streets curved and uneven: "One would say that it is rather fortune than the will of some men using reason which has disposed them this way" (AT 11-12; HR 88). This example occurs in the discussion of the superiority of works done by a single master. And, as noted above, God is not mentioned here as maker of the universe. This would have been the most obvious example of all.

Most of the examples are political or, in the case of planning cities, directly related to the political. And one of the most important considerations leading to the claim that the works of solitary masters are more perfect is that the solitary workman constructs with a single end in view: "Thus one sees that the buildings that a single architect has begun and finished are usually more beautiful and better ordered than those that several have tried to fit together by making use of old walls which had been built for other ends" (AT 11; HR 87).

It is the same with the legislation of human conduct. People who began as half-savage and have been civilized little by little have made their laws as they were constrained to by crimes and quarrels. They cannot be as civilized as those who from the beginning have observed the constitution of a prudent legislator. God is cited as sole legislator for the state of true religion and then Sparta is given as an example of a flourishing political entity: "And to speak of human things, I believe that if Sparta was formerly flourishing, this was not due to the goodness of each of its laws in particular (since many were very strange and even contrary to good morals), but due to the fact that, having been invented by one single man, they all tended to the same end" (AT 12; HR 88).

In the first place, we can surely quarrel with the notion that well-planned cities are more beautiful than the ancient cities that have grown over time, and that buildings which must make use of old walls are less beautiful than others. They may be less functional, but they are often far more beautiful in themselves. In the second place, Sparta and the nation whose ordinances were given by God alone no longer even exist. And Lycurgus is the *legendary* legislator: Sparta may have flourished, then, for different reasons, although in fact, as Aristotle says, the end of all its laws may have been courage (*Politics* 1271b). In any case, the claim that prudence does better than custom and time is contradicted only a little later in Part Two where Descartes speaks of the difficulty of reforming states. Custom (*l'usage*) moderates imperfection, avoids or corrects many imperfections, which prudence could not have so well provided for (AT 14; HR 89).

In political matters at least there are no absolute beginnings. The would-be reformer always comes in in the middle. And unlike the architect, he never has the opportunity to start from nothing. Descartes, in the construction of the method in Part Two and in the search for a firm foundation in Part Four, seems, with respect to the conduct of his own life, to be attempting to start at the beginning, to overcome the limitation of having come in in the middle on his own life, as we all do. He attempts to achieve a divine perspective on himself and, in the redoing of Genesis in Part Five, on all things. But is he a political reformer in spite of his frequent protestations to the contrary? That is, with respect to the matter of pride as rule over others, does Descartes claim the position of (divine) legislator?

Descartes's travels, his observations of various peoples, are in a sense undertaken from the standpoint of the disinterested spectator. He is "spectator rather than actor" (AT 28; HR 99). He comes in in the middle, but as an observer. He is not affected by what is happening: he remains free, detached from the consequences, and above the confusion. We can and indeed are invited to make the comparison with Socrates, who never traveled anywhere (*Crito* 52b). Immediately after Descartes's description of his travels, he concludes Part Three with an account of how he got the reputation of being a "philosopher." This is the confession of ignorance discussed above. So, Descartes acquires his reputation in the same way that Socrates did, by confessing his ignorance. But whereas Socrates is put on trial and dies on account of envy, Descartes could conceivably be offered the most honorable position on earth.

Descartes's travels and detached observations bring him much closer to the Sophists than to Socrates. As we are told in the *Apology*, the Sophists go from city to city. But unlike Descartes, the Sophists affect the cities into which they go. On the other hand, like Descartes, they have no real stake in any particular city. They remain detached and "free." In short, they do not really care what happens in any particular city or what effects their teachings produce in any particular place.

Descartes's life in Holland retains much of the detachment of his life while traveling. In the midst of a busy people, he can live as solitary and withdrawn as in the most far-off desert (AT 31; HR 100). What he has there are the conditions for a tranquil life. He is not a busybody, and no one meddles in his affairs. The comparison with Socrates is unavoidable: Socrates is a busybody, a gadfly attached to this city, Athens, for its good. Socrates lives anything but a solitary life. He questions everyone he meets, both citizens and strangers, but especially fellow citizens. He cares most of all about the condition of the souls of his own. That the life of philosophy is the life of *human* excellence, belonging to man as such and not to any particular city, does not detach Socrates from the here and now of

Athens. He is certainly not unaffected by what happens there: the true cause of his sitting in prison is that the Athenians thought it best to condemn him, and he, in turn, thought it best to obey. Socrates is not the disinterested spectator of the "comedies" that go on in Athens.

But Descartes's detachment from any particular society does not mean disdain for the human as such. Indeed, he seems to imply the opposite: this detachment from any particular society, even to the point of what seems to be avoidance of friendship, goes along with a concern for all mankind. Man as such or all men equally are to be the recipients of his benefits. He has no preferences and no one is excluded. Nevertheless, there is still something "inhuman" about this stance. As I have already noted, the ordinary human ties of family and friends are conspicuously and almost totally absent from the *Discourse*. Descartes's position with respect to other men is presented not as less than human but as divine.

God may have legislated for a particular people, whose nation no longer exists as a nation ruled by the Mosaic Law. But there is a law for all mankind, and it is given by Descartes in the Sixth Part. This is "the law that obliges us to procure, as much as is in us, the general good of all men" (AT 61; HR 119). It is not clear whether Descartes is presenting this as a law that he discovers in nature, that is, as a principle of "natural law," or whether he himself is its sole legislator.[20] The reference to "grossly sinning" against this law surely is meant to give the impression of divine origin.

The law that obliges us to procure as much as is in us the good of all men cannot be a principle to serve as the foundation for any society, even if it is one of the higher principles of the natural law. Society must be particular, that is, it must exclude some. It cannot be concerned with man as such. Descartes's discussions of societies and peoples suggest that, in his view, political entities have no basis in nature. That is, he seems to speak of them only in terms of custom. In matters of the conduct of life, reason results in diversity. But this does not mean that Descartes is politically neutral, that he regards all forms of society as equal. Diversity means imperfection, at least of some societies.

If Descartes has views about what the best society would be, he also insists that he is not a reformer. Of course, this very insistence makes us wonder about the sincerity of his denials: "My design has never been extended further than to try to reform my own thoughts and to build on a property that is entirely my own" (AT 15; HR 90). But if this is strictly true, there would be no reason for the *Discourse*. The initial claim that he wants to be instructed by public opinion is clearly ironic. Perhaps, then, he writes for a few, for whom the doubting of all opinion is not too bold (AT 15; HR 90).

Descartes's design to build on a property entirely his own removes him from the authority of any society. He rejects the foundations already in place. But precisely if the foundations of society are conventions or customs, it is *always* impossible to begin from nothing. The origin of customs must be hidden.[21] They have no claims to natural foundations, as the very diversity of custom testifies. Descartes's account of his travels has the effect of equalizing all societies. But Descartes knows quite well that philosophy does not come out of Persia or China. It begins with the pagan Greeks and is carried on through the medieval schools, and this is how Descartes has access to it. But as we see in Part One, and again in Part Four, Descartes seems to reject completely all that has preceded him. In leaving his books and his country (AT 11; HR 87) he is attempting to begin from nothing, to begin as a man simply and not as a man from this country and these schools.

As we see at the beginning of the Second Part, the "disembodied mind" still needs a warm room in winter. There is, of course, a dependence on the body that cannot be escaped. But this still leaves us with the angel in the machine. Part Two begins with the warm room but with no conversation and no passions. The question, as always with Descartes, comes out to be: Is this angel in a machine a man? Or is it a distortion of the human, a monster of nature? Or finally, is it the elevation of man to the divine?

There is much in the *Discourse* to suggest Descartes's assumption of the divine stance both toward corporeal nature and toward human things. To begin from nothing seems to be only a divine possibility. And this is how Descartes begins philosophy, that is, metaphysics, in the Fourth Part. There is also, as I have discussed, the apparent defiance and then presumption in the explanation of Descartes's task presented in Part Six: man will make himself master and possessor of nature. Finally, the "separation of soul and body," especially evident in what precedes the *je pense, donc je suis*, goes further than any pagan approach to the surpassing of the human.

But if we are correct in trying to see into the shaded areas of this picture, the human, in its more ordinary manifestations, begins to show itself again. That is, what amounts to the annihilation of the human into the machine and the angelic, is in some sense overcome. For Descartes does not, in fact, make an absolute beginning. And philosophy, the activity of the most divine part, is directed now by Descartes to a purely human end.[22]

Descartes's rejection of his books in Part One can perhaps best be understood in terms of the analogy with building that he uses so often. The old building is demolished even to the foundations, but the new building is then constructed on the same "ground." If the new home were not to be on the same ground, the demolition of the old would not be necessary and would make no sense. The Cartesian refounding of philosophy must be understood as a rejection of theology *and thus cannot be seen for what it is apart from this theological ground.*[23] And, as Descartes himself says, one ordinarily saves the parts of the old house to serve in the new.

The human face of the *Discourse* shows itself not only in its ties to a past but also in its direction to an end. In the Sixth Part, Descartes reveals the law that obliges us as much as is in us to procure the general good of all men. And he characterizes the truly virtuous as those who desire in general the good of men. Such men will sacrifice themselves, their time, their money, and perhaps glory, for the good of all. This is how Descartes presents himself, and this is essential to his apology. The goal of the "practical philosophy" is the elimination of human misery. Descartes's task, then, is founded in compassion.[24] And this compassion extends to all men, to man as man. "For I have already gathered such fruits [from the method], that even though in the judgments I make of myself I try always to tend toward the side of mistrust rather than presumption; and, looking over with the eye of a philosopher the diverse actions and enterprises of all men, there is almost none that does not seem to me vain and useless; I do not fail to receive an extreme satisfaction from the progress that I think I have made already in the search for the truth, and to conceive such hopes for the future, that if, among the occupations of *men purely as men*, there is one which is solidly good and important, I dare to believe that it is the one I have chosen" (AT 3; HR 82). [Emphasis added.]

The magnitude of Descartes's self-assertion can be seen in contrast with what the *Apology* and the *Phaedo* reveal about the power of philosophy and what the *Confessions* asserts about human power. But the very possibility for this self-assertion will be shown to rest on theological ground. The most important occupation that belongs to men purely as men presupposes a notion of the divine "occupation."

Truth and Certitude

Descartes presents his life as one entirely occupied with the search for truth. Indeed, he presents it as the search for and the discovery of certitude. This identification of truth and certitude seems to be an undeniable feature of Descartes's thought as a whole and of the story of his life told in the *Discourse*. But the very fact that the *Discourse*, in which this identification so dominates, is itself a "fable," immediately throws the reader off balance in his expectations of what truth and certitude might mean here. For "fables make us imagine many events as possible which are not possible," and those who rule their morals by the examples they find in fables and histories are subject to "conceiving plans that are beyond their strength" (AT 6-7; HR 85).

We have to wonder, if the *Discourse* itself is a fable, that is, if Descartes chooses to present his life in this way, what meaning of "truth" is suggested by this choice. The immediate effects of the realization that the *Discourse* is a fable are doubt and uncertainty. And precisely because the identification of truth and certitude is presented as a kind of first principle of the conduct of his life, we have to wonder whether the possession of truth as certitude is a "result" that is possible or impossible for man. Fables are not composed of propositions of which truth or falsehood can simply be predicated. If they do express truth, this expression is nonpropositional. The effect of fables is the awakening of the mind by their "charm" (AT 5; HR 84).

The First Part of Descartes's story is an explanation of why he left his books and his country. He had been persuaded that the study of letters would enable him "to acquire a clear and assured knowledge of all that is useful for life," and so, he has "an extreme desire" to learn them. But he is thoroughly disappointed and changes his opinion entirely. Instead of clarity and assurance, he is troubled by doubts and errors. The only benefit he derived from his education was the discovery of his own ignorance (AT 4; HR 83). This, of course, is no insignificant benefit, however little Descartes seems to make of it.

The criticism of his education as a whole is reflected especially in his remarks about the study of philosophy: "Philosophy gives the means for speaking with an appearance of truth about all things and of making oneself admired by the less learned" (AT 6; HR 84). Even though philosophy has been cultivated by the most excellent minds over many centuries, there is nothing that is not disputed and, thus, not doubtful (AT 8; HR 86).

Given the character of Descartes's disappointment with letters, the turn that he makes away from the tradition looks like a turn from letters to numbers, from discourse to mathematics. Mathematics pleased him most because of the certitude and evidence of its reasons. And he is astonished that nothing great had been built on its firm and solid foundations (AT 7; HR 85). The method of the Second Part is presented as a method distilled from the best features of geometry and algebra (AT 20; HR 93).

Descartes's task, after his disappointment with his books, is to reject whatever is merely probable as if it were false (AT 8; HR 86). On the one hand, this practice looks like the extreme of safety and carefulness: only what cannot be doubted is to be accepted as true. But, on the other hand, it can appear as extremely reckless, requiring the rejection of much that *may* be true. Descartes's procedure begins from the very questionable, risky, and bold assumption that only the certain may be accepted as true. Once it is admitted that what is probable may be true, one risks the rejection of what may be the most important truths. Descartes recognizes the boldness of his plan when he says in the Second Part that he is not a reformer and is not presenting the method as something all should follow: "But I fear that this may already be too bold for many" (AT 15; HR 90).

Descartes's own practice as he actually writes the *Discourse* is not quite the same as what we might expect from this description of his procedure. If we look at Part One in terms of what he actually does there, we see that the *Discourse* itself is not geometrical in character. Descartes begins from common opinion, specifically the common opinion that *le bon sens* is equal in all men. And in this matter, the common opinion of the philosophers is the same as common opinion as such: reason is the form of the individuals of the human species and therefore must be equal in all. In other words, Descartes actually begins the *Discourse* from universal agreement in an opinion.

In his own assent to this opinion, Descartes is undeniably ironic. But the point to be made here is that he chooses to begin from universal agreement in an opinion that is false and that in the actual writing of the *Discourse* he takes as his starting-point the whole species "man." The expression *le bon sens* is, I think, deliberately ambiguous, reflecting the lack of precision that characterizes common opinion. Descartes begins, then, from a blurring of the distinctions among "judging well," "distinguishing the true from the false," "*le bon sens*," and "reason." This is a blurring of the distinction between theoretical and practical intelligence, and it reflects the imprecision of common opinion with respect to this distinction also. The precision which is supposed to characterize philosophical opinion is parodied in Descartes's use of the terminology of the schools. But in the very statement of the common opinion of philosophers, Descartes displays the contradiction in the philosophical position. If reason is the specific difference and not an accident merely, then it should be the same in all the individuals of the species. But philosophers are the first to deny this equality: it is denied in the claim that philosophy is the highest activity.

The *Discourse* begins, then, from common opinion, even though this beginning is ironic and the opinion itself is quickly rejected. The *Dioptrics* begins from the senses, especially the sense of sight: "The whole conduct of our life depends on our senses, among which that of sight being the most universal and the most noble, there is no doubt that the inventions which serve to augment its power are among the most useful that can be" (AT 81). The conduct of life is, in a sense, the whole concern of the *Discourse*, and here it is said to depend, not on the mind alone, but on the senses.

Opinion and the senses are precisely what he rejects in the method of Part Two and in the refounding of metaphysics in Part Four. They are the first to go in the doubt which regards the probable as false. Part Two presents us with the disembodied mind, the mind free of the pleasures or pains of the body and free of the speech of other men. The first rule of the method identifies the true with the clear, distinct, and indubitable (AT 18; HR 92). Only what is "presented to the mind" so clearly and so distinctly as to be indubitable can be trusted. What is presented clearly and distinctly to the senses cannot be trusted, for even sight can sometimes be deceived. Again, this looks like the extreme of carefulness, the degree of hesitancy we might expect from a man walking alone in the darkness (AT 16-17; HR 91).

The method is presented as mathematical in character, but this is a mathematics that is subtly freed from the imagination and thus from the body. The geometry of the ancients is "always so tied to the consideration of figures that it cannot exercise the understanding without greatly fatiguing the imagination" (AT 17-18; HR 91). Descartes corrects this fault first by the use of lines "because I found nothing more simple nor that I could more distinctly represent to my imagination and to my senses." Then he moves to symbols for the sake of remembering and combining. This move from lines to symbols occurs at the very beginning of the *Geometry*. What is made to appear as a matter of mere convenience is in fact the elimination of the imagination from mathematical thought.

The disembodied mind appears again in Part Four, of course, as the first principle of the philosophy Descartes is seeking (AT 32; HR 101). *Je pense, donc je suis* is a truth that is so firm and so assured as to be unshakeable. Because he can pretend that he has no body, that there is no world or place where he is, he can conclude that he is "a substance whose whole essence or nature is only to think and which, in order to be, has no need of any place and depends on no material thing" (AT 33; HR 101).

But the *je pense* of the first principle is not at all self-evidently true. It is not undeniable that it is I who do the thinking that gets done "in" me. There is, at least equally undeniably, a sense in which my thoughts happen to me. Descartes calls attention to this over and over in the *Discourse* when he speaks about the thoughts we have when we dream (AT 32; HR 101). The third maxim, which says that only our thoughts are entirely in our power thus requires "long exercise, often repeated meditation" in order to accustom ourselves to it. The philosophers who rivaled their gods in happiness did so by "occupying themselves without ceasing in considering the limits prescribed to them by nature" and thus "they *persuaded* themselves . . . perfectly that nothing was in their power except their thoughts" (AT 26; HR 97). [Emphasis added.]

Then, the manner in which Descartes proceeds from this first principle to the most immediate inference (that he is a substance whose whole essence is only to think) is also questionable. He pretends that he has no body and that he is not in any place, but, when he does this, he cannot pretend that he is not. But if he ceased to think, he would have no reason to believe that he is. Descartes's doubt about the existence of his body is a deliberate self-deception. Because it is deliberate it appears to be under his control, but this does not alter the fact that the move from *je pense, donc je suis* to "I am a substance whose whole essence is only to think" is based on the simply false assumption that he has no body, even though that assumption is known to be false.

I am not attempting to show up flaws in Descartes's logic. My point is that the disembodied mind of the Fourth Part must be taken in the spirit of the *Discourse* as a fable. The link between truth and perfect clarity is divine, not human: "Even this that I have just now taken for a rule, namely, that the things we conceive very clearly and very distinctly are all true, is certain only because God is or exists and that he is a perfect being, and that all that is in us comes from him. . . . But if we did not know that all that is real and true in us comes from a perfect and infinite being, however clear and distinct our ideas might be, we would have no reason which would assure us that they had the perfection of being true" (AT 38–39; HR 105). From the fact that God is perfect and that all that is in us is from him, it follows that "our ideas or notions, being real things which come from God, insofar as they are clear and distinct can only be true"

(AT 38; HR 105). That we often have ideas which are false is due to their participation in nothingness: they are confused and obscure because we are not perfect.

But if there were such a link for us between clarity and truth, we would never be deceived. Deception occurs when we are quite "clear" about something that is false. Descartes is treating the existence of falsehood in the same way that the theologians deal with the existence of evil: If God exists, how can there be evil?; If God exists, how can there be falsehood? But in doing so, Descartes is pointing to the necessary link between clarity and truth as something that belongs only to the divine perspective.

The human is not the disembodied mind but the speaker and actor of Part Five. It is this "true man" with appetites and desires, not the thinking thing of Part Four, who seeks the mastery of nature.[25] In distinguishing man from machines and beasts, Descartes is also distinguishing him from the divine. All men can "arrange diverse words and compose from them a discourse by which they make their thoughts understood" (AT 57; HR 116-17) and all men can, in each circumstance, arrange their actions in such a way as to attempt to bring about a desired end, that is, all men can be prudent for themselves (AT 58; HR 117). Of course, both of these endeavors can fail and often do fail.

We see the failure of speech in Part Six where Descartes tells us that often while he explains his opinions to intelligent people they seem to understand him very distinctly. But when they repeat his opinions, they change them so much that he cannot admit to what they say (AT 69; HR 124). Also in Part Six we see the ultimate threat to prudence, for Descartes's deliberations about whether or not to publish are done in the expectation that he will live a normal length of time. But death destroys all plans and makes prudence impotent.

The clock is a much more accurate measurer of time than we are with our prudence. And numbers are far more precise than words. The propositions of arithmetic, unlike the propositions of discourse, are fully comprehensible. After recounting his successes with the method in geometry and algebra, Descartes explains the reason for his success: "In which [claims] I will not perhaps appear very vain to you if you consider that, there being only one truth of each thing, whoever finds it knows as much as can be known; and that, for example, a child instructed in arithmetic, having made an addition following its rules, can be assured of having found, pertaining to the sum he examined, all that the human mind can know" (AT 21; HR 94).

It is in mathematics that the human mind comes closest to the link between clarity and truth. Numbers and mathematical propositions can be taken as wholly transparent. That is, they are what we might call "fully specified." Unlike the words and the propositions of discourse, they do not hide meanings.[26] Of course, Descartes ignores the possibility of mathematics as a science dealing with numbers *in themselves*. The whole question of the mode of existence of mathematical objects is put in the shadows, especially in the shadow of the existence of God. In the Fourth Part, he takes up the existence of bodies and the existence of mathematical objects both in relation to the existence of God. There is nothing in the demonstrations of the geometers which assures him of the existence of their object: "I clearly saw that, supposing a triangle, it was necessary that its three angles be equal to two right angles; but I saw nothing about this that assured me that there was any triangle in the world" (AT 36; HR 103-04). Descartes seems to be identifying existence with existence "in the world" simply and to be limiting his treatment of mathematical "objects" to their relations only.

Mathematics brings man as close as possible to the divine perspective. And it bridges the gap between mind and matter.[27] The most significant manifestation of this bridging is seen in the crafts. In Descartes's discussion of mathematics in Part One, it is clear that mathematics has already shown itself useful in all the arts and in diminishing the toil of men (AT 6, 7; HR 84, 85). The task of making man master and possessor of nature rests on the practical knowledge of the craftsman: "By . . . knowing the force and the actions of fire, water, air, stars, the heavens and all the other bodies that surround us, as distinctly as we know the various crafts of our artisans, we would be able to use them in the same way for all the uses to which they are proper and thus make ourselves masters and possessors of nature" (AT 62; HR 119). The knowledge of the craftsman is not the knowledge of the object in itself but only in relation to other things. The task of making ourselves masters and possessors of nature implies the pursuit of the knowledge of all things only in relation to man, only insofar as they might be useful in achieving man's ends. The lack of precision of *le bons sens* is cleared up; the blurring of the distinctions between theoretical and practical reason is now given a very precise articulation.

The dominion over nature is the imposition of man's infinite will on nature. The divine in man is now understood not as contemplative but as active, not as speculation but as ruling, not as understanding causes but as producing effects. The change from understanding causes to producing

effects is expressed by Descartes when he says that the practical philosophy will be one by which "knowing the force and actions of fire, water,
air, stars, the heavens, and all the other bodies that surround us, *just as we
understand the various skills of our craftsmen,* we could, *in the same way,*
use these objects for all the purposes for which they are appropriate."
[Emphasis added.] The kind of knowledge that the scientist will seek is
the kind of knowledge that the craftsman has. This is not a knowledge of
the "nature" of things but a knowledge directed toward action and production.

God's activity in creating is analogous to (but certainly not identical
with) the activity of the craftsman; the divine activity is no longer like that
of the speculative intellect, but rather like that of the practical intellect.
God knows all things *because* he makes them. What Descartes has done is
to take the notion of God as craftsman and to make it the model for
knowing in the sciences.

We see this carried out in the *Dioptrics* and the *Meteorology.* The
first discourse of the *Dioptrics* concerns light. But Descartes's whole
approach to the subject of light is *not* essentially to know its nature. His
approach is grounded in the useful. The very opening sentence places the
entire discourse within this context: "The whole conduct of our lives
depends on our senses, among which that of sight being the most universal and the most noble, there is no doubt that the inventions that serve to
augment its power are among the most useful that there can be" (AT 81).
He goes on from this beginning to discuss the great utility of the telescope
which in a very short time has already made possible the discovery of new
stars in the heavens and new objects under the earth. The telescope has
opened the way to a knowledge of nature much greater and more perfect
than ever before. But what is shameful is that this very useful invention is
due only to experience and fortune. It is the result of an accident. And
this, Descartes says, is to the shame of the sciences.

This is Descartes's purpose in writing the *Dioptrics*: the perfection of
the telescope, the overcoming of the difficulties that remain in perfecting
the telescope. The execution of the things he will talk about will depend
upon artisans. It is with such practical results, such productions as his end
that he will determine what he says about light. This is the context for the
claim which is decisive here: "There is no need for me to undertake to say
here what is the true nature [of light], and I think that it will suffice for me
to use two or three comparisons that will help to conceive it in the manner
that seems most convenient to me, in order to explain all those of its
properties which experience has made known to us, and then in order to

deduce all the others which cannot be so easily noticed. [I am] imitating in this the astronomers, who, although their suppositions may almost all be false or uncertain . . . nevertheless do not fail to draw from them many very true and very certain results" (AT 83). The understanding of the true nature of light is not at issue here for the end is not the knowledge of true causes but the production of a good effect.

In the *Meteorology*, production becomes the means to attaining knowledge. Descartes comes to know the cause of the rainbow by producing the effect. But to know the cause of the production of a natural thing, that is, to know how to re-produce it, is not necessarily to know its true cause.

The special importance of this discussion is evident from the way Descartes introduces it: "The rainbow is a wonder of Nature so remarkable, and its cause has in all ages been sought out so carefully by fine thinkers, yet so little known, that I could not choose a subject more appropriate to show how, by the method I use, one can arrive at knowledge that those whose writings we have on the subject did not have" (AT 325). Thus his explanation of the rainbow will exhibit the method. It is noteworthy that the rainbow is God's sign of the covenant in Genesis 9:12-17.

Descartes's first step is to bring near what is in the sky. He has observed that a rainbow is produced when the sun shines on water from a fountain. So he makes an imitation of a very large drop of water in order to be able to examine it better. He fills a large round transparent phial with water, controls the angle of the light passing through it, measures the angle of each of the colors. This "wonder of nature" no longer appears marvelous. For we can produce the same effect, we ourselves can cause it, and thus measure it. The discourse on the rainbow moves from wonder to knowledge through production and measuring. (There is, of course, an essential connection between making and measuring.) The conclusion of the discussion of the rainbow is an instance of the task of the *Meteorology*, and of the *Discourse on Method*.

Descartes concludes the discussion of the rainbow by explaining away "the appearance of signs in the sky which cause great admiration (wonder) in those who do not know the reasons for them" (AT 343). Knowledge eliminates wonder. And at the very beginning of the *Meteorology* he tells us that he believes "it is possible . . . to find the causes of everything that is wonderful upon the earth," so that we will no longer have any occasion to wonder at anything we see (AT 231). God does not wonder because nothing is strange to him, and nothing is strange to him because he makes each thing to be what it is.

The analogy between God and the craftsman is perhaps unavoidable. But the failure to distinguish God from the craftsman is the source of Augustine's misery in Book Seven: the identification carries with it the implication that God needs the world. It is only when he abandons the project of controlling, manipulating, and "constituting" the world and God that Augustine is at his proper "place." Now he wonders at his love for God and he trembles at the works of God. In his disinterested love he abandons the anxious search for certitude.

The comparison between Socrates and Descartes is equally revealing. On the day of his death, Socrates is still wondering. This is because Socrates's activity has always been the search for causes, *true* causes, not the production of effects.

Descartes's attempt to conquer nature, with its attendant elimination of wonder, is the attempt to conquer death by purely human means. The certitude of the *je pense, donc je suis* is thus revealed in its ultimate intention.

But, in the end, we must ask whether this making ourselves masters and possessors of nature is one of those impossible things that fables present as possible: the mastery of nature is the mastery of death. Descartes hints at this when he says that medicine may even be able to overcome the enfeeblement of old age. And, if there is some way to make men wiser, it will be through medicine that this will be accomplished. All of this is supposedly made possible by the method, which eliminates all doubt and error. So the *Discourse* promises the overcoming of all evil, all suffering, and all pain.

For all of its "internal" emphasis on mathematical truth, the *Discourse* itself is a kind of poetry, and its truth must be seen with this in mind. Fables "charm." They are meant to exalt the mind, but they may also lead us to attempt things that are beyond our strength. Descartes's promises concerning the great benefits to be conferred by science are always for some distant future. He often mentions, in his account of his deliberations concerning publication, the effect that the good of future generations has on his decision. And as his own preoccupation with death clearly shows, he does not expect that these promises can be fulfilled immediately. He presents himself as subordinating his own life to the striving for this end for others. And those who truly desire the general good of all mankind, that is, those who are truly virtuous, are invited to subordinate their own desires to the working out of these goals. Whether or not the goal of the conquest of nature can be realized, it is presented as good and virtuous. Descartes's "occupation is solidly good and important."

The mastery and possession of nature, and ultimately the conquest of death, are turned toward the light in the picture of Descartes's life. So also, then, is the firm foundation of the philosophy that promises these things.[28] The *je pense, donc je suis* is the point at which philosophy is refounded in certitude. The beginning and the end of this new, practical philosophy, are thus presented in such a way as to throw all the rest into the shadows and to make everything else appear only in relation to them. The whole picture, however, is quite different.

The unqualifiedly certain affirmation of existence, which is the first principle of the philosophy Descartes was seeking, results in the goal of the overcoming of death. It is the certitude of death that allows the certitude of existence to come to light. Descartes's "occupation" is carried out, in the light, and against the shadow of his *pre*-occupation with approaching death.

Transition and Return: From Modern Despair Back to the Beginning

Descartes, at least in the *Discourse on Method*, attempts to provide grounds for hope, hope that death can indeed be conquered. This is neither the Socratic conquest of the fear of death nor the hope of the Christian believer grounded in the certitude of God's compassion. Rather it is hope grounded in the certitude of self-assertion. This search for certitude has led inevitably to philosophical powerlessness and despair.

If we can return to the beginning of philosophy, a way out of this despair may open up. Philosophy has two beginnings: its historical beginning with the pre-Socratics and its always repeated beginning in wonder. The initial philosophical stance, the stance of the disinterested spectator, is an attempt to rise above the human and thus to escape death. But the attempt to escape death presupposes death. In Socrates, philosophy returns to its own origin and becomes a meditation on death. The philosophical life is a preparation for death, the task of Penelope weaving the shroud.

CHAPTER IV

Conclusion: Death and the Disinterested Spectator

Compassion and Distance

To say that philosophy begins in wonder is to claim that the philosopher always begins from the stance of the disinterested spectator. For wonder is indifferent to the consequences for man, and even for the philosopher himself, of what is wondered at. In this way, wonder rises above laughter and tears and trembling: as disinterested and as purely spectator, the philosopher is not affected by what he observes.[1] His passions are unaffected, or more precisely, the passions that manifest themselves in laughter, in tears, and in trembling are given no scope. Wonder itself is a feeling, and when it is sufficiently strong, it seems to leave no room for the others.

The disinterested spectator appears to be inhuman on account of this indifference. Rousseau takes this appearance to its monstrous extreme in his discussion of pity as the source of the social virtues: "Reason engenders vanity and reflection fortifies it; reason turns man back upon himself, it separates him from all that bothers and afflicts him. Philosophy isolates him; because of it he says in secret, at the sight of a suffering man: Perish if you will, I am safe. No longer can anything except dangers to the entire society trouble the tranquil sleep of the philosopher and tear him from his bed. His fellow-man can be murdered with impunity right under his window; he has only to put his hands over his ears and argue with himself a bit to prevent nature, which revolts within him, from identifying him with the man who is being assassinated."[2]

This description presents the philosopher as lacking especially in compassion. This is due to his isolation, his kind of separation from other men: he thinks himself to be above the human and somehow immune to the things that make other men pitiable. In this sense, philosophy comes closer to laughter than it does to tears or to trembling. The distance of the disinterested spectator is like the distance of the spectator at a comedy: the laughter of ridicule is made possible by the presumption that one will never appear ridiculous. Tears and trembling betray a recognition of common powerlessness in the face of what is fearful.

The inhuman appearance of the disinterested spectator is due to his lack of the ordinary human feelings. The feelings that we expect in a good man seem to be absent from him insofar, that is, as he is the indifferent observer. The absence of pity, from the standpoint of ordinary decent human beings, is bestial and monstrous.[3] We begin to see why philosophy might require a defense. In Rousseau's example, the philosopher is, of course, not the murderer: he does not do anything bad. Indeed, he does not *do* anything. He stays in bed, covers his ears, argues with himself a bit, all in a kind of pretense that he does not really see and hear. The philosopher's rejection of the senses is here displayed in a light that is not morally neutral.

When we consider the disinterested spectator as he observes the nonhuman, he himself appears not monstrous but ridiculous. Thales is unaware of his own feet. His eyes are turned to what is above and he is so absorbed in his observations that he forgets everything below his head. His fall into the well does no one any harm (apart from a few bruises to Thales himself who must have been suddenly reminded of his body). And it gives the housemaids a good laugh. Thales is literally brought down.

In the story of Thales's fall, we see that the disinterested observer of the nonhuman appears ridiculous to those observing him. He lacks the ordinary human concern with where his own feet are going. One way of putting this indifference to his own body and its welfare is to say that the element of fear, an essential element of prudence, is absent. But whereas the absence of pity seems monstrous, the absence of fear seems ridiculous, at least in the case of Thales. For Thales appears stupid. He seems not to even know that any danger exists. He is not courageous but careless.

The carelessness of Thales and the carelessness of Rousseau's philosopher are not, of course, the same and do not demand the same kind of defense. In fact, the carelessness of Thales does not seem to need any defense: it can be ridiculous because it is harmless, harmless because there is no obvious connection with anything human. Of course, we would not want all the farmers to be like Thales and we could not tolerate an army of Thaleses. But as long as the ordinary, the many, remain as they are, the indifferent observers of the nonhuman can be allowed. As long as there are housemaids to laugh at him, Thales can be regarded as harmless.

From what has been said thus far, it would appear that the demand for the defense of philosophy arises chiefly from the perception of the non-philosophers that the philosopher is indifferent to them in their suffering. If there is anyone who can improve the life of men it should be the philosopher since he is wise. But the very activity of philosophy isolates him from his own species. The philosopher is not content to be merely human: he seeks to escape, by himself, into the divine. So the many, non-philosophers, who see that he is indeed a man, require an account from him.

As plausible as this conclusion may be, it is not in fact what happens. The paradigmatic case of the defense of philosophy is undeniably that of Socrates. But Socrates is hated not because he remained aloof and isolated but precisely because he did what he did openly, publicly, "in the market-place." In the *Apology* he claims that his wisdom is *human* wisdom, not the more-than-human wisdom of the natural philosophers. His life has not been an escape to the divine but rather a life for Athens as the gift of the god to Athens. Far from being unconcerned about his fellow citizens, he has done nothing but work for their good. Socrates offers himself indiscriminately, to fellow citizen and stranger (23b), to old and young. The *Theaetetus*, which ends with Socrates's going off to arrange something about his trial, begins with his explicit affirmation of his concern for the good of the young, especially the Athenian youth. The indictment brought by the new accusers asserts that he corrupts the young.

The Socratic defense of philosophy is demanded not on account of any disinterestedness or indifference but on account of the public character of Socrates's practice of philosophy. He is a "busybody." Socrates compares himself with the gadfly and thus recognizes and agrees with, to some extent, the common opinion about him. He attributes the demand for his defense to anger and envy (28b), and certainly the *Apology* itself presents us with a display of this anger.

What the case of Socrates reveals is that, either way, philosophy is open to attack. The isolation of the disinterested spectator opens him to the charge of selfishness. The public, Socratic, practice of philosophy provokes anger and envy, expressed in the charge that he is a nuisance, a busybody, and ultimately more than annoying. Socrates is accused of being downright harmful to the city.

Wonder and Death

The fact that philosophy, that is, ancient philosophy, comes under attack from both sides is due, at least in part, to a kind of tension between divine and human, a tension that seems to belong to (ancient) philosophy as such.[4] Socrates's claim that his wisdom is precisely *human* wisdom is rejected in the anger of his fellow citizens, of those whom he especially sought to benefit. The implicit recognition of the claim to the more-than-human, of the extraordinary, in the practice of philosophy (even in the Socratic practice)[5] leads to the execution of Socrates: the many affirm their power over the philosopher by showing that he does in fact die like everybody else, that he is not divine. The extraordinary manner of Socrates's death is thus a second apology and a kind of second-best defense.

The tension between human and divine in the practice of philosophy is there from the very beginning, belongs to philosophy as such, and thus makes philosophy always questionable *to itself*. As we see from the *Phaedo*, philosophy must defend itself, give an account of itself, both to its enemies and to its friends. Further, even in Socrates himself, on the day of his death, this tension forces itself to the surface and is glimpsed in his struggle to make what he says seem true to himself.

The tension inherent in the practice of philosophy is, again, there from the very beginning: it is present in wonder itself. The divine, inhuman side of wonder is seen in the way it results in the stance of the disinterested spectator.[6] But wonder is a feeling. Because it inhibits or suppresses the far more ordinary feelings, like fear and anger, and because it does not prompt action but rather turns into a kind of passivity, it may go unrecognized as a feeling. Wonder is a human feeling and it is pleasant. In great part, it accounts for the pleasure of philosophy.

The way in which wonder turns into the stance of the *disinterested* spectator can be better understood if we compare it with the similar experience of horror. A good example of this horror is the moment of recognition in a tragedy. Both wonder and horror occur when a sudden recognition takes place. This sudden recognition brings on a sudden paralysis, a suspension of even the most ordinary movements. In the staging of a tragedy, this can be displayed, for example, by having the actor suddenly stop walking or talking. And there is, of course, an expression of horror—the mouth open but not speaking, the eyes wide—which conveys the fact that something is being understood for the first time. In tragic recognition, the paralysis even begins as a recoiling from what is seen.

The recoiling that occurs at the instant of recognition, the even momentary paralysis of action in tragedy, allows us to see how wonder can lead to the stance of the spectator. There is a stepping back, a stopping in one's tracks, because of surprise. The horror of tragic recognition is, of course, extremely painful. The specific ingredient that constitutes it, as it is distinguished from other very painful feelings, is the recognition that one has done something horrible, that one has oneself actually brought about something terrible. The deed itself is horrible and those who have not brought it about are also horrified: their horror too has the element of shock. But the recognition in tragedy does have this aspect, that the actors have done it themselves. That they did not *intend* to do what they did is assumed in the recognition itself. They are surprised by what they themselves have brought about.

The wonder in which philosophy begins is pleasant. This pleasure is due in part to the surprise of sudden recognition. But unlike the recognition in tragedy, there is no element of wonder of having oneself brought anything about. The surprise in wonder interrupts the flow of ordinary activity but what is suddenly recognized does not call for any action on the part of the one who sees. Oedipus sets out at once to undo the harm that he has done, or rather to prevent any further harm. The actions that call forth horror cannot be undone and this also constitutes the special character of horror. In philosophical wonder the lack of any requirement for action allows the one who wonders to persist in simply looking.

The disinterested character of this looking has to do with the stepping back caused by surprise. The stepping back, the suspension of motion toward, keeps a distance between the spectator and what he is looking at. In his thought, he is untouched by what would ordinarily make a man recoil. Thus, the question of the immortality of the soul is the perfect question for displaying the nature of philosophy. The philosopher, like everyone else, is moving relentlessly toward death. That Socrates can dispassionately take up the question of the immortality of the soul on the very day of his death cannot fail to create the impression of a disinterestedness that is inhuman. Wonder is a feeling and indeed a human feeling but insofar as it negates or suppresses the more ordinary human responses, it appears as inhuman. In its distance from what it observes, philosophy comes closer to the stance of the spectator at a comedy. This spectator feels himself to be superior and invulnerable. The philosopher takes a stance toward the human which seems to assume this invulnerability: he pretends to a divine posture.

But the movement involved in taking this stance, the movement that rises above the ordinarily human, cannot be made by anything but a man. For there is an essential connection between philosophy and death. The gods do not philosophize, in spite of the fact that philosophy is said to be divine. Perhaps the most obvious reason why the gods (and certainly Augustine's God) do not engage in the activity of philosophy is that they do not need to: their knowledge is such that no transition from wonder to knowledge need take place. This in itself locates philosophy as a human activity. But the fundamental distinction between gods and men is the immortality of the gods. The gods do not philosophize because they do not die and do not fear death. Because philosophy is an attempt to overcome death, it occurs only insofar as man is mortal. It presupposes death in its attempt to overcome death.

Even the wonder in which philosophy begins must be understood in its relation to death. For wonder is a matter of being taken out of the ordinary everyday immersion in means and ends, out of the absorption in accomplishing that is required for the very maintenance of life. This paralysis of action is a kind of rising above the ordinary and above all necessary strivings which men undertake to preserve themselves. Aristotle allows for this relationship between wonder and death in his distinction between philosophy and productive knowledge: "That [philosophy] is not a science of production is clear even from the history of the earliest philosophers. *For* it is owing to their wonder that men both now begin and at first began to philosophize. . . . And a man who is puzzled and wonders thinks himself ignorant. . . . Therefore since they philosophized in order to escape from ignorance, evidently they were pursuing science in order to know, and not for any utilitarian end. And this is confirmed by the facts; for it was when almost all the necessities of life and the things that make for comfort and recreation had been secured, that such knowledge began to be sought" (*Metaphysics* 982b). [Emphasis added.] From one side, then, philosophy looks divine, even from its very beginning in wonder. But insofar as it is necessarily an escape from the pursuit of useful ends, it presupposes human mortality and has it as its necessary condition.

The other characteristic of philosophy which locates it as a human possibility has to do with the transition, or at least the attempt at a transition, from wonder to knowledge. The divine perspective would seem to be that of knowledge simply, without the need for this transition. So, the divine can be said to know but not to philosophize. To say that philosophy begins in wonder is to say that it begins in ignorance or more precisely in the recognition of ignorance. Thus, philosophy may have a divine end and even result in a divine perspective, but its beginning is distinctively human.

The Strange and the Familiar

If we proceed further in the analysis of philosophical wonder, this distinctively human character emerges more clearly. But, at the same time and from the same source, the persistent connection between philosophy and immortality also comes forward. Wonder is a response to the strange, the unusual or unfamiliar. As such, it contains an element of surprise, for part of what it means to characterize something as strange or unfamiliar is that the thing in question was unexpected.

There seem to be two kinds of "things" that can be distinguished as calling forth wonder. On the one hand, unusual natural phenomena, especially those visible in the heavens, make all who see them wonder. Descartes discusses such phenomena in the *Meteorology*: men naturally wonder at what is above them and this wonder is destroyed by knowledge or by an explanation in more familiar terms. Socrates, on the day of his death, wonders at what is also a natural phenomenon, the pleasure and pain he feels in his legs. He finds pleasure "strange" and "wonderfully" related to pain. The natural phenomena that inspire wonder are, of course, sensible phenomena.

The other kind of "thing" that can inspire wonder is a proposition. (In fact, Socrates's account of his youthful "investigation of nature" actually shows him even then beginning from *opinion* about natural things: "Do heat and cold, by a sort of fermentation, bring about the organization of animals, *as some people say*?") Socrates's turn to argument from natural philosophy preserves the beginning of philosophy in wonder. His "method," described at the end of the story of his turn, is very much a matter of dealing with the strange in relation to the familiar: "I assume in each case some argument which I consider strongest and whatever seems to me to agree with this, whether about cause or anything else, I hold as true, and whatever disagrees with it, as untrue" (100a). The procedure here entails examining a proposition against the background of the familiar. We see this immediately in the *Phaedo*: the argument which illustrates the method begins from the existence of the "itselfs" and Simmias regards the existence of the "itselfs" as "most certain." But the method also requires that the starting point, the *logos* provisionally taken to be strongest, be itself examined against some other, higher, *logos*.

The play between familiar and strange in the realm of speech is also seen at the beginning of the dialogue. The prohibition against suicide seems strange to them until Socrates explains it in terms of an account which they accept. But once the prohibition against suicide has been accepted, has become familiar, Socrates's willingness to die begins to seem strange. The strange can only emerge against the background of the familiar. Truth, according to Socrates's description of his method, is a kind of agreement of propositions; the initially strange proposition is shown to agree with the familiar. The procedure of arguing is to work one's way back to a proposition that will be accepted and then to show that the proposition in question agrees with it. So when Socrates, in the last argument, wants them to accept the assertion that the soul is immortal, he begins from "nothing new," from "the same thing [he] has always been saying." He goes back to the most familiar (100b). We see the same procedure displayed in the *Apology* in Socrates's other story about his life. When he first hears the oracle, he is puzzled. He thinks that the god must be mistaken because he knows that he is not wise. But, on the other hand, the god does not lie. So Socrates is confronted with two propositions which seem to contradict each other. Socrates's search, from this point of view, is the attempt to resolve an apparent contradiction. And the contradiction is resolved in this way: Socrates comes to a new understanding of the meaning of 'wisdom'.

With these things in mind, we can begin to identify the characteristics of philosophical wonder that bear most directly on the question of the human and divine in the activity of philosophy. What we see in the case of Socrates, and on the very day he is to die, is that the philosopher gets around to wondering at the most familiar, at what is so close that it usually goes unnoticed. Socrates's first words in the *Phaedo* (after he asks Crito to see that his wife is taken home) have to do with the strangeness of pleasure. One of the most important differences between wonder in general and philosophical wonder is that the wonder that is common to all men concerns the unusual, unfamiliar, and unexpected, whereas the philosopher wonders at what everyone else takes for granted. Yet there would be no wonder without the surprise provoked by the unusual, unfamiliar, and unexpected. What happens in philosophical wonder is that something quite familiar suddenly seems strange, suddenly stands out and seems not to fit in with everything else. That is, something that has been accepted all along and is therefore familiar suddenly comes forward and stands out against the background of the familiar and seems not to agree with what has remained familiar.

What this means is that wonder has as an essential element, indeed as its own beginning, the sudden appearance of the false. The strange proposition does not agree with the familiar and thus suddenly seems to be false. This initial appearance of falsehood is delightful. The disinterested spectator first finds pleasure in this sudden appearance of the strange. (On the other hand, such things as strange phenomena in the sky and monsters inspire terror.) From the origin of philosophy in wonder we are led to the origin of wonder in the appearance of falsehood. Thus, philosophy does not occur without doubt and originates in a kind of doubt.

The strange is immediately suspected of being false because it does not agree with what is still taken for granted. At the same time, its very emergence from the background of the familiar is a kind of assertion of itself, an insistence of its truth. The weight of custom is against its being true but it would never have struck us as strange unless we suspected that it is indeed true.

The suspicion that the strange proposition is true has the further effect of calling the whole bulk of the familiar into question. For if the strange proposition is indeed true, then the whole context from which it has come forward as strange may be false. That is, our most fundamental assumptions must be ultimately called into question. Of course, our most fundamental assumptions do not immediately become questionable, for they are not even easily identified. But wonder does work back toward these assumptions: philosophy is ultimately concerned with the most familiar. Yet philosophy cannot be concerned with the most familiar until the familiar has appeared as strange and thus as somehow false.

The doubt in which philosophy must begin locates philosophy as a human activity. This doubt, if I have described it correctly, is the suspicion that the strange proposition is false and, at the same time, that it is true. Such suspicion or mistrust has to be contrasted with certitude. The condition of certitude is one in which there is no suspicion but only confidence. One of the possibilities of truth or falsehood has been eliminated or was never there at all.

Complete confidence would surely seem to be a better state than doubt. Doubt, at least about some things, is accompanied by anxiety. We see this quite clearly in the *Phaedo* when the objections of Simmias and Cebes have the effect of making those present visibly uneasy. Socrates understands their anxiety to be a mistrust of argument as such and he characterizes the hatred of argument as the greatest evil that can happen to a man. What becomes of the claim, then, that the initial appearance of falsehood (the appearance that constitutes wonder) is pleasant? The doubt felt by those present on the day of Socrates's death and by the hearers of Phaedo's report is painful, produces anxiety, and is accompanied by the desire to arrive at certitude. It is also accompanied by the suspicion that certitude is impossible.

The anxiety produced by the questioning of Socrates's arguments for immortality is foreshadowed by Phaedo's description of his own feelings, presented at the very beginning of the dialogue. He did not feel his usual pleasure in discussion but rather a "strange" mixture of pleasure and pain. The pleasure of philosophy is not always pure. We see this also in the *Theaetetus* where Socrates describes his activity as that of the midwife (149a). Theaetetus is puzzled and anxious. Socrates identifies this anxiety as the beginning of philosophy and compares philosophy to childbirth. What this comparison suggests is pain, labor, urgency, the desire to get through with it.

Philosophy's mixed beginning in wonder points to the desirability of certitude. That is, we are tempted to say that philosophy begins in wonder and should therefore end in certainty. Doubt should be only transitional and should be resolved, the anxiety relieved and overcome. When the labor is over, there is, undeniably, a child. But when Theaetetus is delivered of his assertion about knowledge it must still be examined to determine whether it is true or false.

Philosophy begins in wonder, but in what does it end? In fact, it does not end. Philosophy is "endless toil." The philosopher's "immortality" is his entrapment in an endless task. Like Penelope, he is always unweaving what he has woven. This is the very nature of philosophy. Wonder is endless because the human can never totally and completely rise above the familiar or escape the familiar. When a proposition which first seems strange is woven into the fabric of the familiar (and the familiar adjusted to it) it becomes part of the background against which other propositions show up as strange.

Wonder needs the familiar, presupposes the familiar. In this beginning, philosophy reveals its distinctively human character and shows itself to be a precisely human possibility. Its divine character is not located in any termination of its activity in certitude, in any "end" as completion. Rather, it is always approaching the divine.[7] It is both—it is always, and it is always approaching. So Socrates is still wondering on the day of his death and he dies wondering at his most familiar friends: "You strange men!" His last expression of wonder is at the strangeness of the human. Yet, as Phaedo reveals in his wonder at Socrates (88e), it is Socrates who is extraordinary. These two sides are both human.[8]

The Fable of Certitude

The situation of philosophy, beginning in wonder and never ending, seems to be precisely what Descartes is attempting to overcome. That is, the project of Descartes is the complete escape from the familiar. This is what his doubt is meant to accomplish. He wants to eliminate the background of the familiar, start from nothing, begin again from an unqualifiedly certain proposition. But at least in the *Discourse*, this is a fable.

Certitude is, at least in one sense, pre-philosophical and even anti-philosophical. For the familiar is certain, or rather seems certain. The most familiar is the most certain because it is so trusted, so relied upon, that it goes almost completely unnoticed. It is the last to appear as strange, the strongest holdout against doubt. This link of the certain and the familiar is precisely what philosophy must overcome and, at the same time, what it needs in order to take place at all. The link is expressed in the divided line of the *Republic* at the second stage in the lower section of the line. The activity of the soul that corresponds to the realm of visible things is trust (*pistis*). This is where opinion, as distinguished from knowledge, is located. But "the given" (the familiar) must also be understood as what is most familiar to thought and not only as what is given to the senses. We see this in Socrates's turn to words, away from the investigation of things by means of the senses. He counts on this familiarity as certitude especially, as we have seen, in the last argument for immortality. The "itselfs" have become so familiar to Simmias through repeated discussion that he regards their existence as "most certain." The two "approaches to truth" which are discussed in the *Phaedo* correspond to these two senses of the familiar: the senses and words.

Descartes seems to want a totally new beginning with respect to both kinds of given. This would allow for a new and certain foundation for metaphysics: the whole of the familiar is subjected to doubt all at once so as to arrive at a proposition that is indubitable and thus certain. But as we have seen, Descartes's chief concern in the *Discourse* is certitude in the conduct of life, assurance in action. The context for his project is twofold. As we see in the First Part, it is the given as transmitted in both the philosophical and the theological traditions which must be put aside. In spite of the fact that the best minds over the centuries have pursued it, philosophy provides nothing but doubt and confusion. Theology, on the other hand, is a more-than-human activity and it provides no certitude about salvation.

Descartes's search for certitude can be understood against the background of the medieval uncertainty concerning salvation. The *Discourse* is surely presented (at least on one level) as a kind of triumph of self-reliance which can be seen for what it is in contrast to Augustine's total reliance on God. Augustine's uncertainty about salvation is a mistrust of himself. But there is hope because God is unchangeable and so loved the world, that he gave his only son. Descartes begins from the medieval uncertainty about salvation and strives for a certitude actually grounded in himself. The *Discourse* is not a prayer and it is decidedly not an account designed to persuade toward reliance on God. On the contrary, Descartes concludes very early on that he must rely only on himself, that he is "alone" in the shadows.

If my interpretation of the *Discourse* is near the mark, the certitude from which Descartes begins, on which the *je pense, donc je suis* really rests, is a certitude of power. This is not surprising in light of the medieval background I have just sketched. For Augustine, divine action does not negate human action but there is a most fundamental sense in which what is really happening in human life is not being brought about by human agents. It is to this aspect, the side of human powerlessness, that Descartes is responding in his search for self-reliance.

On the one hand, Descartes's response here seems to be a return to the Stoics, a going back to a pre-Christian mode of thought and action in order to escape the anxiety of Christian uncertainty. The absence of any reliance on God in the *Discourse* would support this analysis. But the third provisional maxim does not square with the project of ruling nature presented in the Sixth Part. Descartes's rejection of theology, as both unnecessary and useless, does not simply lead him back to the ancient position. Ancient philosophy is also uncertain. It is always approaching the divine perspective but never achieving it. It is the *futile* toil of weaving and unweaving. Descartes's occupation is presented as, in the language of the *Phaedo*, a weaving which does not get undone. He augments his knowledge day after day. And his occupation is said to belong to man as man. So, Descartes's rejection of and apparent overcoming of the uncertainty of both faith and philosophy does seem to mean a new beginning. We seem to have in Descartes a starting from nothing that allows him to begin from an indubitable starting point. And this is the starting point for modern philosophy, including the analytic tradition which follows from it.[9]

I have attempted to show that this impression must at least be modified: Descartes's starting point does not arise out of nothing. In one sense, the *je pense, donc je suis* looks back to the Stoic perspective and is based on the distinction between what is in our power and what is not in our power. The total self-reliance of Descartes's first principle is like the Stoic freedom from fortune which allowed them to rival their gods in happiness. But Descartes does not simply return to the Stoic position, in part because he has presented in the *Discourse* a project which calls for the overcoming of the limitations on human power and makes that overcoming possible.

Even in this, Descartes does not at all begin from nothing. The *je pense, donc je suis* is the first principle of what turns out to be a *practical* philosophy. This is a radical change in the nature of philosophy itself. In one sense, a "practical philosophy" would have to be a contradiction in terms. We are not now speaking of one particular branch of philosophy, such as ethics or politics, but of "first philosophy" itself. This fundamental reorientation of philosophy to a practical end, this new beginning of philosophy in power, could not have occurred without Christian theology. I do not mean that it is consistent with Christian theology: indeed, it is a gross distortion.[10] Nor am I claiming that this change followed *inevitably* from that theological background. My claim is that Descartes cannot be understood without reference to the fundamental teachings of Christianity, as they were elucidated in the writings of the theologians.[11]

Philosophy and the Divine: From Disinterested Spectator to Compassionate Actor

My discussion of Augustine, when taken in contrast to my analysis of the *Phaedo*, is meant to bring to light one of Descartes's most important theological presuppositions. The radical change in the nature of philosophy itself, effected by Descartes in the *Discourse*, presupposes a fundamental change in the notion of the divine, a change which appears so strikingly in *The Confessions*. Philosophy must always understand itself in terms of its relationship to the divine. In spite of the fact that Descartes describes his own occupation as one belonging to man as man, his radical reorientation of philosophy presupposes an understanding of the nature of the divine, which makes this change possible.[12]

The difference between the ancient philosophical notion of the divine and the Christian notion which my discussion has emphasized is the difference between the divine as distinterested spectator and the divine as actor. The God of Christianity is not the disinterested spectator of the world. He is its creator and its ruler, even to the fluttering of the leaves of the trees. And as *The Confessions* testifies on every page, God acts in human life, although often in secret ways. What characterizes God's action toward men is his compassion: "You, Lord, abide forever, and you are not angry with us forever, because you have pity on dust and ashes" (VII.8). The Platonists know that "In the beginning was the Word" but not that "the Word was made flesh and dwelt among us" or that "he emptied himself . . . and was found in fashion as a man, and humbled himself, and became obedient unto death. . . . " There is no look of pity in the books of the Platonists. The notion of the divine as actor and as compassionate actor is the presuppostion for Descartes's radical reorientation of philosophy in the *Discourse*.

Philosophy begins with the pre-Socratics as the stance of the disinterested spectator. Ancient philosophy was and was content to be powerless: it does not seek to rule nature but only to understand. And as the *Apology* demonstrates, philosophy was powerless in the face of public opinion. Socrates did not seek to rule in the city during his life and at the end he does not exert sufficient power to conquer the anger of his fellow citizens. Medieval thought, both philosophical and theological, preserves this stance and this powerlessness. We find in Aquinas's *Summa Theologica*, for example, the claim that theology is more a speculative than a practical science.[13] Even though the notion of the divine has changed from disinterested spectator to actor, the activity of theology remains primarily a speculative matter.

In Descartes's *Discourse* we see the change that depends upon this new notion of the divine but which the medieval theologians were unwilling to make. Descartes's criticism of the Scholastic disputations is meant to apply not only to the degeneration that had apparently taken place in this practice but to the whole theological tradition: "And I have never observed that, through the method of disputation practiced in the Schools, any truth was discovered that had previously been unknown" (AT 69; HR 124). Indeed, his rejection of theology in Part One makes clear that theology was "useless," that is, speculative, in that it did not teach anyone how to go to heaven. In the Sixth Part, Descartes explicitly refers to the philosophy taught in the Schools as speculative and describes his own project in contrast to this.

Augustine's *Confessions* is not itself a purely speculative work. But we do see, in his discussions of philosophy and in his own thinking after his encounter with the Platonists, the same unwillingness to reorient human thought from speculative to practical. The "object" of thought, its highest object, is now a divine being who is not a disinterested spectator of the world but its creator and ruler. Yet thought itself does not thereby become practical. There is no "method" for salvation in *The Confessions*.

In order to see both the radicalness of Descartes's change from the tradition and his presuppositions in that tradition, it is necessary to keep in view the two-sidedness of Augustine's position. On the one hand, the question of God's unchangeableness is a speculative question. On the other hand, the unchangeableness of God cannot ultimately be, for Augustine, only a theoretical concern: "For that truly is which remains unchangeably. It is good then for me to cling to God: for if I remain not in him, I shall not be able to remain in myself" (VII.11). On the one hand, the truth of created things is understood only in terms of their having their being from God: "And I looked at other things and I saw how they owe their being to you . . . and all things are true insofar as they are" (VII.15). God is "still working and still remaining." On the other hand, Augustine is most wary of any *human* making: "So men go outside themselves to follow things of their own making, and inside themselves they are forsaking Him who made them and are destroying what they themselves were made to be" (X. 34). Augustine's soul "made for itself a God to fill the infinite distances of all space and it had thought this God to be you, and had placed it in its own heart: thus again becoming the temple of its own idol, a temple abominable to you" (VII.14). On the one hand, the difference between presumption and confession is at least partly expressed in the fact that there are "no look of pity" and "no tears of confession" in the Platonists. And tragedy is criticized because "there can be no real compassion for fictions on the stage. A man listening to a play is not called upon to help the sufferer" (III.2). On the other hand, it is God who is truly compassionate: "You are wounded by no sorrow, yet you love souls far more deeply than we can, and your compassion is more lasting and indestructible than ours" (III.2). *The Confessions* teaches reliance on God for the relief of misery. This is not to say that human action is negated, that man is totally powerless. If so, *The Confessions* itself would be a futile undertaking in its public intention. But the human cannot be surpassed by human power. Death is conquered by Christ who was willing "to let death be common" to him and to us (X.43).

In the Sixth Part of the *Discourse*, Descartes changes philosophy from a speculative to a practical science, that is, from a useless to a useful science. He does this by making paradigmatic the kind of knowledge that is had in the crafts. Production, the human making of which Augustine is so wary, becomes the model for knowing in the sciences. This change is only possible on account of the idea of divine "production," a production which actually constitutes the truth of things. But the theologian is always attempting to distinguish God from the craftsman. We see in Augustine that the failure to make this distinction is at the root of his evil manner of inquiry (VII.5).

The elimination of wonder which is most in evidence in the *Meteorology* is consonant with the notion that the truth to be sought in the sciences is the kind of truth which the craftsman has concerning his productions. Descartes's procedure in investigating the cause of the rainbow is by his own insistence an especially good example of his project.[14] By reproducing the things of nature we come to know them in the way the craftsman knows what he makes. Thus wonder at the things of nature is eliminated: God does not wonder because he makes each thing to be what it is.

Descartes's move to the truth of production goes along with his turn to mathematics. There is, of course, an essential connection between making and measuring. Indeed, there is a sense in which we can say that the arts are entirely a matter of correct measurement. The key here is precision. And we find Descartes criticizing speech for its unavoidable lack of precision. But with mathematical propositions, complete precision is possible. There are no hidden corners of meaning to be patiently uncovered.[15]

The elimination of wonder at natural things and the turn to mathematics is a kind of reversal of the Socratic turn away from natural philosophy. The opening passages of the *Dioptrics* and the *Meteorology* suggest this quite forcefully. Here, too, the return is foreshadowed in Augustine but is never made by Augustine. The philosophers do say many true things about the created world, and Augustine sees the reason for what they say in calculation, in the order of time, and in the visible evidence of the stars; the views of Manes, on the other hand, "did not correspond with what had been established by mathematics and [his] own eyesight" (V. 3). And after his reading of the Platonists, he speaks about the "other things" of creation in terms of a knowledge modelled on clear sight (VII.11.12).

But again, Descartes does not follow inevitably from Augustine nor is he simply faithful to the Augustinian view. The natural philosophers do say much that is true while the ignorant are astonished and full of admiration. But "the proud cannot find [God], however deep and curious their knowledge, not even if they could count the stars and the grains of sand or measure the constellations in the sky and track down the paths of the stars" (V.3). God rules the universe even to the immeasurable fluttering of the leaves of the trees. The astrologers (mathematicians) cannot measure and set down in their tables the small intervals of time between the birth of twins so as to pronounce the truth (VII.6). And even though Augustine speaks of created things in terms of knowledge as "sight" after reading the Platonists, the reading of St. Paul has a wonderful effect on him: "These things did by wonderful means sink into my very bowels, when I read that *least of thy Apostles,* and had considered your works and trembled" (VII.21). The contemplation of the works of God causes him to tremble, and the turning within, prompted by the Platonists, causes him to tremble with love and horror in the presence of and distance from God.

There is, in Augustine, no attempt to control nature by means of knowledge. The knowledge of production is a knowledge aimed at controlling, at exercising power, at imposing one's will. The rule that is exercised both in the *Phaedo* and in Augustine is the rule of soul over body (*Confessions* VII.7). And this is accomplished by speech, not by numbers. Mathematics does not rule the passions. In ruling one's own body the soul rules itself. But in Descartes, we are left with the inevitable "dualism." Yet rule is exercised over body as such.

The rule over body as such is made possible by the reorientation of science in terms of the model of the crafts, of production. This is a reversal of the ancient position, as expressed by Aristotle for example, which in fact begins by distinguishing philosophy from productive science: wonder can only occur as a break with the useful and with the means and ends of production. As we have seen, this very dependence on production as that against which philosophy begins, establishes the link between philosophy and death. Philosophy and the wonder in which it begins presuppose human mortality.

Descartes's concern with the elimination of wonder is very much an attempt to eliminate fear, and in particular the ultimate fear, of death. Those who do not know the causes of things are terrified by what they take to be wonderful, extraordinary phenomena. This kind of wonder is not specifically philosophical wonder for it does not belong to the disinterested spectator. But by reorienting all science to useful ends, Descartes aims at the elimination of wonder and fear of death simply. The activity of the craftsman and the kind of knowledge that he has are not mysterious or strange, because they are useful. And the crafts are primarily and ultimately for the sake of preserving life and preventing death. In Part Six, Descartes holds out the promise of overcoming human misery, even death itself, through the refounding of philosophy as a useful science modeled on production.

Cartesian Presumption, Socratic Victory

Descartes's project cannot but strike us as the greatest defiance, the greatest rebellion against God.[16] Not only the promises of Part Six but the whole of Descartes's project as the search for self-reliance and certitude begin to appear as the struggle against the effects of original sin: sickness, pain, work, death, and the so-called "darkening of the intellect." Descartes, in the attempt to and the expectation of eliminating these conditions, is attempting to do what faith believes that only God can do. From this point of view, Descartes's whole enterprise is one based on the most monstrous pride. This view is only confirmed by the fact that he presents his project not as a matter of pride but as an undertaking of the greatest compassion and indeed, like Redemption, for all mankind. The attempt to exercise this greatest compassion is the greatest presumption.[17]

We find in Descartes no echo of Augustine's anxiety over what he calls "the ambition of the world." For Augustine, good deeds for the sake of other men put one in danger of being proud, of wanting to be loved and feared not on account of God but instead of God. Descartes never worries about this. But the moral struggle recounted in Part Six of the *Discourse* does have its counterpart in Augustine. Descartes presents himself as torn between total selfishness and total self-sacrifice. These are the two poles that pull him back and forth between the alternatives of publishing and not publishing. For his own sake and his own greatest pleasure, he wants to be left alone. But "the law that obliges us to procure as best we can the common good of all mankind" requires that he make his thoughts known and, if he does this, he will inevitably be caught up in controversy. The heart of this difficulty, what makes this a *struggle*, is precisely his recognition that he does not have much time. Because he is mortal, he must choose between interested and disinterested action, or he must make some compromise.

This struggle is, in one sense, foreshadowed in Augustine. On the one hand, *The Confessions* presents a man who is totally concerned with his own salvation and, thus, wholly "interested." As we have seen, even such questions as that of God's unchangeableness are not simply theoretical questions for Augustine. On the other hand, the very nature of man's "place" demands the disinterested love of God. Augustine goes so far in this disinterestedness that Rousseau can speak of "St. Augustine who would have consoled himself with being damned if that were the will of God."[18]

But Augustine's struggle between total self-interest and total disinterestedness is not a source of perpetual torment. It is resolved in his
conversion, in his "chaste" love of God. He can say, "It is good for me to
cling to God," because God is unchangeably good. That is, God does not
put us in the impossible position of wanting our own happiness by nature
and being required by grace to put all concern for happiness aside. Nor
does Augustine's concern for his own salvation make him indifferent to
the sufferings of others. His compassion is for the sinner: "This certainly
is a truer form of compassion, but the pain in it does not give one
pleasure" (III.2). And *The Confessions* is a public confession for the sake
of the "companions in my joy and sharers in my mortality" (X.4). But
Augustine's compassion for other men is only an imitation of the far
more powerful compassion of God: "You have forgiven and covered up
my past sins . . . when the confessions of these past sins are read and
heard, they rouse up the heart and prevent it from sinking into the sleep of
despair and saying 'I cannot.' Instead they encourage it to be wakeful in
the love of your mercy and the sweetness of your grace" (X.3).

The possible conflict between Augustine's own salvation and his
good deeds towards other men centers around the temptation to pride,
the dangers of a good reputation. But it is resolved on the level of hope
and of trust, not in oneself, but in God. Descartes's dilemma is that his
reputation for knowledge leads him into controversy, which in turn
makes him lose the time he needs in order to pursue knowledge. Specifically, he must decide whether or not to publish. He resolves the conflict
by writing and publishing the *Discourse*. In the *Discourse*, the conflict is
presented in terms of the struggle between the desire for "repose" and the
obligation to try to relieve the misery of all mankind, that is, the struggle
between total self-interest and total self-sacrifice.

Socrates, in the *Apology* and the *Phaedo*, discusses his own life in
similar but certainly not identical terms. In his speech to the whole
citizen-body he describes his activity as one of service to the god for the
sake of Athens; he has been a gadfly constantly stinging the city and
waking it from its lethargy. His service to the city has kept him so busy
that he has neglected his own private affairs. Now he is poor on account
of his complete occupation with the good of Athens. There is, of course,
no claim on Socrates's part that he works for the good of all mankind,
although he does refer to his questioning of citizens and strangers alike.
And his questioning concerns human excellence as such, not any excellence peculiar to an Athenian. At the beginning of the *Theaetetus*, we see

also that Socrates does not exclude anyone from the benefits of his activity but he does explicitly say that he cares most of all about Athens. This special concern for Athens is not due to any extraordinary inherent Athenian goodness, but rather to a recognition of the limits imposed by space and time on the effectiveness of a man's activities.

At the beginning of the *Phaedo*, a very deliberate exclusion takes place. When Socrates says that the philosopher would be absurd if he were troubled at the approach of death, Simmias is forced to laugh at the thought that "the many" would, in this case, agree with Socrates: philosophers desire and deserve death. Socrates's response is that "the many" would be speaking the truth but without knowledge, for they do not know in what way the philosopher desires death or deserves death or what kind of death it is. And Socrates concludes: "Let us then speak with one another, paying no further attention to them" (64b). So, too, Crito is told to pay no further attention to the man who is responsible for administering the poison (63e).

Socrates's concern on the day of his death is for his friends, at least those who are present and perhaps those who are absent, like Plato. Indeed, Socrates shows himself to be kind, gentle, and patient with all of their objections and discouragements. Phaedo tells Echecrates that when Socrates saw them becoming mistrustful of argument as such, he rallied and cured them: "I have often wondered at Socrates, but never did I admire him more than then. That he had an answer ready was perhaps not strange; but what astonished me more about him was, first, the pleasant, gentle, and respectful manner in which he listened to the young men's argument" (88e-89a).

Simmias provides the context for the discussion of immortality when he says to Socrates at the beginning of the dialogue: "Do you intend to go away and keep this thought to yourself, or would you let us share it? It seems to me that this is a good which belongs in common to us also" (63c-d). Socrates works hard throughout the discussion and especially in pulling them together into agreement. The emphasis on "agreement" throughout the dialogue is striking, and reaches a peak in the final argument for immortality: "I am speaking this way because I want you to agree with me" (102d). This is the kind of rallying that Phaedo describes to Echecrates.

Finally, in the central hatred of argument section, where the real battle is fought, Socrates exhorts them, and Phaedo in particular, to strive manfully against the notion that there is no soundness in argument and in order to become sound themselves: "You [Phaedo] and the others for the sake of your whole life still, and I because of death itself" (90e-91a). This hint of a distinction between Socrates himself and the others is pushed as far as an open declaration of "selfishness" (91b) and a warning that he may, in his eagerness, deceive himself and them. Yet even this threat is tempered: "But you, if you are persuaded by me, will give little thought to Socrates but much more to the truth; and if you think what I say is true, agree to it, and if not, strive against it with every argument, that I may not in my eagerness deceive myself and you alike and go away, like a bee, leaving my sting in you" (91c).

We do not, then, find in Socrates the same bold struggle between self-interest and obligation to others as total self-sacrifice that we find in Part Six of the *Discourse*. Socrates's busyness in the service of Athens has kept him poor but he does not say either in the *Apology* or in the *Phaedo* that it has kept him from being happy. That is, his public activity is not in conflict with the activity of philosophy: indeed, questioning and answering is the activity to which he turned after his disappointment with natural philosophy.

If the extremes of the conflict between self-interest and benefiting others are not present in Socrates, neither is the extraordinary Cartesian confidence about what philosophy can accomplish. Socrates describes his wisdom as merely human wisdom but his practice is undertaken as an interpretation of a divine command. Descartes's occupation is characterized as purely human, yet he seems to promise much more, to show a much greater confidence in what human beings can accomplish on their own. But Socrates's chief concern is with the soul and Descartes's, at least in the Sixth Part of the *Discourse*, is with the body. Both are ultimately most concerned with death, with the fear of death and with overcoming death.

That Socrates is chiefly occupied with improving the soul and Descartes with improving the body may go a long way toward explaining why Socrates's defense in the *Apology* fails and Descartes's in the *Discourse* succeeds. But Descartes's success is not really a victory for philosophy. What has become perfectly respectable are the sciences, along with mathematics, separated off from philosophy. Even if some initial link between philosophy and science is recognized, even if science is understood to have some philosophical origin in the distant past, the role of philosophy in the beginnings of modern science is thought to be over: this was a beginning made once and for all. There is no return to question any philosophical first principles, no attempt to uncover assumptions. Philosophy now, at least as it appears in the self-understanding of the analytic tradition (which has its origins in Descartes), is at best a rather pathetic, anemic handmaiden of science. It is embarrassed at its own powerlessness.[19]

On the other hand, Socrates does have some success in defending philosophy in the *Phaedo*. The *Apology* as the attempt to rule the anger and envy of "the many" fails. But "the many" are excluded in the *Phaedo*: Socrates is with friends and he is up against the fear of death on one front and the hatred of argument on another. His action in drinking the poison without trembling or turning pale is the real victory over the fear of death and, on that level, the best possible defense of the philosophical life. As Socrates had said in the *Apology*: "I shall give you great proofs of this, not words, but what you esteem, deeds" (32a). I have argued that Socrates's last words, "We owe a cock to Asclepius," are an indication that he thinks he has won the victory over hatred of argument, has "cured" them of this "worst evil."

Idle Talk and Endless Toil

The defense of philosophy in the *Phaedo* is Socrates's defense against the charge that philosophy is "idle talk" (115d), that it is "merely" words. We do not have here the vulgar, angry shouting of the *Apology*. Rather, this charge is brought by the educated, by those who have some acquaintance with philosophy. At worst, they hate argument: they are the disputants who "come to believe that they are the wisest of men and that they alone have understood that there is nothing sound or sure in anything, whether argument or anything else" (90b-c). Socrates perceives that those present are headed toward this condition, toward contempt for words. Many of those present, including the chief interlocutors Simmias and Cebes, are mathematicians. And Echecrates and his unnamed, unnumbered companions are also mathematicians. My discussion of the *Phaedo* was intended to show that on both levels—that of Socrates with Simmias and Cebes, and that of Phaedo with Echecrates—a respect for argument is generated or re-established. In the end, they cannot regard philosophy as "mere words." And although Socrates strives throughout the dialogue for agreement, in the end he encourages them to go back and re-examine their first assumptions, even though they seem most certain.

But even this victory is limited. It is Crito, Socrates's old friend, who seems not to have been truly persuaded. When he asks Socrates "How shall we bury you?" Socrates's reply lets us see clearly the suspicion that philosophy is really only words. Socrates laughed gently and said: "I do not persuade Crito, my friends, that I am this Socrates who is now talking to you and ordering each of the things I said . . . but it seems that this was idle talk to encourage you and myself" (115c-d). Crito is unconvinced on two levels: he still doubts the arguments for immortality and, more importantly, he still really suspects that all argument is only "idle talk."

The charge that philosophy is downright dangerous for a city may, in certain circumstances, be sincerely believed by the accuser. Socrates refers, in the *Apology*, to the public opinion that natural philosophers are atheists. But it is quite clear that the real reasons for the indictment against Socrates are anger and envy, both due to the reputation of Socrates for wisdom. And his activity, as described in the *Apology*, has humiliated many powerful men. That Socrates fails to win an acquittal at his public trial may suggest that there really is very little that can be done to defend philosophy against anger and envy. In the case of Socrates the anger and envy are so strong because his practice of philosophy has been public: he has been indiscriminately questioning anyone he meets. But as he says at the trial, public opinion about philosophers in general is suspicious, even if confused. The only thing to be done in the face of such anger and envy is to stop doing the activity. Again, in the case of Socrates, there is not the alternative of practicing privately: no matter what city he would go to, indeed even in Hades, he would continue the same indiscriminate questioning.

The more dangerous charge against philosophy is the charge that it is idle talk. At least this is the situation today, in places where the university is regarded as a good thing, where free inquiry is said to be highly valued. There is, as there always has been to some degree, the suspicion that philosophy is "mere words." This means that philosophy is regarded as useless and trivial, indeed as trivial because useless. Philosophy as "idle talk" cannot be useful and serious or important: at best it is an amusement and not, in Descartes's terms, an *occupation* "which is solidly good and important." Descartes's success in defending science in the *Discourse* is due in good part to his criticisms of his university studies as useless and, of course, to his reorienting "philosophy" toward practical useful ends. Thus, he can defend his activity as the *most* useful and important occupation of all those possible for man.

The suspicion that philosophy is idle talk, that it is trivial, grows out of the (usually unarticulated) identification of the useful and the important. The truly important is serious, in contrast with the merely amusing. Amusement is good only insofar as it prepares one for further useful occupation, for being seriously busy. So, "serious" means "related to action." Mere words can only be trivial.

Once university education turns toward occupation, toward preparation for useful employment, the tendency to suspect philosophy of being idle talk must accelerate. That is, to the degree that education becomes less liberal, the powerlessness of philosophy becomes more embarrassing, even to many who teach it. But this is, in one sense, a backwards way of seeing the situation. If the importance of the nonuseful had been a strongly held conviction in those who had been liberally educated, the reorientation of the university toward the practical should not have taken place. Even if we leave out of account those who are angered by philosophy, we must still face the conclusion that the defense of philosophy even to its potential friends is very difficult and that victory, if not impossible, is easily reversed.

Philosophy, certainly before its enemies but also even in front of its friends, has no defense *of its own*. The tendency to identify the serious and important with the immediately useful or with the directly useful is so strong that one seems to come close to doing violence to 'important' by saying that the most important is in fact the useless. Because philosophy is useless and because to demand a defense is to demand that it show its usefulness, philosophy is placed in an almost impossible position. It can have no "theoretical" defense because a defense must be in terms of practical value. And as it attempts a defense in terms of its usefulness for action, it is no longer philosophy.

Thus, the *Phaedo* and the *Discourse on Method* are rhetorical, mythical, or in Descartes's description, fables. And the rhetorical character of the *Apology* is undeniable. This is not to say that these works have no philosophical content. But they do show that in order to defend itself philosophy must use the precisely useful art of rhetoric; it must persuade, it must "sing charms."[20] Fables "exalt the mind and form the judgment."

One of the things that happens in these apologetic works is that the rhetorical and poetic are made difficult to distinguish from the theoretical, philosophical. This must happen if the defense is to succeed at all: the reader has to be persuaded. But the task of the reader who does not need this persuasion is to pursue the distinction between the philosophical and the rhetorical or poetic. At the end of the *Phaedo*, Crito cannot distinguish between philosophy and rhetoric. At the beginning, Simmias and Cebes cannot distinguish between philosophy and poetry or myth. Socrates's victory in the *Phaedo*, his "cure," is to save them from slipping into hatred of argument from this failure to distinguish.

What brings them so close to this slip is the urgency of the discussion. Only Socrates remains unchanged on the day he is to die. The others allow the fear of death to sway them, but Socrates holds fast to the life of argument. But the very strong presence of the fear of death points up the rhetorical nature of the dialogue. Phaedo's "report" of Socrates's drinking the poison without trembling or turning pale gives us an instance of persuasion by deed. As Socrates tells the Athenians at his trial, they value deeds more than words. If the assent to the arguments about immortality is based on the evidence of Socrates's certitude, then that assent is brought about by means of persuasion and not because of the truth of the arguments. And Socrates himself, in the course of defending them all against hatred of argument, says that he is not now being philosophical; rather, he is most eager to make what he says seem true to himself. But the others should care more for the truth than for Socrates and should oppose him with all their strength if they think he says something false.

Socrates's actions in the face of death are meant to persuade the hearers not only that these particular arguments are true but, more importantly, that philosophy is not "idle talk." This means that 'serious', as opposed to 'idle', is taken in the sense of having an effect on action. But, as I have tried to show, Phaedo's "report" is mythical. It is not literally true. Phaedo does in his story what Socrates did in the conversation: there is a blurring of the distinction between theoretical and moral excellence. This is the only way philosophy can defend itself against the charge that it is idle talk; it must present itself as having a good effect on action.

In the *Discourse on Method*, Descartes also presents us with a fable. And this fable too begins from a blurring of the distinction between theoretical and practical reason: *le bon sens* is deliberately ambiguous. But Descartes's defense is radically different from Socrates's and Phaedo's defense. Descartes begins from a blurring of the distinction between theoretical and practical but ends with the complete collapse of that distinction. In the *Phaedo*, on the other hand, the distinction is blurred but it is always preserved: separation of soul and body and rule of soul over body are presented as inseparable in the philosopher but as distinct modes of being.

Descartes attempts no defense of the theoretical as such. He completely takes the side of common opinion, which identifies the important with the useful.[21] His references to theoretical activity are in terms of his own private pleasure, harmless but not important. He speaks of the "extreme satisfaction" that he took in advancing in knowledge: "I did not believe that one could receive sweeter or more innocent satisfaction in this life" (AT 27; HR 98). So long as he is engaged in speculative science and the conduct of his own life, he has private pleasure but nothing to share with others and no obligation to write: "But as soon as I had acquired some general notions in physics . . . I believed that I could not keep them hidden away without greatly sinning against the law that obliges us to procure as best we can the common good of all men" (AT 61: HR 119). While he is spending his time on mathematical problems, he lives, in outward appearance, like "those who, having no other task but living sweet and innocent lives, endeavor to separate pleasures from vices and who, to enjoy their leisure without becoming bored, engage in all sorts of honorable diversions" (AT 30; HR 99).

Philosophy is nothing more than an "honorable diversion." It is innocent, harmless, and pleasant, but useless. And "being useful to no one is precisely to be worthless" (AT 66; HR 122). Descartes lives "in outward appearance" in a way no different from the man of leisure who passes the time in harmless, useless speculation. But in fact, his "occupation" is the most "solidly good and important" that man as man can engage in. Whether or not Descartes ultimately identifies the useful with the important, he takes this stand in the *Discourse*; he presents himself in this way in the work which is rhetorical and at the same time a fable.

At the very least, the impatience with philosophy as doubtful, as making no progress, seems undeniably genuine. This impatience is impatience with philosophy as "endless (futile) toil." It is quite common in modern philosophy and is usually accompanied by the determination to bring philosophy to an end, to break out of the cycle of weaving and unweaving, to have done with it once and for all. In the Letter of Dedication that precedes the *Meditations*, Descartes presents himself as refounding philosophy and then as immediately bringing it to an end: his proofs surpass in truth and obviousness the demonstrations of geometry. The questions concerning God and the soul should never have to be raised again.[22]

The impatience of modern philosophy with philosophy as endless toil reaches a kind of peak in Kant who gives it an articulation which expresses not only impatience but even embarrassment: "If [metaphysics] is a science, how does it happen that it cannot, like other sciences, obtain universal and permanent recognition? If not, how can it maintain its pretensions and keep the human understanding in suspense with hopes never ceasing, yet never fulfilled? Whether then we demonstrate our knowledge or our ignorance in this field, we must come once for all to a definite conclusion respecting the nature of this so-called science, which cannot possibly remain on its present footing. It seems almost ridiculous, while every other science is continually advancing, that in this, which pretends to be wisdom incarnate, for whose oracle everyone inquires, we should constantly move round the same spot, without gaining a single step."[23]

Modern philosophy (insofar as it is the search for certitude) is not content with "moving round the same spot." It wants to accomplish something. That is, it regards (all previous) philosophy as "idle talk." And so we must ask whether modern philosophy is itself philosophy at all. Or is this impatience and embarrassment due to an acceptance of the common opinion that philosophy has been "mere words," not serious, and not important? And is the breaking out of the cycle of "endless toil" really a rejection of philosophy as it begins in wonder and a move to assured foundations which are in fact theological presuppositions?

Weaving the Shroud

In the ancient self-understanding of philosophy, we can locate something that is at the heart of the activity of philosophy and that gives rise to the suspicion that philosophy is trivial. Aristotle specifically distinguishes philosophy from production by tracing the beginning of philosophy to wonder. Philosophy began only when the necessities of life had been secured: "All the sciences, indeed, are more necessary than this, but none is better." Philosophy is best because it is "free"; it alone exists "for its own sake." This escape from the necessary and the utilitarian as such, this freedom, is thought to be above the human: "Hence also the possession of it might be justly regarded as beyond human power; for in many ways human nature is in bondage, so that according to Simonides 'God alone can have this privilege,' and it is unfitting that man should not be content to seek the knowledge that is proper to him" (*Metaphysics* 982). The knowledge proper to man is useful knowledge.

Philosophy's escape from bondage, its god-like freedom, give it the appearance of play and of play simply. From the standpoint of production and of action in general, philosophy can only look like mere amusement. This appearance is due in part to the character of wonder itself. For wonder seems to be a kind of deliberate self-deception. The philosopher is puzzled by things that no one else is puzzled by. He seems to pretend that he does not know what he does in fact know, what he must surely know because *everyone* knows it. So, wonder seems to be a game, a diversion. And philosophy as an endless task never gets definitively beyond wonder: wonder is not simply a *temporal* beginning.

We are thus led back to the question of whether wonder is serious or not. Is the sudden appearance of falsehood, the doubt that is essential to wonder, serious or not? But what does serious mean here? Must it retain its connection with the useful?

There is, I think, an important difference between the doubt which lies at the beginning of the beginning of ancient philosophy and the doubt from which modern philosophy begins. Or at least this comparison can be made between Socrates and Descartes. Socrates's doubt is serious in a way that Descartes's doubt is not. This is why Descartes's doubt can be definitively overcome and Socrates's doubt cannot. Descartes makes a radical distinction between action and thought, a distinction of a kind and degree of completeness not made by Socrates: "I had for a long time noticed that as far as morals are concerned, it is sometimes necesssary to follow opinions that one knows to be quite uncertain, just as if they were indubitable . . . but because then I desired to be occupied with only the search for truth, I thought that it was necessary that I do exactly the contrary, and that I should reject as absolutely false all of that in which I could imagine the least doubt" (AT 31; HR 100-01).

Descartes's doubt is much like gambling. For a moment everything is thrown, deliberately, into a state of uncertainty. There is the pretense of risk, the momentary pleasure of uncertainty. But this uncertainty is quickly resolved and it is known all along that it will be resolved. Nothing is *really* at risk; the anxiety is self-induced so that it can be resolved. This kind of game emulates the frivolity of the gods.

But Descartes's distinction between action and thought also points up the element of self-deception which lies at the heart of action. Action requires that we pretend to know what we do not know. We must act as if an opinion is certain. This aspect of action is revealed in Socrates's questioning of politicians, poets, and craftsman. They think they know what they do not know. Socrates's decision to remain in prison is based on an "opinion" about what is best, but this opinion is not mistaken for knowledge. Philosophy has the advantage: "But, gentlemen of the jury, the good craftsmen seemed to me to have the same fault as the poets: each of them, because of his success at his craft, thought himself very wise in other *most important* pursuits and this error of theirs overshadowed the wisdom they had, so that I asked myself, on behalf of the oracle, whether I should prefer to be as I am, with neither their wisdom nor their ignorance, or to have both. The answer I gave myself and the oracle was that it was to my advantage to be as I am" (22d-e). [Emphasis added.]

Wonder paralyzes action. The urgency of action requires a decisiveness that is really a pretense of certitude. The distinterested spectator "does" nothing, but action is blind. And action, precisely the most urgent action, is against death. Philosophy begins as an escape from death and thus presupposes mortality. Then it returns to its conditions and becomes a meditation on death. Socrates's discourse about death on the day of his death is both a diversion from death, a passing the time while waiting to die, and an unblinking, steady looking at death: "I do not think that anyone who heard us now, even if he were a comic poet, would say that I am talking idly and speaking about things which do not concern me." The gods are frivolous and do not philosophize because they do not die and have no fear of death.

The *Phaedo* speaks of the immortality of the soul and even of the philosopher's soul in communion with the divine after death. But the *Phaedo* speaks mythically and is itself a myth. Descartes's *Discourse* seems to promise the conquest of death, the immortality of the body. But it is a fable. Neither of these works is literally true. The immortality promised in each is an imitation of *this* life. Augustine's *Confessions* is not a myth or a fable. But neither is it propositional speech: it is a prayer. And the immortality it promises is not an imitation.

What is being shown to us in the *Phaedo* is philosophy as a holding-action against the fear of death. This is philosophy as an "endless task," Penelope weaving and unweaving while she waits. The web is in fact a shroud (*Odyssey* XXIV.130-37). What is being shown to us in the *Discourse* is a certitude of existence grounded in the certitude of death, a seizing of power away from endless philosophical doubt and the unresolvable uncertainty of salvation. This is a breaking out of the circle of endless toil and taking a stand on one's own ground. But modern philosophy, insofar as it is the search for certitude, can only end in "the despair of one who has the misfortune to be in love with philosophy." *The Confessions* shows us both doubt and certitude: "I know that you are not in any way subject to violence, whereas I do not know in my own case what temptations I can and what I cannot resist." But "there is hope" (X.5). This hope is possible only because God is both unchanging and compassionate. The unchangeable Word was made flesh and let death be common to him and to us. It is in the prayer of Augustine that word and thing come closest.

Those who must escape the despair of modern philosophy find themselves returning to the beginning as if to home. There, Philosophy is allotted her sublimer task, the preparation for death. But for this task, she needs her own Muses. Philosophy herself cannot console.

Notes

Notes to the Introduction

1. Boethius, *On the Consolation of Philosophy,* trans. W. V. Cooper (Chicago: Gateway-Regnery, 1981) 8.

2. Boethius, 18.

3. Edmund Husserl, *Ideas,* trans. W. R. Boyce Gibson (London: Allen; New York: Humanities, 1976) 29.

4. Gilbert Ryle, "Systematically Misleading Expressions," *Proceedings of the Aristotelian Society,* New Series 32 (1932): 169-70.

Notes to Chapter I

Shortly after this book was in the publisher's hands, Ronna Burger's fine study *The Phaedo: A Platonic Labyrinth* (New Haven: Yale UP, 1984) appeared. I was pleased to find that she and I are in agreement on many aspects of the *Phaedo.* But because my own work had been completed before I saw her interpretation, specific references to her book do not appear in the notes.

1. Cf. Eva Brann, "The Offense of Socrates: A Re-reading of Plato's *Apology,*" *Interpretation: A Journal of Political Philosophy* 7.2 (1978) 17-18: "The conversations of the *Crito* and the *Phaedo* are the deliberately positive complements to the oratory of the *Apology.*"

2. The expression translated here as "about things which do not concern me" is *peri prosechonton.* The more literal sense of *prosechonton* (from *prosechō*) is 'present', or 'near at hand'. Within the immediate

221

context of the *Phaedo*, the "near at hand" is, of course, Socrates's own death. But if my interpretation of the *Phaedo* is correct, the Socratic practice of philosophy always presupposes death as "the near at hand."

3. On the distinction between plot and action, see John Jones, *On Aristotle and Greek Tragedy* (New York: Oxford UP, 1962) 24-29. Jones discusses plot as *muthos*.

4. As the very word *pathos* indicates, there is a sense in which the passions simply "happen" to us. See E. R. Dodds, *The Greeks and the Irrational* (Berkeley: U of California P, 1951) 185. The question is, of course, to what extent it is possible to resist and control the passions. Their elimination is not a real possibility.

5. For example, Aristotle, *Metaphysics* 983a, *Ethics* 1177b.

6. There is a further difficulty with this particular proof: "Let us see with regard to all these, whether it is true that they are all born or generated only from their opposites, in case they have opposites, as for instance, the noble is the opposite of the disgraceful." Plants and animals do *not* have opposites. They are, rather, obvious instances of "like from like."

7. Even A. E. Taylor, who insists that the *Phaedo* is an accurate report, admits that the three arguments do not hold up. See his *Plato: The Man and His Work* (Cleveland and New York: Meridian-World, 1956) 184. His reasons for this conclusion are, however, different from my own.

8. Dodds, *Irrational* 139: "The *psyche* is spoken of as the seat of courage, of passion, of pity, of anxiety, of animal appetite, but before Plato seldom if ever as the seat of reason; its range is broadly that of the Homeric *thumos*."

9. Indeed, the same passage from Homer, in which Odysseus speaks to his heart, is used by Socrates in the *Republic* to show that the soul does have parts (441b-c). See Dodds, *Irrational* 213.

10. The Socrates of the *Phaedo* does bring Oedipus to mind, for example, Socrates's bound legs. This comparison is especially vivid in the story of Socrates's turn away from natural philosophy: he is blinded and turns to words. The analysis of *Oedipus* that suggested this comparison to me is that of Bernard M. W. Knox, *Oedipus at Thebes* (New Haven:

Yale UP, 1957), espec. ch. 3. I will not pursue the comparison with Oedipus, but will limit myself to those heroes and poetic characters actually named in the dialogue.

11. The expression that Socrates uses to refer to Penelope's work is *anēnuton ergon*. *anēnuton* means both 'endless' and 'futile'. The distinction between "endless" and "futile" is crucial to my interpretation of the *Phaedo*. I will use "endless task" or "futile task" with reference to Penelope and to philosophy depending upon the context.

12. See Jacob Klein, *A Commentary on Plato's* Meno (Chapel Hill: U of North Carolina P, 1965) 126; and Kenneth Dorter, *Plato's* Phaedo: *An Interpretation* (Toronto: U of Toronto P, 1982) 5, 9.

13. Aristotle, *Meta.* 983a.

14. Ibid. 987b.

15. Compare Robert Leet Patterson, *Plato on Immortality* (University Park: Pennsylvania State UP, 1965) 88: "The famous tripartite division of the soul is figurative, not to be taken literally, and . . . concerns only the functions of the embodied soul; whereas, in itself, the soul is simple."

16. Compare Taylor 176: "There can be no doubt that Plato intends the reader to take the dialogue as an accurate record of the way in which Socrates spent his last hours on earth, and the topics on which he spoke with his intimate friends in the face of imminent death. . . . We are therefore bound to accept [Plato's] account of Socrates' conduct and conversation on the last day of his life as in all essentials historical, unless we are willing to suppose him capable of a conscious and deliberate misrepresentation recognizable as such by the very persons whom he indicates as the source of his narrative. This supposition is to my own mind quite incredible." My own view is in accordance with Klein, *Meno* 126: "The Socratic dialogue, entitled *Phaedo*, is from beginning to end a mythological mime." A myth cannot properly be characterized as a "conscious and deliberate misrepresentation."

17. Compare Dorter 136: "The question apparently represents so elementary a misunderstanding as to make us wonder why Plato inserted it at all, until one notices that Socrates' reply ends in a note of concern. . . . What might Socrates have thought potentially disturbing in this

naive contrast . . . ? Perhaps the fact (unnoticed by the questioner himself) that the hypothesis of forms is precisely unable to account for generation?"

18. Cf. E. R. Dodds, ed., Euripides, *Bacchae*, 2nd ed. (Oxford:
Clarendon, 1960) xliv.

19. Cf. Knox 127: "The search for truth, guided by intelligence,
produces knowledge. 'To know' (*oida, eidenai*) is a word built into the
very fabric of Oedipus' name and ironically emphasized in line after line
of the play."

20. Dodds, *Irrational* 69: [Plato carefully distinguished] "the Apol-
line mediumship which aims at knowledge, whether of the future or of the
hidden present, and the Dionysiac experience which is pursued either for
its own sake or as a means of mental healing."

21. See John Burnet's edition of the *Phaedo* (Oxford: Clarendon P,
1911) 53, note on 73b1. But compare Klein, *Meno* 127n55.

22. See Burnet 1: Pythagoras may have assumed the name of *philosophos* for the first time at Phlius, where the discussion between Phaedo
and Echecrates takes place; 19, note on 61d7: Simmias and Cebes are
pupils of Philolaus, one of the most distinguished of the later Pythagoreans. See also Klein, *Meno* 126-27.

23. Apollo, who dominates the *Phaedo*, is often represented with his
arm outstretched forming a right angle with his body. On the west pedi-
ment at Olympia, Apollo, with his arm thus extended, is represented as
controlling the fight between the drunken centaurs and the Lapiths. See
Bernard Ashmole, *Architect and Sculptor in Classical Greece,* Wrightsman Lectures 6 (New York: New York UP, 1972) 44 (and pl. 48): "[Apol-
lo] is not taking part in the fight: the movement of the arm is symbolic,
and he must be thought of as invisible to the combatants, but swaying the
conflict by his commanding gesture. The expression of the face is deliberately impassive: stern but calm." The centaurs are associated with Dionysus.

24. See Sir Thomas L. Heath, *The Thirteen Books of Euclid's* Elements, 2nd ed. (New York: Dover, 1956) 3: 1. The discovery of the
irrational is due to the Pythagoreans. Heath quotes the first scholium on
Book X of the *Elements*: "The first of the Pythagoreans who made public
the investigation of these matters perished in a shipwreck." The scholium
conjectures that the authors of this story "perhaps spoke allegorically,

hinting that everything irrational and formless is properly concealed and, if any soul should rashly invade this region of life and lay it open, it would be carried away into the sea of becoming and be overwhelmed by its unresting currents."

25. Cf. *Apology* 40a and *Phaedo* 68d.

26. Compare Patterson 113: "If a particular *begins* to participate in a Form, it must have existed *before* it begins so to do. But in the case of soul, this would mean that the soul existed *before* it was alive; and if life be an essential attribute of soul, this would involve a flat contradiction. Here, I think is the kernel of Plato's argument; and it seems to me that the argument is sound."

See also Klein, *Meno* 146: If one analyzes the argument in terms of different kinds of being, "the demonstration amounts to nothing." The soul, like three and odd and snow and fire could also be "extinguished" and perish at the approach of death.

27. See Klein *Meno* 137ff.: Klein discusses the claim that Socrates "does not separate clearly the downward and the upward motion of the *dianoia* and merges the meaning of 'supposition' with that of 'source' in his use of the term *hypothesis*. These ambiguities are tied to the general mythical character of the dialogue."

28. The "learning is recollection" argument moves up the divided line, skipping over mathematicals.

29. See *Theaetetus* 152e, 180-81a. The view that "all things are changing" is attributed to Protagoras and to all philosophers except Parmenides.

30. Klein, *Meno* 133: Klein identifies Socrates's turn to words with "exchanging questions and answers with himself and others."

31. See Burnet 91, note for 90c5: "The language of this sentence is just that which is elsewhere used of the followers of Heraclitus. . . . Now, in the *Theaetetus* Plato makes Socrates say that Protagoras justified his [Man is the measure of all things] by basing it on the doctrine of Heraclitus."

32. The term that is here translated as 'contentious' is *philoneikos*: love of victory is contrasted with love of wisdom, *philosophos*. The *antilogikoi* are lovers of victory, that is, "the contentious." See Richard Lewis Nettleship, *Lectures on the* Republic *of Plato* (1897; New York: St.

Martin's, 1968) 281: Dialectic as the search for truth is contrasted with "reasoning used merely for the purpose of gaining a victory in argument." The latter is *antilogikē*.

33. See *Theaetetus* 157b: "All things are changing" makes speech impossible.

34. Compare Dorter 94: "Socrates has here abandoned his usual philosophical role of a non-partisan examiner of things in favor of that of an advocate determined to make what he believes to be true *seem* as true as possible. He believes that there is a meaningful sense in which we can be called immortal and he is determined not only to give the proofs of this (which could be compatible also with a non-partisan role) but also to make it seem as likely as possible by unphilosophical means as well, and thus his love of victory here is *contrasted* with the disinterested love of wisdom, philosophy."

35. Klein, *Meno* 149, says of the third argument: "The conclusion of the *logos* was uncertain. The *logos* failed because its motion took, unexpectedly, a turn downwards, towards the level on which Death can be even perceived to 'approach' a man. On this level, the brave assertion of the soul's 'departure' becomes a manifestation of human excellence. That is what the *action* presented in the dialogue *shows*. . . . Human excellence itself demands that the effort of the *logos* continue. Immediately after Simmias and Cebes raise their gravest objections, Socrates enjoins his hearers forcefully to forgo forever any 'misology.'"

36. Phaedo uses the same word (here translated as 'uncomfortable') as Socrates uses at 91b to say that, even if the arguments are false, he will be less "unpleasant" for those present.

37. Cf. *Theaetetus* 169b: Here the metaphor for Socrates's activity is wrestling. Theodorus, in a playful exchange with Socrates, says: "You will not allow anyone who approaches you to depart until you have stripped him, and he has been compelled to try a fall with you in argument." Socrates's response is especially significant in terms of the imagery of the *Phaedo:* "There, Theodorus, you have hit off precisely the nature of my complaint; but I am even more pugnacious than the giants of old, for I have met with no end of heroes; many a Heracles, many a Theseus, mighty in words has broken my head; nevertheless I am always at this rough exercise, which inspires me like a passion."

38. See Klein, *Meno* 137: "Throughout the dialogue the invisibility

of *noēta* is related by way of a pun to Hades."

39. See Burnet: 66, note on 78d1.

40. Not the least of these difficulties is the whole question of "participation," which Phaedo, who is in no hurry, passes over in a few lines (102a-b).

41. See *Parmenides* 135b-c: If one were to deny the *eidē*, "he will have nothing toward which his *dianoia* may turn" and will thus utterly destroy the power of discoursing." See Klein, *Meno* 136.

42. Nettleship 281-82: "In what he says of reasoning, Plato, we observe, starts with the conception of certain objective differences of kind, differences which are there whether we recognize them or not; it is the function of true reasoning to discover and follow them. The differences embodied in ordinary language, the terms of which form a sort of classification of things which is in use amongst ordinary men, are often not real, or at least not the most real differences; they only go a little way in. True logic is therefore a perpetual antagonism to, and criticism of, the ordinary use of words and the ordinary manner of discussion; it is the knowing how to use words rightly, that is how to use them so that they shall conform not to the fancies of the speaker, but to the real distinctions of things, the real system of the world."

43. Cf. Klein, *Meno* 149: "But what he has to tell is not a new version of *peri physeōs historia* but a part of the *historia peri psychēs*: it is a topography or, more exactly, an oecography of the soul."

44. Cf. Aristotle, *De Anima* 413a20-30.

45. Klein, *Meno* 133: According to Klein, the "story of nature" responds to the question about cause "without discriminating between its possible meanings."

46. I use the term 'method' not in order to suggest that Socrates has a "method" in the modern, that is, Cartesian, sense, but because it is almost a transliteration from the Greek. Later, it will be useful to see how Socrates's audience is inclined to accept a "way" which seems similar to the procedure of mathematics.

47. Nettleship 286: "Dialectic, Plato tells us in the *Republic* (533b) is the method, and the only method, which attempts systematically to arrive at the definition of any given thing. The process of defining a given

thing is there (implicitly) represented as consisting in taking it away from, and holding it apart from, every other thing with which it is combined or to which it is akin. But this process of abstraction is only the other side of the process of concretion, which sees in what ways a given form or principle is in fact combined with others."

48. Compare Burnet 109, note on 100a2: Burnet claims that the word *erga* is equivalent to *onta* and *pragmata* and is used here because it is the standing opposite to *logoi*. My translation is eccentric but I think it may be justified by the wider context. Penelope is said to be at an endless (or futile) "work" (*ergon*). I take 'action' in the sense of 'work' but with the understanding that work need not be production. In the case of Penelope, the work is not, ultimately, production.

49. See Martin Heidegger, *The Basic Problems of Phenomenology*, trans. Albert Hofstadter (Bloomington: Indiana UP, 1982) 283-86 for his discussion of the good as the "sun," as "light." In the divided line of the *Republic* and in the allegory of the cave, the philosopher is able to look at the "sun." See Nettleship 238: "The line must be conceived of as beginning in total darkness at one end, and passing up to perfect light at the other." The light of the *Phaedo*, though, is a half-light. In addition to the eclipse metaphor, there are the specific references to dawn and dusk at the beginning and end of the dialogue. And in the hatred of argument section, Socrates says to Phaedo: "Call me to help you, as your Iolaus, while there is still light" (89c).

50. Dorter 94: The terms 'convince' and 'conviction' (*pistis*) appear more than fifty times in the dialogue.

51. Socrates uses the same word, which I have translated as "charms," here and at 77e. I have preferred 'charm' to 'incantation' because it seems to me that 'charm' allows for an ingredient of deception and even self-deception.

52. Compare Dorter 8: "Socrates is not a disinterested investigator here but the champion of a cause. He considers it of great importance to convince his audience, at an emotional as well as rational level, that man is not cut off from eternity and that death is therefore not to be feared, for he considers belief in a meaningful sense of immortality to be a basis for morality." Dorter takes "charms" as incantations for the sake of the child within us, that is, as meant for the emotions, in support of, but not essential to, the rational arguments. But see Klein, *Meno* 148: "Are not the *logoi* of the dialogue a series of such 'incantations'?"

53. James Craig La Drière, "Voice and Address," *Dictionary of World Literature*, ed. Joseph T. Shipley (Boston: The Writer, Inc., 1943) 617: "Since, as Aristotle observed (*Rhet.*, III, 1358a-b), the speaker's end in ordinary speech is in the addressee and the addressee therefore largely determines the character of the speech, each of these varieties of address has its inevitable effect upon the attitude of the speaker, which, reflected in the details of the speech, becomes either explicitly or implicitly a part of its meaning."

54. See *Theaetetus* 167e: Socrates emphasizes to Theodorus (also a mathematician) that mere disputation must be distinguished from dialectic.

55. Theaetetus, who has also been studying mathematics, begins by identifying wisdom and knowledge (145e). But his failure to define knowledge has perhaps made him wiser. Also, Theaetetus's first definition of knowledge ("knowledge is perception"), which seems so strange coming from a mathematician, makes sense if there is a preference for "sight" among mathematicians.

56. See Dorter 116: Dorter claims that the stages of Socrates's autobiography correspond to the divided line of the *Republic*.

57. See Nettleship 247: "Thus *eikasia* is conjecture, and the next stage, *pistis*, is so called because it contrasts with *eikasia* in regard to certitude. *Pistis* is a feeling of certainty." 249: "[*Dianoia*] was a word obviously applicable to the state of mind of which the scientific man is the best instance. . . . Plato gives us two characteristics of this state, without showing us the connexion between them: (a) It deals with sensible things, but it employs them as symbols of something which is not sensible; (b) it reasons from 'hypotheses.' Arithmetic and geometry are the most obvious types of *dianoia* in both these respects." 278: [Dialectic is] "the art or process of discourse, of asking questions and giving answers."

58. Klein, *Meno* 148: The arguments are incantations but are ineffective "unless supported by evidence more powerful than the evidence they by themselves are able to supply. This supporting evidence is there, in the very *drama* presented by Phaedo. We witness Socrates's behavior during the long hours before he drinks the draught. For it is not only the content of the *logoi*, their cogency and insufficiency, that mark the struggle with Fear of Death, it is also, and more so, the adult sobriety, the serenity in gravity and jest, imposed by Socrates on the conversation. *Philosophia* is present. We witness its *ergon*. And it is the final scene that

illuminates the working and failing, of that *logos* we were concerned about, the one prompted by Cebes' gravest objection. The friends surrounding Socrates are made to apprehend directly the slow and gradual approach of Death bringing cold and rigor in its wake."

59. See *Apology* 32a: Socrates introduces his claim and his proofs that he prefers death to doing injustice in this way: "I shall give you great proofs of this, not words but what you esteem, deeds." In this sense, the audience for the *Apology* and the audience in the *Phaedo* are alike.

60. Nettleship 147n1: "The state of 'right opinion' described in Books III and IV [of the *Republic*] with its attendant virtue of courage, i.e., tenacity, is a state of *pistis*."

61. See Burnet 1.

62. Cf. Dorter 89: "Phaedo is a representation of the possibility of release from bondage both in the literal sense and in the sense—present throughout the *Phaedo*—in which philosophy is a liberation from bondage to the physical. This latter 'liberation' is what must be accomplished if misology is to be overcome."

63. At the end of the *Apology*, Socrates brings to mind another instance of endless toil, that is, Sisyphus. In the course of discussing the two alternatives of what death might be, he tells what he would do in Hades: "And the greatest pleasure would be to pass my time in examining and investigating the people there, as I do those here, to find out who among them is wise and who thinks he is when he is not. What price would any of you pay, judges, to examine him who led the great army against Troy, or Odysseus, or Sisyphus . . . ?" (41b-c).

64. Plato is mentioned, that is, has Phaedo mention him, as an absent "third." Echecrates asks if Aristippus and Cleombrotus were there and Phaedo replies that they were "said to be in Aegina" (59c). Phaedo volunteers the information that Plato was absent. The theme of "three" and "third" is also played out at the end of the dialogue in a manner that is especially suggestive for the question of truth as it is raised in the dialogue. There are three coverings and three uncoverings, some explicit and some which are not specified but which are nevertheless made known. Phaedo says that he covered his face because of his tears (117d). He never says that he uncovered his face, but he must have, if he witnessed what followed. Socrates uncovered his face, which had been covered, in order to say his last words to Crito (118). And the attendant uncovers Socrates

after he is dead, implying that Socrates had re-covered himself after saying his last words. In this sequence of coverings and uncoverings, Phaedo's uncovering and Socrates's covering are "there" but not said. They are half-hidden.

65. With respect to this question, Brann writes 19-20: "For the first and last time Plato himself irrupts into his own work (38a). Socrates hears him raise his voice to suggest a sober and sensible money penalty, to subvert as it were, Socrates' own proud and derisory proposals. The suggestion is very much like a rebuke, and Socrates accepts it. It is as if in this work, in which Plato does not so much speak through Socrates but represents himself as spoken to by him, Plato is recording something he had heard in court which must have cast its shadow over the other dialogues, and so over the whole philosophical tradition. He has heard that *Socrates' activity is publicly indefensible.*"

Notes to Chapter II

1. See Peter Brown, *Augustine of Hippo: A Biography* (Berkeley and Los Angeles: U of California P, 1967) 175: "The *Confessions* are one of the few books of Augustine's where the title is significant. *Confessio* meant, for Augustine, 'accusation of oneself; praise of God' (*Serm.* 67,2). In this one word, he had summed up his attitude to the human condition."

2. Thomas Prufer, "Notes For a Reading of Augustine, *Confessions*, Book X," *Interpretation: A Journal of Political Philosophy* 10 (1982) 198: "The *Confessions* are a dialogue between one man and God; they have the form of solitary prayer, not of speech with others about being as it shows itself through city and cosmos."

3. Prufer 198-99: "Man is freely confessing abyss in the image and likeness of the freely revealing hidden God. . . . We turn away from the speaking and the listening, the seeing and the being seen of citizenship and become strangers to each other in the hidden thoughts of the heart, being witnessed by the eyes of the Lord and moved in imitation of the Word to a new rhetoric: public witness or *confessio* before others."

4. Michael B. Foster, *Mystery and Philosophy* (London: SCM Press, 1957) 41n1: "In the Greek mysteries the initiate was not allowed to reveal to the uninitiated what he had seen. This was profanation. The very word is derived from *mueō*, 'to keep the mouth shut'. Why is there not a similar

prohibition in the New Testament, but the Christian is told to preach the Gospel to every creature? Because to reveal or not to reveal is not held to be in his power, but in God's."

5. Robert J. O'Connell, *St. Augustine's Early Theory of Man, A.D. 386-391* (Cambridge: Harvard UP, 1968) 5: "Augustine could have drawn many of his Platonic ideas from translations of Plato's *Phaedo* and *Timaeus* which were extant and accessible."

6. The words that I am translating as "mock" and "laugh" and "scorn" are all compounds of *ridere*.

7. See Knox 67ff., 116, 147.

8. It is here that my own position on the question of Augustine's Platonism begins to work out, not as a taking of one side in the debate or as the reconciliation of both sides, but as a rejection of the terms in which the debate is carried on. My own view is that, as he writes *The Confessions*, Augustine is *not* a Platonist and is not unaware of or confused about what his own position is with respect to Platonism.

Henri-Irénée Marrou, *Saint Augustin et la fin de la culture antique*, 4th ed. (Paris: Boccard, 1958) xiii n1, claims that the two fundamental works on the question "What was the part of Christianity and of neo-Platonism in the conversion of Augustine?" are the rival theses of Alfaric and Boyer (the "debate" mentioned above). Charles Boyer, *Christianisme et Néo-Platonisme dans la Formation de Saint Augustin*, 2nd ed. (1920; Rome: Officium Libri Catholici, 1953), 172-73 maintains that "The supposed 'opposition' between Augustine's Christianity and neo-Platonism never seemed like one to him. In his mind the philosophical elements were fused with the Christian premises in an orderly and indivisible unity which received its form from the principle of authority." According to Boyer 81, the parallel between the Prologue of St. John and the neo-Platonic writings in Book Seven, Chapter Nine of *The Confessions* is Augustine's way of expressing how the Gospel *completes* Plotinus.

Prosper Alfaric, *L'Evolution intellectuelle de Saint Augustin* (Paris: Nourry, 1918), 361 maintains that, for Augustine, Catholicism was a simple form of neo-Platonism. In commenting on Book Seven of *The Confessions*, Alfaric is forced to regard Augustine's account as "most improbable" (378-79). Thus we must look to the writings from the time immediately after the conversion to see what Augustine *really* thought then (399). What this shows is that Augustine adopted Platonism before his adherence to Christianity and he became Christian only because he judged Christianity to conform to Platonism (380-81). Augustine underplays the role of neo-Platonism in his conversion account in *The Confessions* because he is now a bishop and monk. Even the "moral" conversion of Book Eight is due to the influence of neo-Platonism (395).

More recently, Robert J. O'Connell has argued that: "Augustine is . . . presenting us with an organic and progressive vision which may best be described as a Christian-Platonist religious philosophy" (*Early Theory* 48). In his *St. Augustine's* Confessions: *The Odyssey of Soul* (Cambridge: Harvard UP, 1969) 188, O'Connell poses the question "Platonism or Christianity?" and answers that: "The two, for Augustine, are substantially at one. The images of both must be made to alternate, then interweave and fuse until their fundamental identity is established."

Of *The Confessions* in particular O'Connell writes: "Augustine seems on the whole content that the series of reflections (done for the most part in his early writings) through which he attempted to elaborate a Plotinian synthesis of the biblical faith, has, by the time of the *Confessions,* issued in a satisfactory view of the soul, its origin, destiny, and place in the universe" (*Odyssey* 81). Augustine's confidence in Plotinus's neo-Platonism accounts for the failure of his thought in *The Confessions,* a failure due mainly to "a radically defective theory of sensibility" (*Early Theory* 288).

With respect to Augustine's "tendency" to "inform" all other sources with a selective Plotinianism, O'Connell interprets what is happening in Book Seven of *The Confessions*: "In the Seventh Book of the *Confessions,* Augustine introduces his account of his Platonic readings with an *apologia* (VII, 13-15) designed to show that he is clearly aware both of the agreement and occasional disagreement—*ibi legi . . . ibi non legi*—between the *platonici* and the Bible. This illustrates the method whereby he read both Plotinus and Scripture, from his earliest works up to and including the *Confessions*. What strikes him is the series of coincidences between the two. . . . When he discovers the same term or image in both Plotinus and the Bible, he is often rather too easily convinced that Plotinus' expression is saying much the same thing as a 'spiritual exegesis' of Scripture will yield. To ask whether he drew a term from the Bible, rather than from Plotinus, is to bring an either-or question to an intellectual development running on a different track entirely. Augustine's is far more a 'both-and' mind; what interests him is what he finds both in philosophy and in Scripture. What is important is the fresh creation that emerges once he has gone to work on such correspondences" (*Early Theory* 18). And, explicating Book Seven, Chapter Thirteen of *The Confessions,*

O'Connell writes: "He is about to present his view of reality at the time he conceived and composed the *Confessions*, a view that weaves biblical and Plotinian themes together into an amalgam resulting from a creative process which it took him years to bring to term" (*Odyssey* 75). O'Connell also claims that Augustine is unaware of a tension within his own thought: "The metaphysical underpinning of the *Confessions* represents a twilight struggle between an emanationism in which the soul can be thought of as 'fallen' and 'distant' from God and a fundamentally different view in which nothing can be 'distant' from the Omnipresent. It is doubtful, though, whether Augustine ever really gauged the terms and importance of that struggle" (*Early Theory* 284-85).

But, on the question of Augustine's infatuation with Platonism, see Brown 104: "The mood passed in a matter of a few months. . . . All this shows how a man's character is decided not only by what actually happens in his life, but, also, by what he refuses to allow to happen."

9. Compare Marrou (305), who claims that only neo-Platonism enabled Augustine to conceive of incorporeal being; his inability had been the great obstacle to his conversion. But see Jacques Maritain, "St. Augustine and St. Thomas Aquinas," *St. Augustine: His Age, Life, and Thought*, ed. M. C. D'Arcy et al. (1930; Cleveland and New York: Meridian-World, 1957) 207: Augustine "repeats and enforces the lesson that the soul will only succeed in finding God by a return and progression *ad intus*, by a withdrawal from things and the senses in order to dispose itself for ascents in its own inmost self. For it is a question of meeting, in the depths of the heart, him who abides there as in His temple, and in whom the heart can find rest, not indeed the God of philosophers and scholars, who may be attained without faith, nor even the God of theologians, who may be attained without charity, but the God of Saints, the life of our life offering Himself to us by grace and in love."

10. Although *expaveram* means that he had been 'terrified' or 'affrighted' (OLD), I have here followed both Warner and Watts in translating it as 'trembled.'

11. Marrou 233: From Augustine's perspective, there is no place for the world and the science which explores it. Augustine's philosophy is one of the soul and God.

12. Commenting on Augustine's account of his mother's death, O'Connell (*Odyssey* 108) cannot help contrasting Augustine and Plotinus: "And yet so different here from the Plotinus who, 'ashamed of being in the body . . . could never be induced to tell of his ancestry, his parent-

age, or his birthplace'. . . . There is defiance, but also a measure of discomfort in Augustine's divergence from Plotinus on this point. The latter is surely more consistent with his theory of man as soul, fallen into the body, when he refuses to speak of his parentage. Augustine feels this discrepancy keenly." This is how O'Connell must account for "what modern readers must be tempted to consider a wearisome and apparently pointless meditation on the sorrow that tormented him at her death."

Brown 27 cites Porphyry's *On the Life of Plotinus* to the effect that Plotinus "seemed ashamed of being in the body."

13. Both the Manichees and the philosophers understand the soul to be in some sense, or in some part, divine. See Brown 50: "The Manichees were austere men. They were recognizable, at the time, by their pale faces; and in modern literature, they have been presented as the purveyors of the bleakest pessimism. Yet they reserved this pessimism for only one side of themselves. They regarded the other side, their 'mind', their 'good soul', as quite untarnished: it was, quite literally, a crumb of the divine substance." See also O'Connell, *Early Theory* 31-33, 93, 100, 110. Foster's treatment of this question is exemplary: "For biblical theology God is beyond nature, and therefore all elements of nature, whether of human or of cosmic nature, are equal in not being God. There can be no hierarchy of divine and non-divine elements in nature nor in human nature. . . . The self dies in order to rise with Christ, whereas in Greek philosophy it becomes conscious of its own divinity" (91). On the question of the divinity of the soul for the Platonists, compare Brown 100. Brown attributes Augustine's realization that the soul is not divine to his reading of the Platonists.

14. Foster 46: "Repentance is consciousness of sin; perhaps we have thought of sin too much as moral, not enough as intellectual failure. Perhaps we have to recognize something like repentance in the sphere of the intellect. This would be alien to our main philosophical tradition which has inherited from Greek philosophy the belief in the divinity of the intellect."

15. Foster 83: "We are accustomed to take it for granted that prayer must be for objects which it lies outside our power to produce. This is obvious. Is it perhaps also the case that prayer must be for objects which it lies outside our power to *specify*?"

16. Prufer 197: "Aristotle's exclusion of action from the most primary sense of being, because of its excellence called 'god,' leaves a space of unsupported human action, the space of human possibility. . . . For

Augustine this space is taken up into a new sense of the divine: God does the unexpected and the unrepeatable; he is artificer and governor."

Robert E. Meagher, *An Introduction to St. Augustine* (New York: New York UP, 1978), 19: "In Greek understanding, human being is essentially defined by its relationship to divine being. The human activity of disclosure images, in word, the divine activity of disclosure." The divine activity itself is not creative (18). And there is no friendship of the human and the divine: they do not speak to each other in the act of contemplation.

17. Marrou 196: 'Astronomy' and 'astrology' were interchangeable terms.

18. Foster 41: "God in the Bible (1) is hidden, in contrast to the 'unhiddenness' of Being for Greek philosophy; (2) he makes himself known, but by an act of will, or grace: it is not his nature to be unhidden."

19. See Erich Przywara, "St. Augustine and the Modern World," trans. E. I. Watkins, M. C. D'Arcy et al., *St. Augustine: His Age, Life, and Thought* (1930; Cleveland and New York: Meridian-World, 1957), 278: Przywara contrasts Kierkegaard's "negative concupiscence, the reverence which 'maintains its distance' from God in order to 'safeguard self,'" with Augustine's chaste fear. "Augustine, therefore, says without hesitation that 'the fear lest He come' is the fear of 'the adulterous woman' . . . whereas the sole 'fear of the chaste woman' is the 'fear lest He forsake her.' The fear of which God approves is chaste fear, the fear which is aware of the presence of God within, but for that very reason utters its awestruck *'non sum dignus.'* It is a 'fear lest He delay,' as it is a 'fear lest He depart,' because love's knowledge of the infinite distance between God and man always trembles with the knowledge that God in no way comes within the scope of man's calculation, far less can be held in his grasp." Przywara also contrasts the Hegelian "lust of the intellect" (277), the lust "to make God captive in the concept, and thus to manipulate Him," with Augustine's chaste love. To love chastely means that man should love God alone and for His own sake; he quotes Augustine: "'God wishes to be loved disinterestedly, that is to be loved chastely, not to be loved because He gives something besides Himself but because He gives Himself' (*Enarr. in Psalm.*, LII, viii.)." But Augustine "also protests against an 'absorption of God' within the boundary of the subject: 'Love God disinterestedly, grudge Him to none.'" Augustine thereby deliberately emphasizes the disinterested worship of divine praise. "In other words, for Augustine 'chaste love' is not only pure in the sense that God is its

exclusive object; it is also pure because it is the reverend awe which worships a transcendent Deity. It is the 'chaste love' of the 'disinterested worship' expressed by the psalmist's words, 'I will freely sacrifice to Thee.'"

Meagher 198 refers to the passage in *De Trinitate* 12.9.14 where Augustine speaks of "the fornication of fantasy."

20. Augustine's story of the theft of the pears may have its significance in the parallel with Genesis: "So all men who put themselves far from you and set themselves up against you, are in fact attempting awkwardly to be like you" (II.6).

21. Augustine even prefers to think that God is changeable than to think that he himself is not what God is. So the first important step of the change that takes place in Book Seven is to become certain of God's unchangeability (chapters 2, 3, 4).

22. See Robert Sokolowski, *The God of Faith and Reason: Foundations of Christian Theology* (Notre Dame, Ind.: Notre Dame UP, 1982) 84-5.

23. Brown 179: "It was most unusual to insist, as Augustine does, that no man could ever sufficiently search his own heart. . . . Augustine's sense of the dangers of identifying himself exclusively with his conscious good intentions, underlies the refrain that so shocked Pelagius: 'command what You wish, but give what You command.' (*Conf.*X,29). For 'I cannot easily gather myself together so as to be more clean from this particular infection: I greatly fear my hidden parts, which Your eyes know, but not mine. . . . Behold, I see myself in You, my truth . . . but whether I may be like this, I just do not know. . . . I beseech You, God, to show my full self to myself.' (*Conf.*X,37)."

24. Brown 102-03: The pagan Platonists of Augustine's time regarded the Christian myth of redemption as a barbarous innovation. But "these differences . . . were only symptoms of an even more profound tension over an issue that coincided only partially with the confessional division between pagan and Christian. The issue was one of spiritual autonomy: to what extent could a man be expected to work out his own salvation by his own power alone? Plotinus had been definite on this issue: his last words had been, 'I am striving to give back the Divine in myself to the Divine in the All.' . . . The Platonists had always felt able to offer a vision of God that a man might gain for himself, by himself, through the unaided rational 'ascent' of his mind to the realm of ideas."

25. Brown 150: "Like a single cloud that grows to darken the whole sky, this sense of the force of past habit deepens in Augustine. *Consuetudo carnalis*, 'a force of habit directed towards the ways of the flesh,' will stand like a black bar, framing his description of every contemplative experience in the *Confessions.*"

Brown 147 quotes Augustine, "'Whoever thinks that in this mortal life a man may so disperse the mists of bodily and carnal imaginings as to possess the unclouded light of changeless truth, and to cleave to it with the unswerving constancy of a spirit wholly estranged from the common ways of life—he understands neither What he seeks, nor who he is who seeks it.' (*de cons. evang.* IV,x,20)"

26. Meagher claims (292) that the human word is not essentially creative but disclosive.

27. O'Connell (*Early Theory* 68) translates *manu veritate* as "truth-hand" and characterizes the expression as "sheer juxtaposition of two ablatives, one correcting the other almost to the point of cancellation, almost to the strain and rupture Plotinus produces when he calmly suggests we 'now eliminate the corporeal mass of the hand'—and thereby shatters his image before our gaze." My own account is meant to show that Augustine's use of corporeal and spatial terms to talk about God is a making of images and a shattering of them, a kind of breaking of idols. But the particular image is chosen very deliberately to suggest something. In this case, it seems to me that the image of the hand suggests the link between God's "making" and truth. O'Connell however, in commenting on Augustine's imagery, claims that "most of the linkages here were forged in the depths of Augustine's poetic unconscious." (69).

Brown 37: "The great advantage of the education Augustine received was that within its narrow limits, it was perfectionist. The aim was to measure up to the timeless perfection of an ancient classic. . . . Every word, every turn of phrase of these few classics, therefore, was significant. The writer did not merely write: he 'wove' his discourse (*Conf.* XII,xxvi,36); he was a man who had weighed the precise meaning of every word (*de beata vita*,iv,31)."

28. Heidegger, *Basic Problems,* e.g., 98, 101, 102, 105. In discussing the "Thesis of Medieval Ontology," Heidegger does not distinguish between creation and production. But this is precisely the crucial distinction.

Cf. Sokolowski 33: "The most fundamental thing we come to in Christianity, the distinction between the world and God, is appreciated as not being the most fundamental thing after all, because one of the terms of the distinction, God, is more fundamental than the distinction itself. In Christian faith, God is understood not only to have created the world, but to have permitted the distinction between himself and the world to occur. He is not established as God by the distinction (whereas pagan gods are established by being different than other things). No distinction made within the horizon of the world is like this, and therefore the act of creation cannot be understood in terms of any action or any relationship that exists in the world."

29. Meagher 25: "Human being's controlling speech and the world of its making are quite provisional. Whatever human being names and makes of things, that is what they are for human being; whereas, whatever God names and makes of things, that is what they are, simply." Meagher (197) quotes *De Trinitate* 12.9.14: "'For the soul, loving its own power, slips from what is whole and common to what is partial and private.'" Meagher comments that "Any . . . personal rendering of the whole must be forced and reinforced upon the whole, which means that power replaces wisdom as definitive of human being's posture toward the whole." 198: "Within the context of a life of power, the mind's word is purely creative, creative of a would-be whole and of a particular life within that whole, both of which are uniquely one's own." Of a life in accordance with one's own will, Meagher (200) claims: "Such a word cannot be spoken in public. Such a life has no public or communal significance."

30. Brown 167 quotes Dodds, "Augustine's *Confessions*," *Hibbert Journal* 26 (1927-28) 471: "Plotinus never gossiped with the One as Augustine gossips in the *Confessions*." See also Marrou 176. Meagher 284: "Aristotle and Augustine concur that human being's highest and most proper work belongs to mind's contemplative capacity, the mind's capacity for true beholding. Aristotle sees the worthiest object of pure beholding to be the first being, with which there can be no fellowship, from which there is no response to our devotion; for this God is too remote (*polu choristhentos*) from human being" (*Nicomachean Ethics* 8.7). Prufer 197: "Augustine is paradigmatic for the theological form of mind in contrast to the Greek philosophical form."

31. Brown 176: "But if denial of guilt was the first enemy, self-reliance was the last. The massive autonomy of Plotinus is now thrown into the sharpest relief by Augustine's new preoccupation with confession." Przywara 258: For Augustine "the only right path for the soul is

fundamentally the path of decisive self-surrender to God, not a forcing of God but the worship of Him as one 'always greater'; above all, no subjective state of any kind whatsoever, but the 'praise of God' as 'the highest work of man.' . . . It is the radical transcendence of 'clearness' 'evidence,' as a subjective principle in 'evident knowledge of the Divine Majesty.'" For Augustine (263), "there is no anxious search for assurance. . . . There is here no anxiety, and this is but the logic of the Catholic denial of an absolute assurance of salvation, to know in what state I may really be. I must forget myself completely in the praise of God." "The characteristic tendency of Lutheranism to make everything centre in the salvation of man, soteriological anthropocentrism, is overcome by the fundamental Catholic orientation, God in Himself and His glory" (272).

32. Brown 164-65: "The *Confessions* . . . is not a book of reminiscences. They are an anxious turning to the past. The note of urgency is unmistakable. . . . Death and disillusionment . . . stood between Augustine and his rich past."

Notes to Chapter III

1. Richard Kennington, "René Descartes," *History of Political Philosophy*, eds. Leo Strauss and Joseph Cropsey (Chicago: Rand, 1963) 385: "The form of the *Discourse* is . . . that of an autiobiography of the first and final founder of philosophy."

2. See Descartes, *Œuvres philosophiques*, ed. Ferdinand Alquié (Paris: Garnier, 1963), I, 568nl.

3. Etienne Gilson, Texte et Commentaire, Descartes, *Discours de la Méthode* (Paris: Vrin, 1947) 111–12: Gilson notes that fables may have a moral significance. But, in Descartes's characterization of the *Discourse* itself as a fable, Gilson sees no reservation about the work as a straightforward account of events (99).

4. Desmond M. Clarke, *Descartes' Philosophy of Science* (University Park: Pennsylvania State UP, 1982) 180–81, claims that the *Discourse* was not written as a "coherent or integrated account of scientific mehtod." Rather, it was patched together from earlier writings. "If one assumes that the *Discourse* was compiled in some such way, then it is possible to explain the inconsistencies and repetitions in the text, and to give a plausible account of the disparity between the method outlined in

Part II and the more hypothetical method proposed in Part VI." Clarke (186–92) reads the *Discourse* as the preface to the *Essays*, that is, as dealing with science. This is clear in his discussion of "seeds of truth," which I interpret as moral natural law.

Cf. J.–R. Armogathe, *Theologia Cartesiana: L'Explication physique de L'Eucharistie chez Descartes et dom Desgabets,* International Archives of the History of Ideas 84 (The Hague: Nijhoff, 1977) 48: The metaphysics of the *Discourse* is merely auxiliary to the physics.

5. See Giambattista Vico, *The Autobiography of Giambattista Vico,* trans. Max Harold Fisch and Thomas Goddard Bergin (Ithaca: Cornell UP, 1944) 113: "We shall not feign here what René Descartes craftily feigned as to the method of his studies simply in order to exalt his own philosophy and mathematics and degrade all the other studies included in *divine* and human erudition. Rather, with the candor proper to a historian, we shall narrate plainly and step by step the entire series of Vico's studies, in order that the proper and *natural causes* of his particular development as a man of letters may be known." [Emphasis added.]

6. The word 'comedy' could mean any kind of drama, not necessarily connected with the comedy of laughter, but not excluding it either. Descartes may be suggesting here a kind of amused contemplation.

7. My discussion of the passions is limited to what Descartes says in the *Discourse*. But it is noteworthy that so much emphasis is placed on wonder and generosity in *The Passions of the Soul*. Kennington 381: "In place of that wonder at the fundamental perplexities that confront the mind that was the beginning of philosophy for the ancients, Descartes substitutes astonishment at a hitherto undreamed-of possibility of human 'creativity' that will banish wonder."

8. Gilson, Commentaire 85: Descartes often transposes the moral method of Stoicism into a scientific method.

9. Gilson, Commentaire 96: Gilson takes the phrase "purement hommes" to mean "simplement hommes," that is, man without any extraordinary assistance from heaven.

10. Gilson, "Augustinian Metaphysics" 295: Augustine, like Descartes, had doubted, but "not only as a matter of method and exercise, but really and painfully." And later (303), Augustine begins from doubt, but his doubt is neither methodical and intentional nor a pretense, like the doubt of Descartes.

11. Kennington 385: The third rhetorical feature of the *Discourse,* "its popularization of philosophy, becomes intelligible when one learns in what sense the founder is in need of non-philosophers." 380: "Only in the *Discourse on Method* (1637) does Descartes offer an account of the beginning and end of his philosophy, of all the parts and their true order. Nevertheless, this writing is customarily depreciated today because of its popular character. Yet precisely its popular rhetoric is the first sign that the *Discourse* alone treats the peculiar difficulty of Descartes' supreme goal: the 'perfect moral science' will come into full existence only by an unprecedented political cooperation between philosophy and the public."

12. See Descartes, *OEuvres Philosophiques* I, 649n3.

13. Gilson, Commentaire 252: With respect to Descartes's claim that the Stoics rivaled their gods in happiness, Gilson takes this as a reference to the Stoic claim that the wise man is as happy as God himself.

Julien-Eymard d'Angers, "Sénèque, Epictète et le Stoïcisme dans l'œuvre de René Descartes," *Revue de Théologie et de Philosophie* 3ème ser. 4 (1954) 176: In the works which follow the *Discourse,* Descartes does not accuse the Stoics of pride, even though this accusation was common among Christians, who attributed the errors of the Stoics to their pride.

Bernard Roland-Gosselin, "St. Augustine's System of Morals," *St. Augustine: His Age, Life, and Thought,* eds. M. C. D'Arcy et al. (1930; Cleveland and New York: Meridian-World, 1957), 230–31: "The Stoics . . . exalted the human will to such a pitch as to turn it into a divine power. . . . Augustine had no difficulty in showing that the wisdom of the Stoics is unhuman through being superhuman."

14. Jean-Marie Beyssade, *La Philosophie Première de Descartes: Le Temps et la coh*érence de la métaphysique (Paris: Flammarion, 1979) 178: Beyssade understands Descartes in the *Discourse* as holding the view of the will expressed in the provisional moral code, that is, the will only desires what the understanding presents as possible.

15. Gilson, Commentaire 246–47: Commenting on Descartes's statement that *only* our thoughts are in our power, Gilson interprets this to mean that external events are in our power only to the extent that they depend on our thought. In support of his interpretation, Gilson quotes from a letter to Mersenne of December 3, 1640, in which Descartes responds to Mersenne's question concerning the view of Saint Augustine

and Saint Ambrose that our hearts and our thoughts are not in our power. Descartes says that he agrees with them with respect to the sensitive part of the soul. He denies that he has said that all our thoughts are in our power but only that, if there is anything absolutely in our power, it is our thoughts. The will is not absolute with respect to power over corporeal things.

16. There is no "Christian physics." Any controversy with the Church into which Descartes might be drawn would have to be due ultimately to implications of his physics for Christian beliefs about God and the soul.

17. See Thomas Aquinas, *Summa Theologica* 1.2, q.95, a.2.

18. See Thomas Aquinas, *Summa* 1.2, q.91, a.2. Also see q.94, a.4: "The practical reason . . . deals with contingent matters, in which are human actions: and therefore, although there is a certain necessity in the general principles, the more one descends to specific details, the more one encounters defects."

19. Kennington 386: "The fruits of the tree of knowledge will undo the consequences of the Fall in the garden, or, more precisely, will effectively deny its truth. The *Discourse* culminates then in a promise of a heaven on earth."

20. Kennington 386: This law is "the only categorical obligation ever asserted by Descartes."

21. Kennington 384: Descartes agrees "with the classic view that opinion is the element of society, the binding ligament that gives it unity and motion. Publication of his private reform would necessarily raise the question, therefore, of whether he intended a public reformation: again he agrees with the classics that philosophic questioning when made publicly tends to erode the element of opinion in which society lives." Since "the schools are the authoritative repository of the opinions that are the 'foundations' of nations, Descartes' reformation is indeed to be public."

22. Foster 61: "The note which has recurred through all these descriptions of modern science is universal humanism. Scientific language is technical, an instrument of man; scientific evidence is communicable to man as man; the experimental method of science is a method of commanding nature to answer man's questions; the aim of modern science is man's mastery over nature."

23. Jacob Klein, *Greek Mathematical Thought and the Origin of Algebra,* trans. Eva Brann (Cambridge and London: MIT P, 1968) 119: Of the "new science" whose foundations were laid in the sixteenth and seventeenth centuries, Klein writes: "Here the 'natural' foundations are replaced by a *science already in existence,* whose 'knowledge' is mocked—but whose place within human life as a whole is placed beyond all doubt. *Scientia* herself appears as an inalienable human good, which may indeed become debased and distorted, but whose worth is beyond question. On the basis of this science, whose fundamental claim to validity is recognized, the edifice of the 'new' science is now erected, but erected *in deliberate opposition to the concepts and methods* of the former."

120: "Now that which especially characterizes the 'new' science and influences its development is *the conception which it has of its own activity.* It conceives of itself as again taking up and further developing Greek science, i.e., as a recovery and elaboration of 'natural' cognition. It sees itself not only as the science *of* nature, but as a *'natural'* science—in opposition to *school* science. Whereas the 'naturalness' of Greek science is determined precisely by the fact that it arises out of 'natural' foundations, so that it is defined at the same time in terms of its distinction from, and its origin in, those foundations, the 'naturalness' of modern science is an expression of its *polemical attitude toward school science.* This special posture of the 'new' science fundamentally defines its horizon, delimits its methods, its general structure, and, most important, determines the conceptual character of its concepts."

Jean-Luc Marion, *Sur la theologie blanche de Descartes: Analogie, création des vérités éternelles et fondement,* Philosophie d'aujourd'hui (Paris: PUF, 1981) 18: Marion believes that Descartes's metaphysics, which excludes revealed theology from its domain, is actually always secretly governed or at least concerned with it. Armogathe 54: Despite his desire to avoid controversy, Descartes recognizes the relevance of his principles to theology.

24. The specific nature of what I here call "compassion" is what Descartes calls "*générosité.*" I refer to it as compassion because of the connections and contrasts with Augustine's God, connections and contrasts that I will develop in the last chapter. Kennington 381–82: "Descartes replaced the distinction made by the ancients between the passions and the virtues with the distinction between good and bad passions." The

supreme passion is *générosité*. Geneviéve Rodis–Lewis, *La Morale de Descartes*, Initiation philosophique (Paris: PUF, 1957) 85: Générosité corresponds to magnanimity. 88: The generous man is completely master of himself and combines in himself the independence of the Stoic wise man and a passionate sensitivity. 82: The third rule of the provisional moral code finds a deeper significance as an expression of generosity. True generosity depends on the will, on firmness of resulution.

25. Donald Phillip Verene, "Technological Desire," *Research in Philosophy and Technology* 7 (1984) 105–11: Verene discusses the claim that "the infatuation with technique is based on the phenomenon of human desire."

26. Foster 54: "Modern scientific knowledge requires for its expression a univocal language. . . . Scientific language is technical language. This means it is like an instrument in the hands of the user. Words are 'instruments' which men use, and of which the user can determine the meaning. Modern science is the expression of a distinctive attitude to nature. In contrast to contemplation, it expresses an attitude of human mastery not of submission."

27. See Klein, *Algebra* 202–03.

28. Rodis-Lewis 97.

Notes to Chapter IV

1. Werner Jaeger, *Aristotle: Fundamentals of the History of His Development*, trans. Richard Robinson, 2nd ed. (Oxford: Clarendon, 1948) 432: Plato's pupil Heraclides said that "Pythagoras was the first to use the words 'philosophy' and 'philosopher' and to explain the nature of the philosopher by means of the famous comparison with the 'pure' spectators of the games at Olympia."

2. Jean-Jacques Rousseau, *The First and Second Discourses*, trans. Roger and Judith R. Masters (New York: St. Martin's, 1964) 132.

3. Desiderius Erasmus, *The Praise of Folly*, trans. Clarence H. Miller (New Haven and London: Yale UP, 1979) 45: Folly speaks of the Stoic, Seneca, who removed all emotion from his wiseman: "But by doing this he is left with something that cannot even be called human; he *fabricates*

some new sort of divinity that has never existed and never will." 45–46: Of the Stoic philosophers, Folly says, "Who would not flee in horror from such a man, as he would from a monster or a ghost—a man who is completely deaf to all human sentiment, who is untouched by emotion, no more moved by love or pity than 'a chunk of flint or a mountain crag.'" Benedict de Spinoza, *The Ethics, The Chief Works of Spinoza*, trans. R. H. M. Elwes, 2 vols. (New York: Dover, 1955) 2: 221–22: "He who is moved to help others neither by reason nor by compassion, is rightly styled inhuman, for he seems unlike a man" (Porposition L).

4. Boethius 4: Describing philosophy's appearance to him, Boethius says that: "One could but doubt her varying stature, for at one moment she repressed it to the common measure of a man, at another she seemed to touch with her crown the very heavens: and when she had raised higher her head, it pierced even the sky and baffled the sight of those who would look upon it."

5. See *Apology* 31b.

6. See Edmund Husserl, "Philosophy and the Crisis of European Humanity," *The Crisis of European Sciences and Transcendental Phenomenology*, trans. David Carr, Studies in Phenomenology and Existential Philosophy (Evanston: Northwestern UP, 1970) 285: Husserl contrasts the mythical–practical attitude with the "theoretical" attitude, the attitude of wonder. "Man becomes gripped by the passion of a world-view and world-knowledge that turns away from all practical interests and, within the closed sphere of its cognitive activity, in the times devoted to it, strives for and achieves nothing but pure *theoria*. In other words, man becomes a nonparticipating spectator, surveyor of the world; he becomes a philosopher."

In explaining the historical origin of philosophy in the pre-Socratics, Husserl analyzes the movement from mere wonder (a variant of curiosity) to *theoria* (the fully disinterested seeing of the world). "Incipient theoretical interest, as *thaumazein*, is obviously a variant of curiosity, which has its original place in natural life as an intrusion into the course of 'serious living', either as a result of originally developed life-interests or as a playful looking-about when one's quite immediate vital needs are satisfied or when working hours are over."

292: Husserl argues that philosophy must begin as cosmology: "Natural man (let us consider him as man in the prephilosophical period) is directed toward the world in all his concerns and activities. The field of his life and his work is the surrounding world spread out spatio-temporally around him, of which he counts himself a part. This remains the case in the theoretical attitude, which at first can be nothing other than that of the nonparticipating spectator of the world, whereby the world loses its mythical character. Philosophy sees in the world the universe of what is, and the world becomes the objective world as opposed to representations of the world, those which vary according to nation or individual subject; thus truth becomes objective truth. In this way philosophy begins as cosmology." Yet Socrates, in the *Theaetetus* (174b) claims that the story of Thales is equally applicable to *all* philosophers.

Jaeger 431: Jaeger says of Socrates's comments on the Thales story in the *Theaetetus*, "It is strange that this praise of geometry and astronomy is here sung by Socrates, whom Plato had once in the *Apology* made to say that of such high matters he understood neither much nor little but just precisely nothing."

7. Foster 34: "The special character of Greek philosophy is that it continued in wonder. Its end was *'theoria'*, wondering contemplation of the divine, in which mystery was not dispelled but more fully revealed. Whereas the end of some modern philosophy, like that of modern science but pursued in a different way, is to put us out of wonder."

8. Heidegger, *"Antigone"* 100.

9. Przywara 257: "From Kant to Hegel speculation follows the road of that forceful Lutheran defiance which seeks to take the world and God by storm. It is evident that the goal to which this path between Scylla and Charybdis leads is but the return in an aggravated form of that confusion which the method of 'assurance' attempted to overcome—uncertainty of life, a restless dissatisfied motion hither and thither as Descartes depicts it so vividly in the opening pages of his *Discours de la Méthode.* . . . More terribly true than he knew had now proved Descartes's description of man: 'I am, as it were a mean between God and nothingness' willing to be God, and being nothing." 264: "The Cartesian 'clear and distinct' expresses almost verbally the tendency which was to give birth in the modern world to what is known as the Enlightenment and Classicism." Foster 22 and n3: Contemporary analytic philosophy "represents a tradition which has dominated European philosophy since the Renaissance." Foster claims (n3) that "Mystery is excluded by Descartes' doctrine of 'clear and distinct perception,' since this implies that anyone who understands a thing at all understands it wholly."

Heidegger and some thinkers in the existentialist tradition do understand themselves as rejecting the modern obsession with certitude. They also are concerned with death and can be said to meditate on death. Whether their kinds of meditation are *preparation* for death is another question.

10. Przywara 254–55: After discussing similarities between Descartes and Augustine, Przywara discusses what he takes to be of "decisive significance." Descartes's search for assurance, especially as displayed in the *Meditations,* "is a search for assurance against malicious deceptions from without, includes indeed a lengthy consideration of the possibilities of such deception on the part of God, or at least of some demonic power. That is to say, we recognize every feature of that terrified longing for assurance characteristic of Luther's religious attitude, here transferred to the domain of philosophy and therefore producing the same results, the same exclusive trust in the individual's interior experience: 'the man who walks alone,' 'to study . . . in myself.' That which is unconsumed in the furnace of doubt is not truth in itself, but 'conceiving very clearly and very distinctly,' that is to say, subjective 'certitude . . . in the understanding alone when it possesses clear perceptions.' "

Maritain 211: Maritain claims that "philosophical Augustinianism seems to be naturally allied to an exaggerated philosophism, obvious in the Cartesian school." The *Meditations* "resemble the *De Trinitate* as much as a dark-room does the eye of a poet. Descartes's 'courageous and attractive' spiritualism, the Cartesian *cogito* (which has quite another range than the *si fallor sum*), the ontological argument, the theory of idea-pictures, of thought-substance . . . far from being authentic forms of Augustinian spiritualism, these are merely the residues of its rational disaggregation."

Gilson, "Future" 304: "The *sum* of St. Augustine affirms at one stroke the existence of man—not only of one half of him, destined to struggle desperately to rejoin the other half." Prufer 199–200: Prufer speaks of Cartesian solitary mind as a "residue after the truncation and destruction of the theology which was the condition of the genesis of this form of mind. . . . Uprooted from eternal and necessary self-sufficient mind enjoying goodness, both freedom from natures and power over natures, which could be otherwise, and the glory befitting generosity and benevolence toward those who would be nothing without them, are monstrous fictions."

11. My claim does not depend upon Descartes's having read St. Augustine and *The Confessions* in particular. On the question of the extent of Augustine's influence on Descartes, see Marion 16. Marion claims that Descartes did read things which he denies having read ("la coquetterie d'auteur"). He hypothesizes that Descartes had a much more precise knowledge of the medieval tradition than he admits. Cf. Geneviève Lewis, "Augustinisme et cartésianisme," *Augustinus Magister*, Congrès International Augustinien, 2 vols. (Paris: Etudes Augustiniennes, 1954) 2:1087. Gilson, "Future" 293: "Whether Descartes did or did not study St. Augustine, the fact remains that his method condemned him to follow in metaphysics the road of St. Augustine. . . . The converse is not true . . . the metaphysic of St. Augustine does not condemn the Augustinian to follow the Cartesian method."

12. Foster 33: "The revelation (unveiling) of the divine to human contemplation: this is what the Greek mystery religions were, and this is what Greek philosophy also was." 34-35: For Greek philosophy, "contemplation was the union of the divine element in man with the divine nature of the universe. . . . It is different from the Christian theology of Creation, according to which God *created* the world and man, so that both nature and man are creatures and not divine." Jaeger 451: Dicaearchus criticized Aristotle's notion of God as having no other object of thought than himself: "Since even a man who was entirely occupied in the contemplation of himself would be blamed as a heartless being, the idea of a God who contemplates himself is absurd." Jaeger cites Dicaearchus as an instance of the claim that the essence of man is in action not contemplation. Meagher 27: "In the modern tradition, the human word, in its desires, aspirations, and assertions, remains nevertheless faithful to its ancient roots in that the human word remains defined by the divine word, understood as disclosive light and as creative power. What is definitively modern is the claim and the experience of the identity of the human word and the divine word. The tradition of modern Western thinking has single-mindedly and single-heartedly meditated upon human being, appropriating to those reflections all the ancient divine names and powers." According to Meagher, "characteristically modern thinking is defined by its atheism."

13. Thomas Aquinas, *Summa* 1 q.1, a.4.

14. AT 6: 325.

15. Foster 54: "Modern scientific knowledge requires for its expression a univocal language. . . . Scientific language is technical language. This means it is like an instrument in the hands of the user. Words are 'instruments' which men use, and of which the user can determine the meaning. Modern science is the expression of a distinctive attitude to nature. In contrast to contemplation, it expresses an attitude of human mastery not of submission."

16. Marion 411: The infinite will makes God and man alike. But free will does not unite us to God: it makes us independent of God. 407-09: Descartes is not the first to make the will the locus of the likeness to God. Marion cites St. Bernard, William de Saint Thierry, Richard de Saint-Victor. But Descartes's predecessors held the will to be privileged because of the love of God. Descartes's account is quite different.

17. What I have been referring to as "compassion" with respect to Descartes's moral teaching is what he calls "*générosité*." I use 'compassion', both in order to avoid the English sense of 'generosity' and in order to assert a connection between the divine compassion and Descartes's '*générosité*'.

Rodis-Lewis 90: According to *The Passions of the Soul*, the generous ("*généreux*") regard nothing as greater than doing good to other men. They are not indifferent to the sufferings of others, but the pity they experience is not bitter. Marion 428: According to Marion, the "self-satisfaction" experienced in generosity can exempt man from being subject to God. 412: Generosity permits man to imitate the divine self-sufficiency. Kennington 389: Generosity "is awareness of one's identity in the quality of one's will or resolutions."

Julien-Eymard d'Angers 195-96: The Stoic distinction between what depends on us and what does not depend on us is linked to Cartesian generosity. Rodis-Lewis 95-96: There is a deep kinship between St. Paul's charity and Descartes's generosity. But charity is due to grace, whereas generosity is not.

18. Rousseau, "Deuxième Promenade," *Rêveries, Œuvres complètes*, Bibliothèque de la Pléiade (Paris: Gallimard, 1959) 1: 1010.

19. See Nino Langiulli, rev. of *Philosophy and the Mirror of Nature*, by Richard Rorty, *Interpretation: A Journal of Political Philosophy* 13 (1985) 141-42: Rorty's "complaint with Analytic Philosophy should not be primarily with its attempt to be a surrogate for epistemology but rather

with its being *ashamed to be philosophy* in the court of science and technology, and with its professionalization to the point of trivialization."

20. Boethius 20, 42: Philosophy uses rhetoric and music. 74: Philosophy has been "singing" to him with her soft and sweet voice.

21. Kennington 391: "The 'universal doubt' that method demands is so far from doubting the view that the good is the useful that it is in fact based on this view, and the useful is needed by all societies always."

22. AT 9: 4, 6-7. See also George Berkeley, *Treatise Concerning the Principles of Human Knowledge* (Indianapolis: LLA-Bobbs, 1957) 6: "Upon the whole, I am inclined to think that the far greater part, if not all, of those difficulties which have hitherto amused philosophers and blocked up the way to knowledge, are entirely owing to ourselves—that we have first raised a dust and then complain we cannot see." David Hume, *An Inquiry Concerning Human Understanding,* ed. Charles W. Hendel (Indianapolis: LLA-Bobbs, 1955) 20: "But this obscurity, in the profound and abstract philosophy, is objected to, not only as painful and fatiguing, but as the inevitable source of uncertainty and error." G. W. Leibniz, *Monadology and Other Philosophical Essays,* trans. Paul Schrecker and Anne Martin (Indianapolis: LLA-Bobbs, 1965) 14: Once the "philosophical grammar" is achieved, "then when a controversy arises, disputation will no more be needed between two philosophers than between two computers," and 19: "Once this is achieved, anyone who in his reasoning and writing is using characters of this kind, will either never fall into error or, if he does, he will always discover his errors himself by the simplest examination." Thomas Hobbes, *The Elements of Law, Natural and Politic,* ed. Ferdinand Tönnies, 2nd ed. (New York: Barnes, 1969) 1: "And seeing that true knowledge begetteth not doubt nor controversy, but knowledge; it is manifest from the present controversies, that they which have heretofore written thereof, have not well understood their own subject." John Dewey is critical of the modern quest for certainty. See his *The Quest for Certainty: A Study of the Relation of Knowledge and Action,* Gifford Lectures 1929 (New York: Minton, Balch and Co., 1929) 128: The quest for certainty becomes "the search for methods of control." But Dewey claims that modern philosophy inherits the search for certainty from ancient thought (51).

23. Immanuel Kant, *Prolegomena to any Future Metaphysics,* trans. Paul Carus, rev. James W. Ellington (Indianapolis: Hackett, 1977) 1-2.

Works Consulted

Alfaric, Prosper. *L'Evolution intellectuelle de Saint Augustin*. Paris: Emile Nourry, 1918.

Aquinas, Saint Thomas. *Summa Theologica*. 5 vols. Madrid: Biblioteca de Autores Cristianos, 1962.

Aristotle. *The Basic Works of Aristotle*. Ed. Richard McKeon. New York: Random, 1941.

Armogathe, J-R. *Theologia Cartesiana: L'Explication physique de l'Eucharistie chez Descartes et dom Desgabets*. International Archives of the History of Ideas 84. The Hague: Nijhoff, 1977.

Ashmole, Bernard. *Architect and Sculptor in Classical Greece*. Wrightsman Lectures 6. New York: New York UP, 1972.

Augustine, Saint. *Concerning the City of God against the Pagans*. Trans. Henry Bettenson. Ed. David Knowles. Middlesex: Penguin, 1972.

———. *Confessions*. Trans. William Watts. The Loeb Classical Library. 2 vols. Cambridge: Harvard UP, 1912.

———. *The Confessions of St. Augustine*. Trans. Rex Warner. New York and Toronto: NAL, 1963.

Berkeley, George. *A Treatise Concerning the Principles of Human Knowledge*. Indianapolis: LLA-Bobbs, 1957.

Beyssade, Jean-Marie. *La Philosophie Première de Descartes: Le temps et la cohérence de la métaphysique*. Paris: Flammarion, 1979.

Boethius. *On the Consolation of Philosophy*. Trans. W. V Cooper. Chicago: Gateway-Regnery, 1981.

Boyer, Charles. *Christianisme et Néo-Platonisme dans la formation de Saint Augustin*. 2nd ed. Rome: Officium Libri Catholici, 1953.

Brown, Peter. *Augustine of Hippo: A Biography*. Berkeley and Los Angeles: U of California P, 1967.

Burger, Ronna. *The Phaedo: A Platonic Labyrinth*. New Haven: Yale UP, 1984.

Clarke, Desmond S. *Descartes' Philosophy of Science*. Studies in Intellectual History. University Park: Pennsylvania State UP, 1982.

D'Arcy, M. C., et al. *St. Augustine: His Age, Life, and Thought*. 1930. Cleveland and New York: Meridian-World, 1957.

Descartes, René. *Œuvres de Descartes*. Eds. Charles Adam and Paul Tannery. 11 vols. Paris: Cerf, 1904.

———. *Œuvres philosophiques*. Ed. Ferdinand Alquié. 2 vols. Paris: Garnier, 1967.

———. *The Philosophical Works of Descartes*. Trans. Elizabeth S. Haldane and G. R. T. Ross. 2 vols. New York: Cambridge UP, 1955.

Dewey, John. *The Quest for Certainty: A Study of the Relation of Knowledge and Action*. Gifford Lectures 1929. New York: Minton, Balch, 1929.

Dodds, E. R. *The Greeks and the Irrational*. Berkeley, Los Angeles, London: U of California P, 1951.

Dorter, Kenneth. *Plato's Phaedo: An Interpretation*. Toronto: Toronto UP, 1982.

Erasmus, Desiderius. *The Praise of Folly*. Trans. Clarence H. Miller. New Haven and London: Yale UP, 1979.

Foster, Michael B. *Mystery and Philosophy*. London: SCM Press, 1957.

Gilson, Etienne. Texte et Commentaire. *Discours de la Méthode*. By René Descartes. Paris: Vrin, 1947.

———. "The Future of Augustinian Metaphysics." *St. Augustine: His Age, Life, and Thought*. Eds. M. C. D'Arcy et al. 1930. Cleveland and New York: Meridian-World, 1957. 287-316.

Heath, Sir Thomas L., ed. and trans. *The Thirteen Books of Euclid's Elements*. 2nd ed. 3 vols. New York: Dover, 1956.

Heidegger, Martin. *The Basic Problems of Phenomenology*. Trans. Albert Hofstadter. Bloomington: Indiana UP, 1982.

———. "The Ode on Man in Sophocles' *Antigone*." *Sophocles: A Collection of Critical Essays*. Ed. Thomas Woodard. Englewood Cliffs: Prentice, 1966. 86-100.

Hobbes, Thomas. *The Elements of Law, Natural and Politic*. Ed. Ferdinand Tönnies. 2nd ed. New York: Barnes, 1969.

Hume, David. *An Inquiry Concerning Human Understanding*, Ed. Charles W. Hendel. Indianapolis: LLA-Bobbs, 1955.

Husserl, Edmund. "Philosophy and the Crisis of European Humanity." *The Crisis of European Sciences and Transcendental Phenomenology*.

Trans. David Carr. Studies in Phenomenology and Existential Philosophy. Evanston: Northwestern UP, 1970. 269-299.

Jaeger, Werner. *Aristotle: Fundamentals of the History of His Development*. Trans. Richard Robinson. 2nd ed. Oxford: Clarendon, 1948.

Jones, John. *On Aristotle and Greek Tragedy*. New York: Oxford UP, 1962.

Julien-Eymard d'Angers. "Sénèque, Epictète et le Stoïcisme dans l'œuvre de René Descartes." *Revue de Théologie et de Philosophie* 3ième sér. 4 (1954): 169-196.

Kant, Immanuel. *Prolegomena to any Future Metaphysics*. Trans. Paul Carus, rev. James W. Ellington. Indianapolis: Hackett, 1977.

Kennington, Richard. "René Descartes." *History of Political Philosophy*. Leo Strauss and Joseph Cropsey, eds. Chicago: Rand McNally, 1963. 379-395.

Klein, Jacob. *A Commentary on Plato's Meno*. Chapel Hill: U of North Carolina P, 1965.

———. *Greek Mathematical Thought and the Origin of Algebra*. Trans. Eva Brann. Cambridge and London: MIT P, 1968.

Knox, Bernard M. W. *Oedipus at Thebes*. New Haven: Yale UP and London: Oxford UP, 1957.

La Drière, James Craig. "Voice and Address." *Dictionary of World Literature*. Ed. Joseph T. Shipley. Rev. ed. Boston: The Writer, Inc., 1970: 615-617.

Langiulli, Nino. Rev. of *Philosophy and the Mirror of Nature* by Richard Rorty. *Interpretation: A Journal of Political Philosophy* 13 (1985): 119-142.

Leibniz, G. W. *Monadology and Other Philosophical Essays*. Trans. Paul Schrecker and Anne Martin. Indianapolis: LLA-Bobbs, 1965.

Lewis, Geneviève. "Augustinisme et cartésianisme." *Augustinus Magister*. Congrès International Augustinien. 2 vols. Paris: Etudes Augustiniennes, 1954. 2: 1087-1104.

Marion, Jean-Luc. *Sur la Théologie blanche de Descartes: Analogie, création des vérités éternelles et fondement*. Philosophie d'aujourd'hui. Paris: PUF, 1981.

Maritain, Jacques. "St. Augustine and St. Thomas Aquinas." *St. Augustine: His Age, Life, and Thought*. Eds. M. C. D'Arcy et al. 1930. Cleveland and New York: Meridian-World, 1957.

Marrou, Henri-Irénée. *Saint Augustin et la fin de la culture antique*. 4th ed. Paris: Boccard, 1958.

Meagher, Robert E. *An Introduction to Augustine*. New York: New York UP, 1978.

Nettleship, Richard Lewis. *Lectures on the Republic of Plato*. 1897. New York: St. Martin's, 1968.

O'Connell, Robert J. *St. Augustine's Early Theory of Man, A.D. 386-391*. Cambridge: Harvard UP, 1968.

———. *St. Augustine's Confessions: The Odyssey of Soul*. Cambridge: Harvard UP, 1969.

Patterson, Robert Leet. *Plato on Immortality*. University Park: Pennsylvania State UP, 1965.

Plato. *Apology. The Trial and Death of Socrates*. Trans. G. M. A. Grube. Indianapolis: Hackett, 1975.

———. *Euthyphro, Apology of Socrates, Crito*. Ed. John Burnet. Oxford: Clarendon, 1924.

———. *Meno*. Trans. G. M. A. Grube. Indianapolis: Hackett, 1976.

———. *Phaedo*. Ed. John Burnet. Oxford: Clarendon P, 1911.

———. *Phaedo*. Trans. G.M.A. Grube. 2nd ed. Indianapolis: Hackett, 1980.

———. *The Republic*. Trans. Allen Bloom. New York: Basic, 1968.

———. *Theaetetus*. Trans. Benjamin Jowett. Indianapolis: LLA-Bobbs, 1949.

Prufer, Thomas. "Notes For a Reading of Augustine, *Confessions*, Book X." *Interpretation: A Journal of Political Philosophy* 10 (1982): 197-200.

Przywara, Erich, S.J. "St. Augustine and the Modern World." Trans. E. I. Watkin. *St. Augustine: His Age, Life, and Thought*. Eds. M. C. D'Arcy et al. 1930. Cleveland and New York: Meridian-World, 1957. 251-286.

Rodis-Lewis, Geneviève. *La Morale de Descartes*. Initiation philosophique. Paris: PUF, 1957.

Roland-Gosselin, Bernard. "St. Augustine's System of Morals." *St. Augustine: His Age, Life, and Thought*. Eds. M. C. D'Arcy et al. 1930. Cleveland and New York: Meridian-World, 1957. 225-248.

Rousseau, Jean-Jacques. *The First and Second Discourses*. Trans. Roger and Judith R. Masters. New York: St. Martin's, 1964.

———. *Rêveries. Œuvres complètes*. Eds. Bernard Gagnebin and Marcel Raymond. Bibliothèque de la Pléiade. 4 vols. Paris: Gallimard, 1959. 1: 995-1099.

Ryle, Gilbert. "Systematically Misleading Expressions." *Proceedings of the Aristotelian Society*. New Series 32 (1932): 139-170.

Sokolowski, Robert. *The God of Faith and Reason: Foundations of Christian Theology.* Notre Dame, Ind.: Notre Dame UP, 1982.

Spinoza, Benedict de. *The Ethics. The Chief Works of Spinoza.* Trans. R. H. M. Elwes. 2 vols. New York: Dover, 1955.

Taylor, A.E. *Plato: The Man and His Work.* Cleveland and New York: Meridian-World, 1956.

Verene, Donald Phillip. "Technological Desire." *Research in Philosophy and Technology.* 7 (1984): 99-112.

Vico, Giambattista. *The Autobiography of Giambattista Vico.* Trans. Max Harold Fisch and Thomas Goddard Bergin. Ithaca: Cornell UP, 1944.

Index

A

Alfaric, Prosper, 232
Analytic philosophy, 2, 7, 202, 211, 247, 250
Anaxagoras, 27, 39, 64, 65, 66, 68, 69, 72, 77
Anger, 13, 14, 15, 21, 22, 23, 27, 29, 37, 38, 41, 44, 51, 55, 70, 92, 116, 118, 129, 193, 194, 204, 212, 213
Apollo, 24, 37, 39, 43, 224
Apology, 11, 12, 24, 29, 34, 44, 75, 83, 85, 86, 137, 158, 160, 171, 179, 194, 233
Aquinas, St. Thomas, 204, 243, 249
Argives, 53
Aristophanes, 23
Aristotle, 17, 36, 175, 196, 207, 217, 222, 223, 227, 229, 235, 239, 249
Armogathe, J.-R., 241, 244
Ashmole, Bernard, 224
Astrology, 91, 107, 108, 109
Augustine, St., 85-135, 165, 173, 188, 196, 202, 203, 204, 205, 206, 207, 208, 209, 219, 231, 232, 233, 234, 236, 237, 238, 239, 241, 242, 244, 248, 249
　City of God, 88
　Confessions, 1, 2, 3, 5, 6, 8, 85-135, 165, 179, 203, 204, 205, 208, 209, 219, 231, 232, 233, 238, 239, 240, 249

B

"Bee," 14, 55, 72, 78, 81, 211
Berkeley, George, 251

Beyssade, Jean-Marie, 242
Boethius, 2, 5, 6, 221, 246, 251
Boyer, Charles, 232
Brann, Eva, 221, 231
Brown, Peter, 231, 234, 235, 237, 238, 239, 240
Burger, Ronna, 221
Burnet, John, 224, 225, 227, 228, 230
"Busybody," 138, 159, 176, 193

C

Certitude, 2, 9, 15, 31, 34, 35, 59, 71, 72, 74, 76, 77, 82, 83, 88, 107, 117, 126, 133, 134, 135, 144, 147, 149, 150, 154, 156, 157, 164, 165, 169, 174, 180, 181, 188, 189, 199, 200, 201, 202, 208, 215, 217, 219, 229, 248
"Charm(s)," 7, 8, 73, 74, 75, 76, 127, 139, 180, 188, 214, 228
Cicero, Hortensius, 104, 121, 126, 127, 132
Clarke, Desmond S., 240, 241
Comedy, 12-25, 26, 144, 145, 154, 177, 192, 195, 241
Compassion, 2, 6, 83, 92, 93, 95, 96, 101, 109, 120, 135, 147, 179, 189, 192, 204, 205, 208, 209, 219, 244, 246, 250
Confession, 85, 86, 87, 95, 96, 97, 101, 121, 122, 132, 133, 205, 209
Courage, 9, 15, 36, 55, 57, 78, 81, 83, 89, 163, 175, 192, 222, 230

D

Death, 2, 5, 6, 7, 8, 9, 12, 15, 16, 18, 22, 23, 26, 27, 28, 29, 30, 31, 34, 37, 41, 42, 43, 44, 54, 56, 57, 59, 61, 71, 83, 89, 93, 105, 110, 115, 121,135, 146, 147, 148, 165, 174, 184, 188, 189, 195, 196, 205, 207, 210, 211, 219, 222, 223, 225, 226, 228, 230, 240, 248
Descartes, Rene, 101, 130, 133, 135, 137-189, 197, 201, 202, 203, 204, 205, 206, 207, 208, 209, 211, 213, 214, 215, 216, 218, 240, 241, 242, 244, 247, 248, 249, 250
    cogito, 1, 248
    je pense, donc je suis, 135, 163, 164, 165, 178, 182, 183, 188, 189, 202, 203
    "le bon sens," 137, 138, 142, 159, 181, 185, 215
    Dioptrics, 182, 186, 206
    Discourse on Method, 1, 2, 3, 5, 6, 7, 8, 105, 135, 137-189, 201, 202, 203, 204, 205, 208, 209, 211, 213, 214, 215, 216, 219, 240, 241, 242, 247
    Geometry, 182
    Meditations, 216
    Meteorology, 150, 151, 186, 187, 197, 206
    Passions of the Soul, 241, 250
Despair, 7, 87, 94, 110, 134, 152, 189, 219
Dewey, John, 251
dianoia, 41, 76, 225, 227, 229
Dionysus, 39, 224
Disinterested spectator, 2, 6, 8, 9, 26, 27, 28, 29, 32, 36, 71, 89, 101, 102, 103, 104, 105, 106, 111, 135, 154, 155, 160, 176, 177, 189, 191, 19, 193, 194, 199, 203, 204, 207, 219, 228, 246
Diversion, 7
Divine, 1, 2, 6, 7, 18, 19, 20, 23, 24, 27, 28, 35, 36, 43, 68, 70, 71, 74, 83, 87, 88, 91, 93, 101, 102, 105, 106, 107, 109, 110, 111, 114, 115, 120, 121, 135, 173, 176, 177, 178, 179, 183, 184, 185, 186, 193, 194, 195, 196, 197, 198, 200, 202, 203, 204, 205, 211, 219, 235, 236, 241, 242, 247, 249, 250

Dodds, E. R., 222, 224, 239
Dorter, Kenneth, 223, 226, 228, 229, 230

E

Epicurus, 111
Erasmus, 245
Evenus, 75
Existentialism, 248

F

Fable, 6, 7, 8, 100, 138, 139, 140, 141, 144, 160, 180, 183, 188, 201, 214, 215, 216, 219, 240
Fear 15, 17, 21, 22, 24, 26, 27, 30, 31, 32, 38, 41, 42, 44, 51, 55, 57, 58, 61, 66, 68, 69, 70, 71, 73, 75, 92, 93, 103, 104, 105, 111, 114, 118, 133, 135, 146, 147, 163, 189, 192, 194, 207, 211, 212, 215, 219, 229
"Form(s)," 19, 39, 40, 46, 49, 50, 51, 52, 59, 60, 64, 66, 80, 137, 224
Foster, Michael B., 231, 235, 236, 243, 245, 247, 249, 250

G

"Gadfly," 37, 43, 72, 176, 193, 209
Gambling, 218
Generosity, 241, 244, 245, 248, 250
Genesis, 98, 102, 127, 128, 129, 130, 174, 176, 187, 237
Gilson, Etienne, 240, 241, 242, 248, 249

H

Hatred of argument, 14, 17, 24, 33, 34, 36, 45, 46, 47, 51, 52, 53, 54, 55, 56, 57, 58, 59, 67, 72, 73, 74, 76, 77, 79, 199, 210, 212, 214, 215, 228

Heath, Sir Thomas L., 224
Hegel, G. W. F., 236, 247
Heidegger, Martin, 228, 238, 247, 248
Heracles, 24, 33, 34, 36, 53, 226
Heraclitus, 225
Heroism, 18, 23, 24, 28, 36, 142
History, 138, 139, 140, 141, 142, 180
Hobbes, Thomas, 251
Homer, 21, 41, 222
Hope, 5, 9, 30, 39, 68, 83, 134, 135, 147, 189, 209, 219
Hubris, 36-44, 115
Hume, David, 251
Humility, 114-122, 173-179
Husserl, Edmund, 7, 221, 246

I

Idol, 104, 105, 109, 129, 131, 205, 238
Immortality, 1, 6, 8, 9, 15, 16, 18, 19, 20, 21, 22, 23, 27, 28, 30, 31, 32, 34, 35, 36, 39, 41, 46, 47, 48, 49, 50, 51, 52, 55, 56, 57, 59, 60, 61, 63, 66, 68, 71, 72, 73, 77, 80, 83, 104, 121, 135, 146, 147, 195, 196, 197, 200, 201, 210, 213, 215, 219, 226, 228
Iolaus, 24, 33, 34, 53, 228
Irony, 25, 36-44, 81, 87, 138, 144, 155, 159, 170, 173, 177, 181, 182
Irrational, 38, 39, 40, 41, 55, 58, 70, 71, 94, 95, 101, 224, 225

J

Jaeger, Werner, 245, 247, 249
Jones, John, 222
Julien-Eymard d'Angers, Balzac, 242, 250

K

Kant, Immanuel, 216, 247, 251
Kennington, Richard, 240, 241, 242, 243, 244, 250, 251
Kierkegaard, Søren, 236

Klein, Jacob, 223, 224, 225, 226, 227, 228, 229, 244, 245
Knox, Bernard M. W., 222, 224, 232

L

La Drière, James Craig, 229
Langiulli, Nino, 250
Laughter, 15, 16, 17, 22, 23, 26, 42, 81, 87-101, 144-152, 191, 192, 193
Leibniz, G. W., 251
Luther, Martin, 248
Lutheranism, 240, 247

M

Magnanimity, 115
Manichees, 91, 100, 126, 235
Marion, Jean-Luc, 244, 249, 250
Maritain, Jacques, 234, 248
Marrou, Henri-Irenee, 232, 234, 236, 239
Mathematics, 39, 40, 49, 64, 75, 76, 100, 107, 149, 150, 152, 168, 180, 182, 185, 206, 207, 211, 227, 229, 241
Meagher, Robert E., 236, 237, 238, 239, 249
Misology (see 'Hatred of argument')
Music, 7, 37, 74, 131, 251
muthos, 222
Myth, 6, 8, 17, 19, 20, 22, 23, 29, 30, 36, 37, 43, 45, 50, 75, 78, 214, 215, 219, 223, 225, 237, 246, 247

N

Natural philosophy, 1, 12, 23, 26, 27, 28, 39, 45, 46, 47, 52, 60, 61, 63, 67, 68, 69, 70, 75, 77, 82, 96, 98, 100, 193, 197, 206, 211, 213, 222
Neo-Platonism, 232, 233, 234
Nettleship, Richard Lewis, 225, 227, 228, 229, 230
Nous, 21, 29, 47, 64, 65, 66, 69

O

O'Connell, Robert J., 232, 233, 234, 235, 238
Odysseus, 21, 22, 23, 24, 25, 28, 31, 35, 36, 41, 51, 74, 222, 230
Oedipus, 39, 94, 195, 222, 223, 224

P

Parmenides, 225, 227
Patterson, Robert Leet, 223, 225
Penelope, 23, 24, 25, 28, 29, 31, 34, 35, 46, 57, 73, 74, 125, 189, 200, 219, 223, 228
Philosophy, 1, 2, 6, 7, 8, 9, 11, 12, 13, 14, 15, 16, 17, 18, 20, 23, 24, 25, 26, 27, 28, 29, 34, 35, 36, 37, 41, 43, 45, 46, 47, 55, 57, 60, 69, 70, 71, 72, 73, 74, 75, 76, 77, 82, 83, 88, 89, 95, 100, 101, 104, 106, 114, 121, 132, 135, 147, 160, 171, 172, 173, 174, 176, 178, 179, 180, 182, 189, 191, 192, 193, 194, 195, 196, 197, 198, 199, 200, 201, 202, 203, 204, 205, 207, 211, 212, 213, 214, 215, 216, 217, 218, 219, 223, 230, 233, 234, 235, 241, 242, 245, 246, 247, 248
Philosophy (character in Boethius), 5, 8, 251
phronesis, 77, 78
Physics, 26, 88
pistis, 76, 201, 229, 230
Pity, 15, 16, 22, 23, 36, 54, 78, 89, 93, 95, 96, 97, 101, 120, 121, 129, 191, 192, 204, 205, 222, 246, 250
Plato, 11, 24, 26, 33, 40, 44, 81, 82, 83, 210, 222, 223, 225, 227, 229, 231, 232, 245, 247
  Apology of Socrates, 11, 12, 13, 14, 22, 23, 26, 27, 35, 37, 38, 42, 43, 44, 47, 53, 55, 62, 63, 67, 70, 72, 75, 81, 82, 176, 179, 193, 198, 204, 209, 211, 212, 213, 214, 221, 225, 230, 246, 247
  Meno, 13, 39, 40
  Phaedo, 1, 2, 3, 5, 6, 7, 8, 11-83, 87, 88, 89, 97, 125, 179, 194, 197, 198, 199, 201, 202, 203, 207, 209, 210, 211, 212, 214, 215, 219, 221,

222, 223, 224, 225, 226, 228, 230, 232
  Republic, 22, 28, 31, 40, 41, 49, 51, 70, 76, 201, 227, 228, 229, 230
  Symposium, 2
  Theaetetus, 13, 56, 193, 200, 209, 225, 226, 229, 247
Platonism, 96, 232, 234
Platonist(s), 1, 95, 96, 98, 100, 101, 105, 109, 120, 121, 122, 126, 127, 128, 130, 132, 204, 205, 206, 207, 235, 237
Plotinus, 232, 233, 234, 235, 237, 238, 239
Poetry, 5, 8, 17, 37, 75, 76, 152, 188, 214
Power, 2, 7, 8, 9, 37, 38, 91, 105, 109, 110, 119, 131, 132, 160, 161, 162, 163, 164, 165, 169, 171, 174, 179, 183, 202, 203, 204, 207, 217, 232, 235, 237, 239, 242, 243, 248
Prayer, 6, 8, 86, 106, 114, 148, 173, 202, 219, 231, 235
Presumption, 1, 2, 95, 96, 101, 122, 132, 133, 173, 174, 178, 179, 205, 208
Pride, 83, 96, 100, 114-122, 127, 132, 133, 134, 135, 152, 173-179, 208, 209
Protagoras, 225
Prufer, Thomas, 231, 235, 239, 248
Przywara, Erich, 236, 239, 247, 248
Pythagoras, 224, 245
Pythagorean(s), 40, 75, 78, 224

R

Rainbow, 151, 187, 206
Rhetoric, 8, 73, 74, 75, 83, 86, 127, 131, 132, 152, 214, 215, 216, 231, 242, 251
Rodis-Lewis, Geneviève, 245, 249, 250
Roland-Gosselin, Bernard, 242
Rousseau, Jean-Jacques, 191, 192, 208, 245, 250
Ryle, Gilbert, 7, 221

S

Sickness, 37, 82, 174, 208
Sisyphus, 230
Smile(s), 16, 23, 81, 91
Socrates, 5, 11-83, 86, 87, 88, 89, 173,
   176, 177, 188, 189, 193, 194, 195,
   197, 198, 199, 200, 201, 206, 209,
   210, 211, 212, 213, 214, 215, 218,
   219, 222, 223, 225, 226, 227, 228,
   229, 230, 231, 247
Sokolowski, Robert, 237, 238
sophia, 77
Sophist(s), 1, 12, 42, 52, 53, 56, 57, 58,
   60, 67, 75, 77, 82, 176
Sophistry, 12, 67, 76
Spinoza, Benedict de, 246
Spirited part of the soul, 22, 23, 28, 41,
   42, 44, 55, 69, 70, 71, 74, 88
Stoicism, 147, 152, 157, 163, 174, 202,
   203, 241, 242, 245, 246, 250
Story, 138, 139

T

Taylor, A. E., 222, 223
Tears, 15, 23, 87-101, 144-152, 191,
   192, 205, 230
Thales, 26, 192, 193, 247
Theseus, 24, 226
"Torpedo fish," 14
Tragedy, 12-25, 39, 93, 94, 97, 146,
   194, 195, 205

Trembling, 25, 26, 29, 30, 32, 34, 78,
   87-101, 110, 114, 119, 121, 122, 127,
   131, 144-152, 188, 191, 192, 207,
   212, 215, 236
Truth, 44-83, 86, 87, 90, 91, 97, 100,
   101, 105, 122-135, 137, 138, 141,
   153, 155, 157, 158, 159, 165, 179-
   189, 198, 199, 205, 206, 211,·215,
   216, 218, 224, 226, 238, 247, 248

U

Uncertainty, 2, 31, 32, 35, 45, 58, 59,
   92, 93, 107, 119, 133, 134, 135, 164,
   180, 202, 218, 219

V

Verene, Donald Phillip, 245
Vico, Giambattista, 241

W

Wonder, 7, 8, 13, 16, 17, 25, 79, 87-
   101, 102, 103, 113, 131, 144-152,
   187, 188, 189, 191, 194, 195, 196,
   197, 198, 199, 200, 201, 206, 207,
   217, 218, 241, 246, 247